A NEW LATIN PRIMER

WORKBOOK

A New Latin Primer
Workbook

Mary C. English

Georgia L. Irby

New York :: Oxford

OXFORD UNIVERSITY PRESS

Oxford University Press is a department of the University of Oxford.
It furthers the University's objective of excellence in research,
scholarship, and education by publishing worldwide.

Oxford   New York
Auckland   Cape Town   Dar es Salaam   Hong Kong   Karachi
Kuala Lumpur   Madrid   Melbourne   Mexico City   Nairobi
New Delhi   Shanghai   Taipei   Toronto

With offices in
Argentina   Austria   Brazil   Chile   Czech Republic   France   Greece
Guatemala   Hungary   Italy   Japan   Poland   Portugal   Singapore
South Korea   Switzerland   Thailand   Turkey   Ukraine   Vietnam

For titles covered by Section 112 of the US Higher Education
Opportunity Act, please visit www.oup.com/us/he for the
latest information about pricing and alternate formats.

Published by Oxford University Press
198 Madison Avenue, New York, New York 10016
http://www.oup.com

ISBN of *A New Latin Primer Workbook*: 978-0-19-026698-1

Printing number: 9 8 7 6 5 4 3 2 1

Printed in the United States of America
on acid-free paper

Contents

Preface	vii
NLP Introduction: Pronunciation	1
NLP 1. Present Tense	3
NLP 2. First and Second Declension Nouns and Adjectives	9
NLP 3. Third Declension Nouns and Adjectives	17
NLP 4. Vocative Case, Imperatives, and Personal Pronouns	27
NLP 5. Genitive Case	35
NLP 6. Dative Case	43
NLP Review A (Lessons 1–6)	51
NLP 7. Accusative, Ablative, and Locative Cases	71
NLP 8. Imperfect Tense	79
NLP 9. Future Tense	87
NLP 10. Fourth and Fifth Declension Nouns	99
NLP 11. Irregular Verbs	105
NLP 12. Personal, Reflexive, and Intensive Pronouns, and Pronominal Adjectives	113
NLP Review B (Lessons 7–12)	123
NLP 13. Perfect, Pluperfect, and Future Perfect Tenses	147
NLP 14. Numbers	155
NLP 15. Demonstrative and Indefinite Pronouns	161
NLP 16. Relative Pronouns, Relative Clauses, and Interrogative Pronouns	171
NLP 17. Passive Verbs: Present, Imperfect, and Future Tenses	181
NLP 18. Passive Verbs: Perfect, Pluperfect, and Future Perfect Tenses	191
NLP Review C (Lessons 13–18)	201
NLP 19. Comparatives and Superlatives of Adjectives and Adverbs	221
NLP 20. Impersonal Verbs and Fiō	227
NLP 21. Deponent Verbs	235

NLP 22. Participles   247

NLP 23. Ablatives Absolute   255

NLP 24. Indirect Statement   263

NLP Review D (Lessons 19–24)   271

NLP 25. Correlatives   293

NLP 26. Present and Imperfect Subjunctives   301

NLP 27. Perfect and Pluperfect Subjunctive and Cum Clauses   309

NLP 28. Purpose Clauses   317

NLP 29. Result Clauses   325

NLP 30. Indirect Commands   333

NLP Review E (Lessons 25–30)   339

NLP 31. Indirect Questions   357

NLP 32. Fear Clauses   365

NLP 33. Relative Clauses with the Subjunctive   371

NLP 34. Conditionals   377

NLP 35. Gerunds and Gerundives   383

NLP 36. Future Passive Periphrastics, Supines, and Other Subjunctive Clauses   389

NLP Review F (Lessons 31–36)   395

Answer Key for Crossword Puzzles and Word Searches   413

Preface

WE RECOGNIZE THAT there are many approaches to teaching and learning languages. We have thus designed this companion workbook to *A New Latin Primer* to feature a variety of drills, additional practice sentences, directed English-to-Latin translation practice, and word games to reinforce grammar, vocabulary, and culture. The workbook includes one lesson for each corresponding lesson in the main text (including the Introduction) plus six Review Lessons (one for every six lessons of *NLP*). The Review Lessons offer a précis of the concepts covered in the previous six lessons (with simple examples in English and Latin to illustrate those concepts), a consolidated list of required vocabulary, additional grammar drills, additional passages of authentic Latin for translation practice, and a crisscross puzzle whose clues are drawn from the passages, examples, and cultural essays of the six *NLP* lessons.

We invite students and teachers to use these exercises in full or to select from them as it seems best. Teachers may choose to assign portions of each set of exercises, for example, or only those exercises that drill new forms; others may wish to reserve some exercises for quizzes or for review later in the semester. The additional passages in the Review Lessons can be employed in the same manner—as review, as sight translations, or as quiz or test passages. Students should find the additional drills and practice sentences helpful in consolidating their understanding of challenging concepts. Many of the translation sentences in the Workbook are intended to be light-hearted, and we encourage students to devise their own contexts for these sentences and to compose their own practice sentences or more formal compositions. Although Latin composition usually receives short shrift in our over-packed, hyper-digitalized lives, it remains one of the best ways to come to understand Latin's beautiful complexities.

This workbook has its genesis in requests for more drills and practice from Georgia Irby's Beginning and Intermediate Latin students at William and Mary, Fall 2013–Spring 2015. It represents many long conversations, extra study sessions, and collaborations with these fine Latin scholars, including Joe Ayanian, Dereck Basinger, Megan Bland, Emily Condos, Laura Cooley, Aaron Finkle, Rachel Greenfield, Susannah Haury, Vicky Ma, Molly Martien, Erin Miao, Daniel Mollenkamp, Paige Newsome, Alex Olson, Joseph Palame, Kristen Roper, Sheila Palmer, Jason Scott-Sheets, and Ben Zhang, and also Grace Albrecht, Callie Angle, Sara Barlow, Ashley Brenton, Lindsey Carter, Max Danielson, Alex DiLauro, Rochelle Evans, William Gaskins, Joel Harrison, Justin "Wolf" Jones, Donna Kinney, Joe Maniaci, Matt Nickele, Sam Nussbaum, Francesca Orfila, Jasmane Ormond, Rebecca Peng, Anna Richmond, Daniel Roth, Sarah VanKirk, and Lauren Visokay. We would also like to thank Jessamyn Rising for her rigorous proofing and salutary recommendations (including the perhaps not-so-serious suggestion of the limerick, which Georgia Irby took as a personal challenge). It is to these very special students that we dedicate this workbook.

Introduction: Pronunciation

1A. Divide the following Latin words into syllables, mark the accents, and pronounce each word.

Marcus	namque
Flāvia	premis
Clōdius	habitant
nōminis	bene
Rōmānōrum	amīcus
coniugem	virginibus
praesidium	consiliīs
opera	populōrum
esse	sine
etiam	fuerat

Present Tense

1A. Identify the conjugation of the following Latin verbs.

Verb	Conjugation
accipiō, -ere, accēpī, acceptus: take, receive	
āmittō, -ere, āmīsī, āmissus: send away, let go, lose	
amō, -āre, -āvī, -ātus: like, love	
audiō, -īre, -īvī, -ītus: hear	
capiō, capere, cēpī, captus: take, seize, capture	
conveniō, -īre, -vēnī, -ventus: come together, meet	
dō, dare, dedī, datus: give	
doceō, -ēre, docuī, doctus: teach, instruct	
faciō, -ere, fēcī, factus: make, do	
fugiō, fugere, fūgī: flee, escape, run away	
habitō, -āre, -āvī, -ātus: live, dwell	
invideō, -ēre, -vīdī, -vīsus: envy, be jealous	
mittō, mittere, mīsī, missus: send, let go	
prohibeō, -ēre, -uī: hold back, restrain, hinder	
relinquō, -ere, relīquī, relictus: leave behind, desert, abandon	
sciō, -īre, -īvī, -ītus: know	
sum, esse, fuī, futūrus: be	
teneō, -ēre, tenuī, tentus: hold, maintain, detain	
videō, -ēre, vīdī, vīsus: see, look at, watch	
vīvō, -ere, vixī, victus: live, be alive	

1B. Following the paradigms in *NLP* 1, conjugate the following verbs in the present tense. Translate each form.

verb: **habitō, -āre, -āvī, -ātus:** live, dwell

conjugation _____

PRESENT	Latin	Translation
Singular		
1st		
2nd		
3rd		
Plural		
1st		
2nd		
3rd		

verb: **videō, -ēre, vīdī, vīsus:** see

conjugation _____

PRESENT	Latin	Translation
Singular		
1st		
2nd		
3rd		
Plural		
1st		
2nd		
3rd		

verb: **vīvō, -ere, vixī, victus**: live
conjugation _____

PRESENT	Latin	Translation
Singular		
1st		
2nd		
3rd		
Plural		
1st		
2nd		
3rd		

verb: **fugiō, fugere, fūgī**: flee
conjugation _____

PRESENT	Latin	Translation
Singular		
1st		
2nd		
3rd		
Plural		
1st		
2nd		
3rd		

verb: **veniō, -īre, vēnī, ventus**: come
conjugation _____

PRESENT	Latin	Translation
Singular		
1st		
2nd		
3rd		
Plural		
1st		
2nd		
3rd		

1C. Give the person and number of the following verbs. Translate each form.

Verb	Person	No.	Translation
scīs			
vident			
fugitis			
dō			
habitās			
amant			
sum			
capimus			
mittunt			
audit			
sumus			
docet			

1D. Keeping the same person, convert the singular forms to plural and the plural forms to singular.

Verb	Person and No. of Given Form	Translation of Given Form	Conversion	Translation of Converted Form
capit				
vidēs				
fugimus				
dant				
docētis				
amō				
habitātis				
est				
sciunt				
mittō				
audit				
sum				

1E. Give the requested forms of the following verbs. Translate each form.

Verb	Requested Form	Latin Form	Translation
amō	3rd person singular		
doceō	1st person plural		
dō	3rd person plural		
videō	2nd person plural		
fugiō	Infinitive		
sum	3rd person plural		
habitō	3rd person singular		
sciō	1st person singular		
mittō	1st person plural		
capiō	2nd person singular		
audiō	Infinitive		
sum	2nd person singular		

1F. Translate the following English sentences into Latin. Use the rubric below each sentence as a guide.

We see.

Person and number _____

Latin present tense ending _____

Dictionary entry of Latin verb _____

Conjugation _____

Latin translation _____

I love.

Person and number _____

Latin present tense ending _____

Dictionary entry of Latin verb _____

Conjugation _____

Latin translation _____

She knows.

      Person and number _____

      Latin present tense ending _____

      Dictionary entry of Latin verb _____

      Conjugation _____

      Latin translation _____

You (plural) live.

      Person and number _____

      Latin present tense ending _____

      Dictionary entry of Latin verb _____

      Conjugation _____

      Latin translation _____

1G. Fill in the blanks with correctly formed Latin verbs from *NLP* 1 required vocabulary. You may use each verb only once. The names are featured in the passages from *NLP* 1. There is no "right" answer.

      Polucarpus et Stronius *(3rd plural)* _____ hīc.

      Nihil *(3rd plural)* _____.

      Epaphra *(3rd singular)* _____et_____.

      Omnēs *(3rd plural)* _____.

      Note: **omnēs**: they all

First and Second Declension Nouns and Adjectives

2A. Identify the declension of the following nouns.

Noun	Declension
animus, -ī, m: soul, mind	
cūra, -**ae**, f: care, concern, trouble	
dictum, -ī, n: word	
digitus, -ī, m: finger	
prōmissum, -ī, n: promise	
fēmina, -**ae**, f: woman	
collum, -ī, n: neck	
principium, -iī, n: beginning	
quadriiugī, -**ōrum**, m (plural): a team of four horses	
patria, -**iae**, f: fatherland, country	

2B. Decline the following noun-adjective pairs.

Case	animus, -ī, m + magnus, -a, -um	prōmissum, -ī, n + certus, -a, -um	vīta, -ae, f + vester, vestra, vestrum
Singular			
Nominative			
Genitive			
Dative			
Accusative			
Ablative			
Vocative			
Plural			
Nominative			
Genitive			
Dative			
Accusative			
Ablative			
Vocative			

2C. Identify the following nouns by case, number, and gender.

Noun	Case	No.	Gender
animus			
fēminārum			
undam			
agrī (3 answers)			
animōrum			
fēminā			
vīta (2 answers)			
virō (2 answers)			
vīna (3 answers)			
animīs (2 answers)			
vīnum (3 answers)			
animī (3 answers)			
patriīs (2 answers)			
vītae (4 answers)			

2D. Give the requested forms for the following nouns.

Noun	Requested Form	Latin Form
annus	Nominative singular	
puella	Genitive singular	
ager	Accusative singular	
poēta	Ablative singular	
vir	Vocative singular	
unda	Dative plural	
animus	Dative singular	
patria	Accusative plural	
vīnum	Genitive plural	
fēmina	Nominative plural	

2E. Keeping the same case, convert the singular forms to plural and the plural forms to singular.

Noun	Case and No.	Conversion
fēminam		
annō (2 cases)		
patriae (Genitive)		
undā		
undae (Dative)		
anime		
poētārum		
puellīs (Ablative)		
vītīs (Dative)		
vīna (2 cases)		

2F. Conjugate the following verbs in the present tense. Translate each form.

verb: **teneō, -ēre, tenuī, tentus**: hold, maintain, detain
conjugation _____

PRESENT	Latin	Translation
Singular		
1st		
2nd		
3rd		
Plural		
1st		
2nd		
3rd		

verb: **faciō, -ere**, **fēcī**, **factus**: make, do
conjugation _____

PRESENT	Latin	Translation
Singular		
1st		
2nd		
3rd		
Plural		
1st		
2nd		
3rd		

verb: **relinquō, -ere, relīquī, relictus**: leave behind, desert, abandon

conjugation_____

PRESENT	Latin	Translation
Singular		
1st		
2nd		
3rd		
Plural		
1st		
2nd		
3rd		

2G. Give the person and number of the following verbs. Translate each form.

Verb	Person	No.	Translation
relinquunt			
tenēs			
facit			
estis			
mittimus			
doceō			
vidēmus			
habitātis			
fugiunt			
audīs			

2H. Translate the following sentences into Latin. Use the rubric below each
sentence as a guide.

I am taking my possessions.

     Person and number of "I am taking" _____

     Latin present tense ending _____

     Dictionary entry _____

     Conjugation _____

     Latin translation of verb _____

     Is "possessions" a subject or direct object? _____

     Case, number, and gender of "possessions" _____

     Dictionary entry _____

     Declension _____

     Latin translation of "possessions" _____

     What English noun does "my" modify? _____

     Case, number, and gender of "my" _____

     Dictionary entry _____

     Declension _____

     Latin translation of "my" _____

     Latin translation of entire sentence _____

     _____

Miserable minds know evil things.

     Person and number of "know" _____

     Latin present tense ending _____

     Dictionary entry _____

     Conjugation _____

     Latin translation of verb _____

Is "minds" a subject or direct object?_____

Case, number, and gender of "minds"_____

Dictionary entry_____

Declension_____

Latin translation of "minds"_____

What English noun does "miserable" modify?_____

Case, number, and gender of "miserable"_____

Dictionary entry_____

Declension_____

Latin translation of "miserable"_____

Is "evil things" a subject or direct object?_____

Case, number, and gender of "evil things"_____

Dictionary entry_____

Declension_____

Latin translation of "evil things"_____

Latin translation of entire sentence_____

_____

2I. Give the Latin forms for the following English phrases. Then recombine the **double-underlined** letters to spell a toponym that is associated with Ovid.

you (singular) do: __ __ __ __ __

for the poets: __ __ __ __ __ __

of life: __ __ __ __ __

fields (Accusative): __ __ __ __ __

we hold: __ __ __ __ __ __ __

ANSWER: __ __ __ __ __

Third Declension Nouns and Adjectives

3A. Give the declension and stem of the following nouns.

Noun	Decl.	Stem
Rōma, -ae, f		
arma, -ōrum, n (plural)		
beneficium, -iī, n		
caput, capitis, n		
cīvitās, -ātis, f		
corpus, corporis, n		
frāter, frātris, m		
populus, -ī, m		
bellum, -ī, n		
oppidum, -ī, n		
māter, mātris, f		
praedō, -ōnis, m		
necessitās, -ātis, f		
nōmen, nōminis, n		
opus, operis, n		
forma, -ae, f		
pastor, -ōris, m		
pater, patris, m		
pax, pācis, f		
pectus, pectoris, n		

Noun	Decl.	Stem
plebs, plēbis, f		
rex, rēgis, m		
aurifex, aurificis, m		
sanguis, sanguinis, m		
scelus, sceleris, n		
stirps, stirpis (-ium), m/f		
tribūnal, tribūnālis (-ium), n		
urbs, urbis (-ium), f		

3B. Identify each of the following words as a noun or an adjective. Then give the declension and stem of each word.

Word	Part of Speech (Noun or Adjective)	Decl.	Stem
forma, formae, f			
virīlis, virīle			
pax, pācis, f			
vester, vestra, vestrum			
ācer, acris, acre			
arbitrium, -iī, n			
infēlix (**infēlicis**)			
pectus, pectoris, n			
aurifex, aurifīcis, m			
cīvitās, -ātis, f			
castra, castrōrum, n (plural)			
meus, mea, meum			
levis, leve			

3C. Decline the following noun-adjective pairs.

Case	rex, rēgis, m + magnus, -a, -um	uxor, -ōris, f + bonus, -a, -um	rūs, rūris, n + dēvius, -a, -um
Singular			
Nominative			
Genitive			
Dative			
Accusative			
Ablative			
Vocative			
Plural			
Nominative			
Genitive			
Dative			
Accusative			
Ablative			
Vocative			

Case	sanguis, sanguinis, m + immensus, -a, -um	forma, -ae, f + ācer, acris, acre	imperium, -iī, n + omnis, omne
Singular			
Nominative			
Genitive			
Dative			
Accusative			
Ablative			
Vocative			
Plural			
Nominative			
Genitive			
Dative			
Accusative			
Ablative			
Vocative			

3D. Give the requested forms for the following nouns.

Noun	Requested Form	Latin Form
imperium	Nominative singular	
soror	Nominative plural	
regnum	Ablative singular	
frāter	Vocative plural	
rex	Genitive plural	
corpus	Dative plural	
urbs	Genitive singular	
scelus	Accusative singular	
pater	Dative singular	
ignis	Accusative plural	

3E. Identify the following noun forms by declension, case, number, and gender. For ambiguous forms, give all possibilities.

Latin Form	Decl.	Case	No.	Gender
regnum (3 answers)				
nōminis				
capitī				
patrem				
corpore				
frātrum				
rēgēs (3 answers)				
scelerum				
imperia (3 answers)				

Latin Form	Decl.	Case	No.	Gender
populōrum				
sorōribus (2 answers)				
urbium				
uxor (2 answers)				
nōmina (3 answers)				
puellā				

3F. Keeping the same case, convert the singular forms to plural and the plural forms to singular.

Form	Case and No.	Conversion
sorōrum		
mātribus (2 cases)		
ignem		
frātrī		
scelera (3 cases)		
capitis		
urbīs		
regnī		
rex (2 cases)		
imperiō (2 cases)		

3G. Identify the declension of the following adjectives and give the requested forms.

Adjective	Decl.	Requested Form	Latin Form
dēvius, -a, -um		Vocative singular masculine	
virilis, -ē		Accusative plural neuter	
sollicitus, -a, -um		Genitive singular feminine	
infēlix (infēlicis)		Ablative singular masculine	
fatens (fatentis)		Dative plural feminine	
insons (insontis)		Nominative singular feminine	
exsanguis, -e		Genitive plural masculine	
gelidus, -a, -um		Ablative plural neuter	
trahens (trahentis)		Dative singular neuter	
immensus, -a, -um		Accusative singular masculine	
cupidus, -a, -um		Nominative singular feminine	
infēlix (infēlīcis)		Vocative singular masculine	
insons (insontis)		Accusative plural neuter	
violātus, -a, -um		Dative plural feminine	
ūniversus, -a, -um		Ablative singular masculine	
rēgius, -a, -um		Genitive singular feminine	
fatens (-entis)		Dative singular neuter	
sollicitus, -a, -um		Ablative plural neuter	
virīlis, -e		Accusative singular masculine	

3H. Give the correct form of the specified adjective to modify each of the following nouns. Translate the resulting phrases.

Noun	Case, No., Gender	Adjective	Latin Form	Translation
agrī (plural)		**omnis**		
poētam		**Rōmānus**		
puellārum		**brevis**		
urbem		**bonus**		
nōminibus		**magnus**		
frātrēs (Acc.)		**malus**		
patrēs (Nom.)		**noster**		
imperiō (Dat.)		**tuus**		
corpus		**miser**		
uxōrī		**certus**		
populōs		**vester**		
regnum		**longus**		

3I. Conjugate the following verbs in the present tense. Translate each form.

verb: **regnō, -āre, -āvī, -ātus**: reign, rule

conjugation _____

PRESENT	Latin	Translation
Singular		
1st		
2nd		
3rd		
Plural		
1st		
2nd		
3rd		

verb: **condō, -ere, condidī, conditus**: build, found, establish

conjugation _____

PRESENT	Latin	Translation
Singular		
1st		
2nd		
3rd		
Plural		
1st		
2nd		
3rd		

verb: **exiliō, -īre, -uī**: jump out

conjugation _____

PRESENT	Latin	Translation
Singular		
1st		
2nd		
3rd		
Plural		
1st		
2nd		
3rd		

3J. Translate the following sentences into Latin. Use the rubric below each sentence as a guide.

The body is big, the mind good.

Person and number of "is" _____

Latin present tense ending _____

Dictionary entry _____

Latin translation of verb _____

Is "body" a subject or direct object? _____

Case, number, and gender of "body" _____

Dictionary entry _____

Declension _____

Latin translation of "body" _____

What English noun does "big" modify? _____

Case, number, and gender of "big" _____

Dictionary entry _____

Declension _____

Latin translation of "big" _____

Is "mind" a subject or direct object? _____

Case, number, and gender of "mind" _____

Dictionary entry _____

Declension _____

Latin translation of "mind" _____

What English noun does "good" modify? _____

Case, number, and gender of "good" _____

Dictionary entry _____

Declension _____

Latin translation of "good" _____

Latin translation of entire sentence _____

_____

I endorse my brother as king.

Person and number of "I endorse" _____

Latin present tense ending _____

Dictionary entry _____

Conjugation _____

Latin translation of verb _____

Is "brother" a subject or direct object? _____

Case, number, and gender of "brother" _____

Dictionary entry _____

Declension _____

Latin translation of "brother" _____

What English noun does "my" modify? _____

Case, number, and gender of "my" _____

Dictionary entry _____

Declension _____

Latin translation of "my" _____

Syntactic function of "king" _____

Case, number, and gender of "king" _____

Dictionary entry _____

Declension _____

Latin translation of "king" _____

Latin translation of entire sentence _____

_____

3K. A limerick to translate.

Habent lupam duō puerī

mātrem. Ūnā habitant laetī.

Sē vocant misera

nōmina et mala.

Nunc ūnus est rex omnis regnī.

Notes: **lupa, -ae**, f: wolf; **duō**: two; **puer, puerī**, m: boy; **ūnā**: together; **laetus, -a, -um**: happy; **sē**: each other; **nunc**: now; **ūnus, -a, -um**: one.

Vocative Case, Imperatives, and Personal Pronouns

4A. Decline the following noun-adjective pairs.

Case	modus, -ī, m + dulcis, -e	opus, operis, n + doctus, -a, -um	Mūsa, -ae, f + tener, tenera, tenerum
Singular			
Nominative			
Genitive			
Dative			
Accusative			
Ablative			
Vocative			
Plural			
Nominative			
Genitive			
Dative			
Accusative			
Ablative			
Vocative			

4B. Give the requested forms of the following nouns.

Noun	Requested Form	Latin Form
opus	Accusative singular	
puer	Vocative singular	
virgō	Ablative singular	
libellus	Vocative singular	
modus	Genitive plural	
praesidium	Nominative plural	
lingua	Dative plural	
amor	Vocative plural	
verbum	Genitive singular	
carmen	Dative singular	
decus	Accusative plural	
Mūsa	Ablative plural	

4C. Give the correct form of the specified adjective to modify each of the following nouns. Translate the resulting phrases.

Noun	Case, No., Gender	Adjective	Latin Form	Translation
amor (Vocative)		novus		
amor (Nominative)		magnus		
puerō (Dative)		doctus		
verbō (Ablative)		sanctus		
carminum		sacer		
Rōmae (Genitive)		noster		
virginēs (Vocative)		tener		
opere		gravis		
decoribus (2 cases)		meus		
libellōs		dulcis		

4D. Identify the following noun forms by declension, case, number, and gender. For ambiguous forms, give all possibilities. Give the correct form of **novus, -a, -um** and **gravis, -e** to modify each form.

Latin Form	Decl.	Case	No.	Gender	novus, -a, -um	gravis, -e
decus (3 answers)						
linguā						
libellō (2 answers)						
praesidiī						
puer (2 answers)						
verbīs (2 answers)						
carmina (3 answers)						
decore						
virginēs (3 answers)						
puerī (3 answers)						
libellōrum						
dīs (2 answers)						

4E. Conjugate the following verbs in the present tense. Translate each form.

verb: **moveō, -ēre, mōvī, mōtus**: move

conjugation _____

PRESENT	Latin	Translation
Singular		
1st		
2nd		
3rd		
Imperative		
Plural		
1st		
2nd		
3rd		
Imperative		

verb: **dīcō, -ere, dixī, dictus**: say, speak (of), mention, call, appoint

conjugation _____

PRESENT	Latin	Translation
Singular		
1st		
2nd		
3rd		
Imperative		
Plural		
1st		
2nd		
3rd		
Imperative		

4F. Give the person, number, and mood of the following verbs. Translate each form.

	Person	No.	Mood	Translation
premō				
dīcunt				
sumus				
movet				
scītis				
audīs				
cape				
mittunt				
facite				
vīvimus				
rogās				
gerit				
agitis				
habētis				

4G. Give the requested forms of the following verbs. Translate each form.

Verb	Requested Form	Latin Form	Translation
premō	3rd person singular		
dīcō	singular Imperative		
cantō	2nd person plural		
moveō	singular Imperative		
rogō	2nd person singular		
vocō	plural Imperative		
agō	Infinitive		
gerō	1st person plural		
faciō	3rd person plural		
sum	Infinitive		
fugiō	plural Imperative		
videō	1st person singular		

4H. Translate the following English phrases into Latin.

1. of consecrated works _____

2. a clever maiden (Nominative) _____

3. for a delicate boy _____

4. with a sweet song _____

5. for our defenses _____

6. sacred words (Accusative) _____

7. She hears a new little book. _____

8. Rome knows the works of the Muses. _____

9. We speak of love and also glory. _____

10. Just now you (plural) control the defenses. _____

4I. Translate the following sentences into coherent English.

1. Et puerī et puellae carmina dulcia cantant.

   _____

2. Matre cum tuā dīc, ō male vir.

   _____

3. Ā certīs praesidiīs virginēs Rōmānās modo absolvitis.

   _____

4. Ō rex brevis, bella magna diū gerimus.

   _____

5. Cūr opera misera hīc nōn relinquis, ō poēta?

   _____

6. Omnēs in patriam mittite.

   _____

7. Rex in regnō cum uxōre habitat.

   _____

8. Ō Mūsa sacra, ā marī fuge.

   _____

4J. Translate the following sentences into Latin. Use the rubric below each sentence as a guide.

O mothers, be good!

Syntactic function of "mothers" _____

Case, number, and gender of "mothers" _____

Dictionary entry _____

Declension _____

Latin translations of "mothers" _____

Is "be" an indicative or imperative verb? _____

Dictionary entry _____

Latin translation of "be" (note the number) _____

_____

What implied noun does "good" modify? _____

Case, number, and gender of "good" _____

Dictionary entry _____

Declension _____

Latin translation of "good" _____

Latin translation of entire sentence _____

_____

Sing (singular) sweet words!

Is "sing" an indicative or imperative verb? _____

Dictionary entry _____

Latin translation of "sing" _____

Is "words" a subject or direct object? _____

Case, number, and gender of "words" _____

Dictionary entry _____

Declension _____

Latin translation of "words" _____

What English word does "sweet" modify? _____

Case, number, and gender of "sweet" _____

Dictionary entry _____

Declension _____

Latin translation of "sweet" _____

Latin translation of entire sentence _____

_____

4K. Fill in the blanks with correctly formed Latin words from *NLP* 1–4 required vocabulary. You may use each word only once. There is no "right" answer.

Dī magnī! (*accusative noun*) _____

(*accusative adjective*) _____

diū (*1st person plural verb*) _____.

Nunc aut (*accusative noun*) _____

aut (*accusative noun*) _____

(*1st person plural verb*) _____.

Sed populī Rōmānī ad (*accusative noun*) _____

cum (*ablative noun*) _____

(*3rd person plural verb*) _____.

Genitive Case

5A. Decline the following noun-adjective pairs.

Case	fīlia, –iae, f + brevis, -e	regnum, -ī, n + sacer, sacra, sacrum	multitūdō, multitūdinis, f + tantus, -a, -um
Singular			
Nominative			
Genitive			
Dative			
Accusative			
Ablative			
Vocative			
Plural			
Nominative			
Genitive			
Dative			
Accusative			
Ablative			
Vocative			

5B. Give the requested forms of the following nouns.

Noun	Requested Form	Latin Form
pars	Ablative plural	
consilium	Genitive singular	
iuvenis	Accusative singular	
frons	Dative plural	
coniunx	Vocative singular	
dux	Vocative plural	
castitās	Ablative singular	
fīlia	Accusative plural	
multitūdō	Dative singular	
dolor	Genitive plural	

5C. Give the correct form of the specified adjective to modify each of the following nouns. Translate the resulting phrases.

Noun	Case, No., Gender	Adjective	Latin Form	Translation
castitātem		multus		
ducī		tantus		
multitūdinum		novus		
dolōribus (2 cases)		vester		
consiliō (Dative)		dulcis		
modō (Ablative)		brevis		
iuvenēs (Nominative)		doctus		
frontēs (Accusative)		tener		
pars (2 cases)		meus		
fīlia (2 cases)		gravis		

5D. Identify the following noun forms by declension, case, number, and gender. For ambiguous forms, give all possibilities. Give the correct form of **tantus, -a, -um** and **brevis, -e** to modify each form.

Latin Form	Decl.	Case	No.	Gender	tantus, -a, -um	brevis, -e
amōrī						
capita (3)						
bellī						
linguae (4)						
animus						
urbium						
fātō (2)						

5E. Conjugate the following verbs in the present tense. Translate each form.

verb: **putō, -āre, -āvī, -ātus**
conjugation _____

PRESENT	Latin	Translation
Singular		
1st		
2nd		
3rd		
Imperative		
Plural		
1st		
2nd		
3rd		
Imperative		

verb: **scrībō, -ere, scrīpsī, scrīptus**

conjugation_____

PRESENT	Latin	Translation
Singular		
1st		
2nd		
3rd		
Imperative		
Plural		
1st		
2nd		
3rd		
Imperative		

5F. Give the person, number, and mood of the following verbs. Translate each form. (N.B. Infinitives do not have person and number—just translate them!)

Form	Person	No.	Mood	Translation
condemnāre				
scrībite!				
colis				
venīre				
mittis				
scrībunt				
putā!				
es				
condemnō				
venīmus				
sum				
putat				
esse				
mittitis				

5G. Give the requested forms of the following verbs. Translate each form.

Verb	Requested Form	Latin Form	Translation
condemnō	singular Imperative		
putō	1st person plural		
colō	2nd person plural		
scrībō	plural Imperative		
veniō	3rd person plural		
dīcō	2nd person singular		
agō	3rd person singular		
sum	1st person plural		
faciō	Infinitive		
audiō	1st person singular		

5H. Translate the following English phrases into Latin.

1. of such great leaders (feminine) _____

2. for spouses _____

3. on behalf of chastity _____

4. for the sake of grief _____

5. out of the city _____

6. You (plural) now write. _____

7. She just now cultivates. _____

8. to consider _____

9. I think for a long time. _____

10. We come nevertheless. _____

5I. Translate the following sentences into coherent English.

1. Consilium rēgis magnum audītis.

   _____

2. Dux populōrum Rōmānōrum bellum gerit.

   _____

3. Prō praesidiō urbis tantīs cum iuvenibus venīmus.

   _____

4. Fīlia castitātis tantae deōs colit.

   _____

5. Puellās scelerum dulcēs omnium nōn iam condemnātis.

   _____

6. Libellōs ducis vestrī malōs putāmus.

   _____

7. Poēta mātris miserae patriam relinquit.

   _____

8. Multitūdō patrum undās maris sacrās pugnat.

   _____

9. Pars puerōrum magna carmina gravia cantat.

   _____

10. Ō puer bone, docta Mūsārum verba decōris grātiā dīc.

   _____

5J. Translate the following sentences into Latin. Use the rubric below each sentence as a guide.

For the sake of your wife you (singular) are cultivating love.

Latin word for "for the sake of" _____

Case taken by this word _____

Case, number, and gender of "wife" _____

Dictionary entry _____

Declension _____

Latin translation of "wife" _____

Person and number of "you are cultivating" _____

Dictionary entry _____

Conjugation _____

Latin translation of "you are cultivating" _____

Syntactic function of "love" _____

Case, number, and gender of Latin "love" _____

Dictionary entry _____

Declension _____

Latin translation of "love" _____

Latin translation of the entire sentence _____

_____

They do not consider virtue worth so much.

Person and number of "they consider" _____

Dictionary entry _____

Conjugation _____

Latin translation of "they consider" _____

Latin translation of "not" _____

Syntactic function of "virtue" _____

Case, number, and gender of Latin "virtue" _____

Dictionary entry _____

Declension _____

Latin noun translation of "virtue" _____

"worth so much" = "of so great a (value)"

Case that renders "of" _____

Adjective that means "so great" _____

Latin translation of "worth so much" _____

Latin translation of entire sentence _____

_____

5K. Give the Latin forms for the following English phrases. Then recombine the **double-underlined** letters to spell the name of one of Rome's most celebrated mothers.

for the sake of the spouse: __ __ __ __ __ __ __ __

__ __ __ __ __ __

we condemn: __ __ __ __ __ __ __ __ __ __

many youths (Accusative): __ __ __ __ __ __ __

__ __ __ __ __ __

of so great a plan: __ __ __ __ __ __ __ __

__ __ __ __ __

ANSWER: __ __ __ __ __ __ __ __

LESSON 6

Dative Case

6A. Decline the following noun-adjective pairs.

Case	genus, generis, n + amīcus, -a, -um	virtūs, virtūtis, f + sacer, sacra, sacrum
Singular		
Nominative		
Genitive		
Dative		
Accusative		
Ablative		
Vocative		
Plural		
Nominative		
Genitive		
Dative		
Accusative		
Ablative		
Vocative		

6B. Give the requested forms of the following nouns.

Noun	Requested Form	Latin Form
terra	Nominative singular	
vox	Genitive plural	
fortūna	Ablative plural	
genus	Nominative plural	
color	Ablative plural	
Dīs	Accusative singular	
mānēs	Vocative plural	
caelum	Dative plural	
mors	Genitive singular	
virtūs	Dative singular	

6C. Give the correct form of the specified adjective to modify each of the following nouns. Translate the resulting phrases.

Noun	Case, No., Gender	Adjective	Latin Form	Translation
terrās		similis		
genera (3)		omnis		
Dītī		sacer		
mānium		noster		
vōcēs (3)		amīcus		
vōcem		gravis		
morte		alius		
virtūtibus (2)		levis		
fortūnārum		tantus		
color		certus		

6D. Conjugate the following verbs in the present tense. Translate each form.

verb: **imperō, -āre, -āvī, -ātus**
conjugation _____

PRESENT	Latin	Translation
Singular		
1st		
2nd		
3rd		
Imperative		
Plural		
1st		
2nd		
3rd		
Imperative		

verb: **crēdō, -ere, crēdidī, crēditus**
conjugation _____

PRESENT	Latin	Translation
Singular		
1st		
2nd		
3rd		
Imperative		
Plural		
1st		
2nd		
3rd		
Imperative		

6E. Give the person, number, and mood of the following verbs. Translate each form. (N.B. Infinitives do not have person and number—just translate those forms!)

Form	Person	No.	Mood	Translation
commendātis				
legunt				
imperā!				
crēdere				
gerite!				
habēs				
agō				
colimus				
docet				
fac!				

6F. Give the requested forms of the following verbs. Translate each form.

Verb	Requested Form	Latin Form	Translation
vīvō	2nd person plural		
commendō	3rd person plural		
imperō	1st person singular		
legō	2nd person singular		
sciō	plural Imperative		
moveō	1st person plural		
crēdō	3rd person singular		
habeō	Infinitive		

6G. Translate the following English phrases into Latin.

1. without fortune _____

2. above the sky _____

3. to/for lineage _____

4. (a man) friendly to the land _____

5. (a thing) similar to death _____

6. voice (Nominative) of the spirits of the dead _____

7. She trusts virtue. _____

8. We command the brothers. _____

9. Give (singular) protection to the mother! _____

10. for the sake of death _____

6H. Translate the following sentences into coherent English.

1. Vīnum mātrī vestrae etiam dātis.

   _____

2. Rex ergō urbem patriae similem capit.

   _____

3. Sorōrī sīc multī frātrēs sunt.

   _____

4. Virtūtem et vītae et mortī legimus.

   _____

5. Mānēs namque puellīs puerīsque tenerīs amīcī sunt.

   _____

6. Virginibus Rōmānīs crēdō.

   _____

7. Dux malus quoque iuvenibus omnibus imperat.

   _____

8. Poēta enim carmina multitūdinī cantat.

   _____

9. Mors miserīs virīs bonō est.

   _____

10. Sī bellum geris, deinde populīs malō opus est.

   _____

6I. Translate the following sentences into Latin. Use the rubric below each sentence as a guide.

Sister, give your brother weapons.

Syntactic function of "sister" _____

Case, number, and gender of "sister" _____

Dictionary entry _____

Declension _____

Latin translation of "sister" _____

Is "give" an indicative or imperative verb? _____

Singular or plural _____

Dictionary entry _____

Conjugation _____

Latin translation of "give" _____

Syntactic function of "brother" _____

Case, number, and gender of "brother" _____

Dictionary entry _____

Declension _____

Latin translation of "brother" _____

What English word does "your" modify? _____

Case, number, and gender of "your" _____

Dictionary entry _____

Declension _____

Latin translation of "your" _____

Syntactic function of "weapons" _____

Case, number, and gender of "weapons" _____

Dictionary entry _____

Declension _____

Latin translation of "weapons" _____

Latin translation of entire sentence _____

_____

I entrust the protection of the city to wretched men (substantive).

Person and number of "I entrust" _____

Dictionary entry _____

Conjugation _____

Latin translation of "I entrust" _____

Syntactic function of "protection" _____

Case, number, and gender of "protection" _____

Dictionary entry _____

Declension _____

Latin translation of "protection" _____

Syntactic function of "of the city" _____

Case, number, and gender of "of the city" _____

Dictionary entry _____

Declension _____

Latin translation of "of the city" _____

Syntactic function of "to wretched men" _____

Case, number, and gender of "to wretched men" _____

Dictionary entry _____

Declension _____

Latin translation of "to wretched men" _____

Latin translation of entire sentence _____

_____

6J. Give the Latin forms for the following English phrases. Then recombine the **double-underlined** letters to spell the name of the Roman "Halloween."

Pluto has: __ __ __   __ __ __ __ __

a painful land: __ __ __ __ __ __   __ __ __ __ __ __

(and) he commands: __ __ __ __ __ __ __

many crowds: __ __ __ __ __ __ __ __ __ __ __

__ __ __ __ __ __

ANSWER: __ __ __ __ __ __ __

NLP Review A (Lessons 1–6)

I: CONCEPTS

IA: Latin Verbs: Present Tense.

- Latin verbs fall into one of four conjugations.
- A verb's conjugation is determined from the verb's infinitive ending: *-āre, -ēre, -ere, -īre.*
- A verb's stem is found by dropping the infinitive ending.

Conjugation	Verb	Infinitive Ending	Stem
First	**amāre**: to like, love	**-āre**	**am-**
Second	**docēre**: to teach, instruct	**-ēre**	**doc-**
Third	**mittere**: to send, let go	**-ere**	**mitt-**
Third (-io)	**capere**: to take, seize, capture	**-ere**	**cap-**
Fourth	**audīre**: to hear	**-īre**	**aud-**

- Verb endings reflect person and number:

Person	Singular	Plural
1st	**-ō/-m**	**-mus**
2nd	**-s**	**-tis**
3rd	**-t**	**-nt**

- Review the irregular verb *sum, esse*:

Person	Singular	Plural
1st	su**m**: I am	su**mus**: we are
2nd	es: you are	es**tis**: you (all) are
3rd	es**t**: he/she/it is	su**nt**: they are

- Most Latin verbs have four principal parts:

amō	I love	1st person singular, present tense
amāre	to love	present active infinitive
amāvī	I have loved, I loved	1st person singular, perfect tense (action is completed)
amātus, -a, -um	having been loved	perfect passive participle (a verbal adjective)

- Review the tables in *NLP* 1 for the connecting vowels of each conjugation (*a, e, i/u, i/iu, i/iu*).
- **IMPERATIVES** express commands. Review the following table (*NLP* 4):

Verb	Singular	Plural	Translation
amō, amāre	**amā**	**amāte**	love!
doceō, docēre	**docē**	**docēte**	teach!
mittō, mittere	**mitte**	**mittite**	send!
capiō, capere	**cape**	**capite**	take!
audiō, audīre	**audī**	**audīte**	listen!

- Review the following **IRREGULAR IMPERATIVES** of very common verbs:

Verb	Singular	Plural	Translation
dicō, dicere	**dīc**	**dīcite**	speak!
dūcō, dūcere	**dūc**	**dūcite**	lead!
faciō, facere	**fac**	**facite**	make! do!
ferō, ferre	**fer**	**ferte**	carry!
sum, esse	**es**	**este**	be!

IB: Latin Nouns.

- Latin nouns have case, number, and gender.
- Gender must be memorized with the noun.
- Latin nouns fall into one of five declensions.
- A noun's declension is found by looking at the genitive singular ending.
- A noun's stem is found by dropping the genitive singular ending (many nouns, especially in the third declension, feature stem changes).

Declension	Noun	Genitive Ending	Stem
1st	**puella, -ae**, f	**-ae**	**puell-**
2nd	**annus, -ī**, m	**-ī**	**ann-**
3rd	**māter, mātris**, f	**-is**	**mātr-**
4th	**lacus, -ūs**, m	**-ūs**	**lac-**
5th	**rēs, - eī**, f	**-eī**	**r-**

- A noun's function in its sentence is determined by case endings:

Case	1st Decl. f/m		2nd Decl. m/f [n]		3rd Decl. m/f [n]	
	Sing.	Pl.	Sing.	Pl.	Sing.	Pl.
Nominative	**-a**	**-ae**	**-us/-r [-um]**	**-ī [-a]**	(varies)	**-ēs [-a/-ia]**
Genitive	**-ae**	**-ārum**	**-ī**	**-ōrum**	**-is**	**-um/-ium**
Dative	**-ae**	**-īs**	**-ō**	**-īs**	**-ī**	**-ibus**
Accusative	**-am**	**-ās**	**-um**	**-ōs [-a]**	**-em** (varies)	**-īs/-ēs [-a/-ia]**
Ablative	**-ā**	**-īs**	**-ō**	**-īs**	**-e/-ī**	**-ibus**
Vocative	**-a**	**-ae**	**-e/-r [-um]**	**-ī [-a]**	(varies)	**-ēs [-a/-ia]**

- A noun or adjective can be in apposition with (or rename) another noun in the same case (often triggered by verbs of calling or naming).

IC: Case Uses (an expanded synopsis of cases appears in Review Lesson B).

NOMINATIVE			
Syntax	**What It Does**	**What to Look For**	**Simple Examples**
Subject	performs the action of the verb		**Frāter sorōrem vīdet.** The <u>brother</u> sees his sister.
Predicate	explains the subject	to be (=)	**Puer est <u>bonus</u>.** The boy is <u>good</u>.

GENITIVE			
"modifies" another noun; "of"			
Genitive of Possession	ownership		**puerī** soror the <u>boy's</u> sister
Subjective Genitive	acts on the noun it modifies	genitive **depends** on noun with implied verbal quality	opus **puellae** the work <u>of the girl</u> (the girl **does** the work)
Objective Genitive	receives "action" of noun it depends on	genitive **depends** on noun with implied verbal quality	amor **libellī** love <u>of a little book</u> (the little book **receives** the love)
Partitive Genitive	part of the whole	genitive **depends** on a number/quantity	multitūdō **puellārum** a crowd <u>of girls</u>
Genitive of Value/ Worth (not very common)	gives value or expresses esteem	genitive **is** a number/quantity	nōmen **magnī** a name <u>of great value</u>
Genitive of Material/Quality	explains "stuff" things are made of	genitive is a physical material or abstract quality	populus **virtūtis** a people <u>of virtue</u>
Genitive of Charge	expresses an accusation or charge	genitive **depends** on a litigious verb; genitive **is** a crime	**Vōs surreptiōnis condemnāmus.** We condemn you <u>of stealing.</u>
Genitive with Special Verbs/ Adjectives	completes special verb/adjective (e.g., remembering, forgetting …)	(+ genitive) in vocabulary entry	**līberī laudis dignī** children **worthy** <u>of praise</u>
DATIVE			
"to/for"			
Indirect Object (I.O.)	indirectly affected by the verb	verb of giving/ saying	**Puer sorōrī libellum dat.** The boy gives a little book <u>to his sister.</u>
Dative of Reference	dative is a person, someone benefiting from or harmed by an action		**Puer sorōrī bellum gerit.** The boy wages war <u>for his sister.</u>

Dative of Purpose	explains purpose of an action or a point of view		**Puer <u>praesidiō</u> bellum gerit.** The boy wages war <u>for</u> (the purpose of) <u>protection</u>.
Double Dative	datives of reference and purpose in the same clause		**Puer <u>sorōrī</u> <u>praesidiō</u> bellum gerit.** The boy wages war <u>**as a protection**</u> <u>for his sister</u>.
Dative of Possession	expresses ownership/ possession	some form of *esse* dative is a person	**Libellus <u>puellae</u> est.** <u>The girl</u> has a little book. (literally: There is a little book to/for the girl.)
Dative with Special Adjectives	completes some adjectives (kind, friendly, dear, pleasing, hostile, near)		**puer <u>sorōrī</u> <u>amīcus</u>** a boy <u>**friendly**</u> <u>to his sister</u>
Dative with Special Verbs	completes some verbs (favor, help, please, trust, believe, persuade, obey, command, serve, resist, pardon, threaten, spare)	technically an I.O. D.O. is inherent in the verb (e.g., the verb can have the sense of a noun)	**Puer <u>sorōrī</u> <u>crēdit</u>.** The boy <u>**trusts**</u> his <u>sister</u>. (i.e., The boy has/shows trust in his sister.)
Dative with Compound Verbs	prefix (*ad-, ante-, con-, in-, inter-, ob-, post-, prae-, pro-, sub-,* or *super-*) + verb	dative is like an I.O.	**Puer <u>sorōrī</u> <u>imperat</u>.** The boys <u>**commands**</u> his <u>sister</u>. (i.e., The boy gives a command to his sister.)
<td colspan="3" align="center">**ACCUSATIVE**</td>
Direct Object (D.O.)	receives the action of the verb		**Frāter <u>sorōrem</u> vīdet.** The brother sees his <u>sister</u>.
Accusative with Some Prepositions	*ad, in, per*		<u>**ad**</u> <u>**urbem**</u> <u>to</u> <u>the city</u>
<td colspan="3" align="center">**ABLATIVE** "by/with/from/because of"</td>
Ablative with Some Prepositions	*ā/ab, cum, dē, ē/ex, in, prō, sine*		**Frāter <u>cum</u> <u>sorōre</u> venit.** The brother comes <u>**with**</u> his <u>sister</u>.
<td colspan="3" align="center">**VOCATIVE** "hey you! yo! on deck! O!"</td>
Direct Address		imperative or 2nd person verb	**Ō puella! Ō puer bone!**

ID: Adjectives.

- Adjectives have case, number, and gender.
- An adjective agrees with the noun it modifies in case, number, and gender.
- Adjectives fall into two categories: one with first/second declension endings and one with third declension endings.
- The category can be determined by looking at the adjective's dictionary ending.
  - if -US/-R, -A, -UM, then the adjective is <u>1st/2nd</u> declension:
    - **bonus** (m), **bona** (f), **bonum** (n)
    - **pulcher** (m), **pulchra** (f), **pulchrum** (n)
      - 2nd declension *masculine* endings modify **masculine** nouns
      - 1st declension *feminine* endings modify **feminine** nouns
      - 2nd declension *neuter* endings modify **neuter** nouns
    - to find the stem, drop the nominative ending from the feminine or neuter form (*pulchr-*)
  - if <u>not</u> -US/-R, -A, -UM, then the adjective is <u>3rd</u> declension:
    - **ācer** (m), **acris** (f), **acre** (n): sharp, fierce (three terminations/ endings)
    - **brevis** (m/f), **breve** (n): small, short (two terminations)
    - **potens** (-entis) (m/f/n): strong, powerful (one termination)
    - to find the stem, drop the nominative ending from the feminine or neuter form of triple and double termination adjectives (*acr-*, *brev-*). Drop the genitive ending from single termination adjectives (*potent-*).

Case	1st Decl. f		2nd Decl. m [n]		3rd Decl. m/f [n]	
	Singular	Plural	Singular	Plural	Singular	Plural
Nominative	-a	-ae	-us/-r [-um]	-ī [-a]	(varies)	-ēs [-a/-ia]
Genitive	-ae	-ārum	-ī	-ōrum	-is	-um/-ium
Dative	-ae	-īs	-ō	-īs	-ī	-ibus
Accusative	-am	-ās	-um	-ōs [-a]	-em [varies]	-īs/-ēs [-a/-ia]
Ablative	-ā	-īs	-ō	-īs	-e/-ī	-ibus
Vocative	-a	-ae	-e/-r [-um]	-ī [-a]	(varies)	-ēs [-a/-ia]

- A **SUBSTANTIVE** is an adjective that functions as a noun (e.g., *bona*: "goods," "property").

IE: Pronouns.

- Pronouns take the place of nouns.
- Pronouns agree with their referents in **number** and **gender** but take their cases according to how they function in their own phrases.
- **PERSONAL PRONOUNS** refer to specific people.

Case	Singular (I/me)	Plural (we/us)	Singular (you)	Plural (you)
Nominative	ego	nōs	tū	vōs
Genitive	meī	nostrum (nostrī)	tuī	vestrum (vestrī)
Dative	mihi (mihī, mī)	nōbīs	tibi (tibī)	vōbīs
Accusative	mē	nōs	tē	vōs
Ablative	mē	nōbīs	tē	vōbīs

II: VOCABULARY *NLP* 1–6

NOUNS

fēmina, -ae, f: woman

fīlia, -iae, f: daughter

fortūna, -ae, f: fortune

lingua, -ae, f: tongue, language

Mūsa, -ae, f: Muse, a goddess of artistic inspiration

patria, -iae, f: fatherland, country

poēta, -ae, m: poet

puella, -ae, f: girl

Rōma, -ae, f: the city of Rome

terra, -ae, f: land

unda, -ae, f: water, stream, wave

vīta, -ae, f: life

ager, agrī, m: field

animus, -ī, m: soul, mind

annus, -ī, m: year

arma, -ōrum, n (plural): arms, weapons

bellum, -ī, n: war (**bellum gerere**: to wage war)

caelum, -ī, n: sky

consilium, -iī, n: plan, counsel, good judgment, advice

deus, -ī, m: god

imperium, -iī, n: command, dominion, power

libellus, -ī, m: little book

modus, -ī, m: way, method, measure, rhythm

populus, -ī, m: people

praesidium, -iī, n: defense, protection, guard

puer, puerī, m: boy

regnum, -ī, n: kingdom, realm, sovereignty

verbum, -ī, n: word

vīnum, -ī, n: wine

vir, virī, m: man, husband

amor, -ōris, m: love

caput, capitis, n: head

carmen, carminis, n: song, poem

castitās, -ātis, f: chastity, virtue

color, -ōris, m: color, hue, complexion

coniunx, coniugis, m/f: spouse,
  husband, wife

corpus, corporis, n: body

decus, decoris, n: honor, glory

Dīs, Dītis, m: Pluto, god of the underworld

dolor, -ōris, m: pain, grief

dux, ducis, m/f: leader, general

frāter, frātris, m: brother

frons, frontis (-ium), m: brow, forehead

genus, generis, n: origin, lineage, kind

ignis, -is (-ium), m: fire

iuvenis, -is, m: youth, young man

mānēs, -ium, m (plural): spirits of the
  dead

mare, -is (-ium), n: sea

māter, mātris, f: mother

mors, mortis (-ium), f: death

multitūdō, multitūdinis, f: multitude,
  number, crowd

nōmen, nōminis, n: name

opus, operis, n: work, task, labor

pars, partis (-ium), f: part

pater, patris, m: father, senator

rex, rēgis, m: king

scelus, sceleris, n: crime

soror, sorōris, f: sister

urbs, urbis (-ium), f: city

uxor, -ōris, f: wife

virgō, virginis, f: maiden, virgin

virtūs, virtūtis, f: valor, manliness,
  virtue

vox, vōcis, f: voice

nihil: nothing

ADJECTIVES

alius, alia, aliud: other, another
  (aliī ... aliī: some ... others)

amīcus, -a, -um: friendly (+ dative)
  (amīcus, -ī, m and amīca, -ae, f:
  friend)

bonus, -a, -um: good; bona, -ōrum, n
  (plural): goods, possessions
  (substantive)

certus, -a, -um: certain, resolved,
  decided

doctus, -a, -um: learned, clever

longus, -a, -um: long, vast, spacious

magnus, -a, -um: great

malus, -a, -um: bad, evil

meus, mea, meum: mine

miser, misera, miserum: wretched,
  unhappy, miserable

multus, -a, -um: great, many

noster, nostra, nostrum: our

novus, -a, -um: new

Rōmānus, -a, -um: Roman

sacer, sacra, sacrum: holy, consecrated,
  accursed

sanctus, -a, -um: holy, sacred, blameless

tantus, -a, -um: so great, so much

tener, tenera, tenerum: delicate, tender,
  soft

tuus, tua, tuum: your (singular)

vester, vestra, vestrum: your (plural)

brevis, -e: short

dulcis, -e: sweet, pleasant

gravis, -e: heavy, serious, painful

levis, -e: light, unambitious, fickle

omnis, -e: whole, entire, every
  (singular), all (plural)

similis, -e (+ dative): like, similar

VERBS

amō, -āre, -āvī, -ātus: like, love

cantō, -āre, -āvī, -ātus: sing, play

commendō, -āre, -āvī, -ātus: commit, entrust

condemnō, -āre, -āvī, -ātus: condemn, blame, disprove

do, dare, dedī, datus: give

habitō, -āre, -āvī, -ātus: live, dwell

imperō, -āre, -āvī, -ātus (+ dative): command, control

putō, –āre, -āvī, -ātus: think, suppose, consider

rogō, -āre, -āvī, -ātus: ask, ask for, endorse

vocō, -āre, -āvī, -ātus: call, summon

doceō, -ēre, docuī, doctus: teach, instruct

habeō, -ēre, habuī, habitus: have, hold, consider, wear

moveō, -ēre, mōvī, mōtus: move

teneō, -ēre, tenuī, tentus: hold, maintain, detain

videō, -ēre, vīdī, vīsus: see, look at, watch

absolvō, -ere, -solvī, -solūtus: release (from), set free (from); complete, finish

agō, -ere, ēgī, actus: do, drive, accomplish, guide, spend, act

capiō, -ere, cēpī, captus: take, seize, capture

colō, -ere, coluī, cultus: inhabit, cultivate, worship

crēdō, -ere, crēdidī, crēditus (+ dative): believe, trust

dīcō, -ere, dixī, dictus: say, speak (of), mention, call, appoint

faciō, -ere, fēcī, factus: make, do

fugiō, -ere, fūgī: flee, escape, run away

gerō, -ere, gessī, gestus: carry on, manage, wear, endure, suffer

legō, -ere, lēgī, lectus: pick, choose, read

mittō, -ere, mīsī, missus: send, let go

premō, -ere, pressī, pressus: press, oppress, control, pursue

relinquō, -ere, relīquī, relictus: leave behind, desert, abandon

scrībō, -ere, scripsī, scriptus: write

vīvō, -ere, vixī, victus: live, be alive

audiō, -īre, -īvī, -ītus: hear

sciō, -īre, -īvī, -ītus: know

veniō, -īre, vēnī, ventus: come

sum, esse, fuī, futūrus: be

PREPOSITIONS

ā/ab (+ ablative): from, away from, by

ad (+ accusative): to, toward, for (the purpose of)

causā (+ genitive): for the sake of

cum (+ ablative): with

ē/ex (+ ablative): out of, from, on account of, by reason of

grātiā (+ genitive): for the sake of

in (+ ablative): in, on

in (+ accusative): into, onto, against

per (+ accusative): through

prō (+ ablative): in front of, for, on behalf of, in place of

sine (+ ablative): without

suprā (+ accusative): above; (as adverb: "previously," "above")

CONJUNCTIONS AND ADVERBS

ac: and in addition, and also, and

atque: and also

aut: or (**aut ... aut**: either ... or)

bene: well

deinde or **dein**: then, next

diū: for a long time

enim: for, indeed

ergō: therefore

et: and (**et ... et**: both ... and)

etiam: as yet, still, but also

hīc: here

iam: now; already (**nōn iam**: no longer)

modo: just now

nam, namque: for, indeed, really

nec: and ... not

neque: and not (**neque ... neque**: neither ... nor)

nōn: not

nunc: now

-que: and

-que ... -que: both ... and

quoque: also

sed: but

sī: if

sīc: thus, in this manner

tamen: nevertheless, nonetheless, however, but

tantum: only

III: ADDITIONAL DRILLS

IIIA. Decline the following noun-adjective pairs. Consult the glossary above for the dictionary entries.

Case	terra + gravis	regnum + similis	iuvenis + malus
Singular			
Nominative			
Genitive			
Dative			
Accusative			
Ablative			
Vocative			
Plural			
Nominative			
Genitive			
Dative			
Accusative			
Ablative			
Vocative			

IIIB. Give the requested forms of the following nouns.

Noun	Requested Form	Latin Form
pars	Nominative plural	
lingua	Ablative singular	
ager	Dative singular	
verbum	Dative plural	
genus	Accusative singular	
castitās	Nominative singular	
color	Genitive plural	
unda	Vocative plural	
puer	Ablative plural	
imperium	Genitive singular	

IIIC. Give the correct form of the specified adjective to modify each of the
following nouns. Translate the resulting phrases.

Noun	Case, No., Gender	Adjective	Latin Form	Translation
sorōrī		**certus**		
puellae (plural)		**dulcis**		
deus		**sacer**		
marium		**magnus**		
uxōrem		**doctus**		
virginibus		**noster**		
patris		**brevis**		
rēge		**novus**		
virō		**gravis**		
anime		**levis**		

IIID. Give the Latin for each of the following English phrases.

      1. a friendly man (Nominative) _____

      2. sweet life (Nominative) _____

      3. of evil voices _____

      4. your (singular) virtues (Accusative) _____

5. in a miserable land _____

6. to/for our crimes _____

7. with an accursed crowd _____

8. to/for your (plural) origin _____

9. with such great fires _____

10. of my chastity _____

11. serious plans (Nominative) _____

12. O Roman poet! _____

13. new weapons (Accusative) _____

14. to/for our grief _____

15. O great songs! _____

16. my leader (Accusative) _____

17. to/for a clever brother _____

18. of short girls _____

19. by all names _____

20. of a similar field _____

IIIE. Conjugate the following verbs. Translate each form.

verb: **cantō**

conjugation: _____

PRESENT	Latin	Translation
Singular		
1st		
2nd		
3rd		
Imperative		
Plural		
1st		
2nd		
3rd		
Imperative		

verb: **teneō**

conjugation: _____

PRESENT	Latin	Translation
Singular		
1st		
2nd		
3rd		
Imperative		
Plural		
1st		
2nd		
3rd		
Imperative		

verb: **gerō**

conjugation: _____

PRESENT	Latin	Translation
Singular		
1st		
2nd		
3rd		
Imperative		
Plural		
1st		
2nd		
3rd		
Imperative		

verb: **sciō**

conjugation: _____

PRESENT	Latin	Translation
Singular		
1st		
2nd		
3rd		
Imperative		
Plural		
1st		
2nd		
3rd		
Imperative		

IIIF. Give the person, number, and mood of the following verbs. Translate each form. (N.B. Infinitives do not have person and number—just translate those forms. Imperatives are second person, but be sure to give the number and translation for those forms.)

Form	Person	No.	Mood	Translation
amat				
movētis				
colimus				
crēde				
venīre				
habitās				
legunt				
sum				
relinquitis				
scīte				
esse				
agunt				
geris				

Form	Person	No.	Mood	Translation
mittō				
commendāre				
es				
docētis				
dīc				
videt				
fugere				
sumus				
faciunt				
capis				
scrībimus				

IIIG. Give the requested forms of the following verbs. Translate each form.

Verb	Requested Form	Latin Form	Translation
commendō	1st person singular		
sum	2nd person plural		
premō	plural Imperative		
dīcō	Infinitive		
teneō	3rd person plural		
vīvō	1st person plural		
rogō	singular Imperative		
mittō	2nd person singular		
doceō	2nd person plural		
audiō	3rd person plural		
veniō	Infinitive		
sum	3rd person singular		

Crossword Puzzle.

Across

1. Ovid's handbook on finding dates at Rome
4. A bald Roman
5. A poetess of elegant Latin verse
9. The mother of Apollo and Diana
12. One of the first consuls at Rome
14. Augustus's selfless sister
15. A prominent Roman lady who runs away with a gladiator
17. Vergil's homeland
19. He travels to the underworld to revive his dead wife
23. Scipio Africanus's famous daughter
27. The Roman king who established the city's infrastructure
28. A Roman poetess, daughter of Cicero's rhetorical rival
29. Cicero's beloved daughter
32. A Roman festival of the dead
36. "City of the Dead"
37. A bleak land on the Black Sea, the site of Ovid's exile
38. Horace's literary patron
40. Raised by a wolf, a boy who founded a great city
41. She had a dream of the "chaste" Venus
44. A place detested by Greek girls
45. The peoples whose daughters became the first Roman wives
47. The religious king at Rome
48. Rome's legal king
52. Ovid's cognomen, meaning "nose"
53. A chaste Roman
54. The Trojan settlement in Italy after the Trojan War
55. A Sabine king
56. Horace's work that includes poems of praise for Augustus
57. The girl loved by Figulus

Down

2. Her son founded the city of Rome
3. Catullus's historian friend
6. She remained loyal to her husband even after he married an Egyptian queen
7. Ovid's collection of letters from heroines to their lovers
8. Catullus's home town
10. The tree of mourning
11. A little girl mourned by Salvius and Heros
13. An impolite man in Pompeii
16. A wealthy ex-slave obsessed with his own death
18. The Trojan hero who survives the war to settle in Italy
20. An Ovidian sculptor who fell in love with a statue
21. The ferryman of the dead
22. The Roman "Halloween"
23. Endorsed as aedile by the goldsmiths of Pompeii
24. A beautiful Flavian lady with an elaborate hairdo
25. One of Catullus's favorite meters
26. A Spanish artist who illustrated Ovid's *Metamorphoses*
30. Augustus's overbearing wife
31. The study of inscriptions
33. Ovid's sad poems from exile
34. The tracks of another man were in his bed
35. One of the three things that makes life worth living
39. Ovid's hometown
41. The queen of Egypt whose children were raised by Augustus's sister
42. A napkin thief
43. She accompanied her husband on campaign in Germany and Gaul
44. A temple near the bookshop that sells Martial's poetry
46. Claudius's debauched queen
49. She was killed by her own father to protect her honor
50. Ovid's Juliet
51. Her rape caused the overthrow of the kings at Rome

IV: ADDITIONAL PASSAGES

1. Ovid, *Amores* 3.15.7. Ovid links his poetic virtuosity to the great Roman poets who preceded him. Meter: elegiac couplets (dactylic hexameter line).

Mantua Vergiliō, gaudet Vērōna Catullō.

Notes: **Mantua, -ae**, f: a town in northern Italy; **Vergilius, -iī**, m: Publius Vergilius Maro (Vergil), author of the *Aeneid*; **gaudeō, -ēre, gavīsus sum**: rejoice (in) (construe *gaudet* as the verb for both halves of the sentence); **Vērōna, -ae**, f: a town in northern Italy; **Catullus, -ī**, m: Gaius Valerius Catullus (Catullus), a prominent poet at Rome in the 50s BCE.

2. *CIL* IV 1881. Pompeii. On a basilica wall.

Virgula Tertiō suō, "Indecens es."

Notes: **Virgula, -ae**, f: a woman's name meaning a "little twig" or "divining rod"; **Tertius, -iī**, m: a man's name meaning "the third"; **suus, -a, -um**: here, "her own" (perhaps an indication that Tertius is Virgula's boyfriend); **indecens (-entis)**: unseemly, impolite.

3. Ovid, *Metamorphoses* 14.775–77. The Sabine king Titus Tatius wages war against Romulus to win back the kidnapped women (see *NLP* 3.5). Tarpeia, daughter of a Roman commander, opens the Roman citadel to the Sabine troops in return for "what the Sabine soldiers were wearing on their left arms." Tarpeia hopes to obtain their gold bracelets; instead, the soldiers kill her with their shields. Meter: dactylic hexameter.

Tatiusque patrēsque Sabīnī

bella gerunt; arcisque viā Tarpēia reclūsā

dignam animam poenā congestīs exuit armīs.

Notes: **Tatius, -iī**, m: (Titus) Tatius, the Sabine king; **Sabīnus, -a, -um**: Sabine; **arx, arcis (-ium)**, f: citadel, fortress; **viā ... reclūsā**: "the path (of the citadel) disclosed" (ablative absolute); **Tarpēia, -ae**, f: daughter of Spurius Tarpeius, commander of the citadel; **dignus, -a, -um** (+ ablative): worthy (of); **anima, -ae**, f: life, soul; **poena, -ae**, f: punishment; **congestīs armīs**: "under heaped up weapons"; **exuō, -ere, -uī, -ūtus**: release, cast off, strip off.

4. Horace, *Carmina* 3.1.1–4. Horace champions the novelty of his poems and poetic style, and he distinguishes himself from those poets who cater to the masses. Meter: Alcaic strophe.

> Ōdī profānum volgus et arceō.
> Favēte linguīs: carmina nōn prius
> > audīta Mūsārum sacerdōs
> > virginibus puerīsque cantō.

Notes: **ōdī**: "I hate" (this verb lacks regular present tense forms); **profānus, -a, -um**: impious, uninitiated; **volgus, -ī**, n: crowd, rabble (note the gender); **arceō, -ēre, -uī**: keep at a distance; **faveō, -ēre, fāvī, fautus** (+ dative): favor, support; **prius**: earlier, previously; **audītus, -a, -um**: heard, listened to; **sacerdōs, -ōtis**, m/f: priest, priestess (in apposition with the subject).

5. Vergil, *Aeneid* 11.576–77. With his daughter Camilla, Metabus escapes from his homeland while his enemies are in hot pursuit. Approaching the Amasenus river, Metabus realizes that he can not cross safely while holding the child. Attaching her to a spear, he launches Camilla across the river as he prays to Diana to keep her safe. Diana grants his request, and, as a sign of his gratitude, Metabus dresses his toddler in wild animal skins, rearing her as a huntress and devotee of the goddess. Meter: dactylic hexameter.

> Prō crīnālī aurō, prō longae tegmine pallae
> tigridis exuviae per dorsum ā vertice pendent.

Notes: **crīnālis, -e**: worn in the hair; **aurum, -ī**, n: gold; **tegmen, tegminis**, n: covering; **palla, -ae**, f: "palla," the long wide outer garment worn by Roman women; **tigris, -idis**, m/f: tiger; **exuviae, -iārum**, f (plural): skin, slough, hide; **dorsum, -ī**, n: back; **vertex, -icis**, m: summit, crown of the head; **pendō, -ere, pependī, pensus**: hang, suspend.

6. *CIL* VII 394 (= *ILS* 3155; *RIB* 842). Maryport. A cavalry unit honors the god of war.

Martī Mīlitārī coh(ors) I Baetasiōrum c(īvum) R(ōmānōrum), cui praeest U[l]pius Titiānu[s] praef(ectus), v(ōtum) s(olvit) l(ibens) l(aeta) m(eritō).

Notes: **Mars, Martis**, m: the Roman god of war; **mīlitāris, -e**: military, of war; **cohors, cohortis (-ium)**, f: troop, company, cohort; **I**: the first (cohort); **Baetasiī, -iōrum**, m (plural): a Germanic tribe who lived between the Rhine and Meuse rivers; **civis, civis (-ium)**, m/f: citizen; **cui**: "over whom" (dative singular); **praesum, -esse, -fuī** (+ dative): be in charge (of), preside (over); **Ulpius Titiānus, Ulpiī Titiānī**, m: a Roman man's name (Ulpius was the emperor Trajan's cognomen, or "last" name for distinguishing individual families within a tribe); **praefectus, -ī**, m: prefect, an officer in the Roman army; **vōtum, -ī**, n: vow, offering; **solvō, -ere, solvī, solūtus**: fulfill; **libens (-entis)**: willing, joyful; **laetus, -a, -um**: cheerful, favorable; **meritō**: deservedly, rightly.

LESSON 7

Accusative, Ablative, and Locative Cases

7A. Decline the following noun-adjective pairs.

Case	mīles, mīlitis, m + hūmānus, -a, -um	aqua, -ae, f + dulcis, -e
Singular		
Nominative		
Genitive		
Dative		
Accusative		
Ablative		
Vocative		
Plural		
Nominative		
Genitive		
Dative		
Accusative		
Ablative		
Vocative		

7B. Give the requested forms of the following nouns. Consult the required vocabulary for the dictionary entries.

Noun	Requested Form	Latin Form
aqua	Ablative singular	
animal	Vocative singular	
hostis	Genitive singular	
proelium	Genitive plural	
eques	Nominative plural	
castra	Ablative plural	
numerus	Accusative plural	
sōl	Ablative plural	
perīculum	Dative plural	
legiō	Accusative singular	

7C. Give the correct form of the specified adjective to modify each of the following nouns. Translate the resulting phrases.

Noun	Case, No., Gender	Adjective	Latin Form	Translation
equī (pl., 2)		similis		
mīles (2)		hūmānus		
tempora (3)		longus		
sermōnem		tōtus		
locō (2)		vester		
rūris		bonus		
officiīs (2)		sacer		
oppidōrum		tantus		
memoriae (sing., 2)		gravis		
signum		levis		

7D. Conjugate the following verbs. Translate each form.

verb: **accipiō, -ere, -cēpī, -ceptus**
conjugation _____

PRESENT	Latin	Translation
Singular		
1st		
2nd		
3rd		
Imperative		
Plural		
1st		
2nd		
3rd		
Imperative		

verb: **constituō, -ere, -stituī, -stitūtus**
conjugation _____

PRESENT	Latin	Translation
Singular		
1st		
2nd		
3rd		
Imperative		
Plural		
1st		
2nd		
3rd		
Imperative		

7E. Give the person, number, and mood of the following verbs. Translate each form. (N.B. Infinitives do not have person and number—just translate those forms. Imperatives are second person, but be sure to give the number and translation for those forms.)

Form	Person	No.	Mood	Translation
fuge				
scīmus				
vīvit				
rogās				
absolvunt				
movēre				
putāte				
legō				
accipis				
constitue				
commendāre				

7F. Give the requested forms of the following verbs. Translate each form.

Verb	Requested Form	Latin Form	Translation
accipiō	Infinitive		
constituō	3rd person plural		
imperō	2nd person singular		
teneō	3rd person singular		
scrībō	2nd person plural		
sum	plural Imperative		
videō	1st person plural		
vīvō	1st person singular		

7G. Translate the following English phrases into Latin. In each case you will use a Latin preposition.

1. concerning the camps _____

2. from the town _____

3. toward the enemies _____

4. with the horses _____

5. without a soldier _____

6. on account of duty _____

7. in battle _____

8. against the legions _____

9. through the countryside _____

10. above the sun _____

7H. Translate the following sentences into coherent English.

1. Imperātor nunc mīlitēs ex castrīs in proelium mittit.

_____

2. Sīc rēgī malō nōn crēdimus.

_____

3. Sorōrēs sermōnēs longōs cum patribus saepe faciunt.

_____

4. Uxōrem tuam fēminam teneram putās.

_____

5. Puella vestrō cum fīliō multōs annōs Rōmae habitat.

_____

6. Brevī tempore populī opera virtūtis magnae per oppidum constituunt.

_____

7. Ō frātrēs, hostēs tantōs fugite.

_____

8. Itaque poēta decore cum doctō dīcit.

_____

9. Ignēs colōribus multīs undique vidēmus.

_____

10. Dux urbem in miseram legiōnibus cum tōtīs bellum gerit.

_____

7I. Translate the following sentences into Latin. Use the rubric below each sentence as a guide.

We flee out the city away from the enemies with the cavalrymen.

Person and number of "we flee" _____

Dictionary entry _____

Conjugation _____

Latin translation of "we flee" _____

Preposition meaning "out of" + case taken _____

Dictionary entry of "city" _____

Declension _____

Latin translation of "out of the city" _____

Preposition meaning "away from" + case taken _____

Dictionary entry of "enemy" _____

Declension _____

Latin translation of "away from the enemies" _____

_____

Preposition meaning "with" + case taken _____

Dictionary entry of "cavalryman" _____

Declension _____

Latin translation of "with the cavalrymen" _____

Latin translation of entire sentence _____

_____

On a long journey, a horse is often a source of great danger to the soldier.

Preposition meaning "on" + case taken _____

Dictionary entry of "journey" _____

Dictionary entry of "long" _____

Latin translation of "on a long journey" _____

Latin translation of "is" _____

Syntactic function of "horse" _____

Dictionary entry of "horse" _____

Correct form of "horse" _____

Case needed for "a source of great danger" _____

Dictionary entry of "danger" _____

Dictionary entry of "great" _____

Latin translation of "a source of great danger" _____

Case needed for "to the soldier" _____

Dictionary entry of "soldier" _____

Latin translation of "to the soldier" _____

Latin translation of entire sentence _____

_____

7J. Give the Latin forms for the following English phrases. Then recombine the **double-underlined** letters to spell the name of the father of the Roman professional army.

Caesar: __ __ __ __ __ __

comes: __ __ __ __ __

to the kingdom: __ __   __ __ __ __ __ __

he cultivates: __ __ __ __ __

he abandons (it): __ __ __ __ __ __ __ __ __

ANSWER: __ __ __ __ __ __

Imperfect Tense

8A. Decline the following noun-adjective pairs.

Case	templum, -ī, n + medius, -a, -um	mens, mentis (-ium), f + pūblicus, -a, -um
Singular		
Nominative		
Genitive		
Dative		
Accusative		
Ablative		
Vocative		
Plural		
Nominative		
Genitive		
Dative		
Accusative		
Ablative		
Vocative		

8B. For each of the following nouns, select the adjective that agrees in case, number, and gender. Then translate the resulting phrases. You may use each adjective only once.

Adjective bank: **mediam, altīs, dulcīs, gravēs, omnī, pūblicā, breve, similium**

Noun	Case, No., Gender	Adjective	Translation
viā			
templum			
portae			
studiōrum			
līberī			
formās			
noctem			
mentibus			

8C. Conjugate the following verbs. Translate each form.

verb: **parō, -āre, -āvī, -ātus**

conjugation _____

PRESENT	Latin	Translation
Singular		
1st		
2nd		
3rd		
Imperative		
Plural		
1st		
2nd		
3rd		
Imperative		

parō, -āre, -āvī, -ātus

IMPERFECT	Latin	Translation
Singular		
1st		
2nd		
3rd		
Plural		
1st		
2nd		
3rd		

verb: **sūmō, -ere, sumpsī, sumptus**

conjugation _____

PRESENT	Latin	Translation
Singular		
1st		
2nd		
3rd		
Imperative		
Plural		
1st		
2nd		
3rd		
Imperative		

IMPERFECT	Latin	Translation
Singular		
1st		
2nd		
3rd		
Plural		
1st		
2nd		
3rd		

8D. Give the person, number, and mood of the following verbs. Translate each form. (N.B. Infinitives do not have person and number—just translate those forms. Imperatives are second person, but be sure to give the number and translation for those forms.)

Form	Person	No.	Tense	Mood	Translation
parat					
optābās					
incipiunt					
sūmere					
eram					
docēbātis					
fugite					
tenent					
faciēbāmus					
estis					
mittēbant					
erās					
vīvēbam					
vocābat					
absolvit					
sum					
dīcis					
premēbās					
esse					
constituere					

8E. Give the requested forms of the following verbs. Translate each form.

Verb	Requested Form	Latin Form	Translation
sūmō	1st person plural Present		
appellō	3rd person singular Imperfect		
parō	2nd person plural Imperfect		
commendō	singular Imperative		
sum	3rd person plural Imperfect		
optō	3rd person singular Present		
legō	2nd person singular Present		
incipiō	2nd person singular Imperfect		
imperō	1st person singular Imperfect		
crēdō	Infinitive		
vīvō	1st person singular Imperfect		
sum	2nd person singular Imperfect		
moveō	3rd person plural Present		
agō	1st person plural Imperfect		
sciō	2nd person plural Imperfect		

8F. Translate the following English phrases into Latin.

1. We were calling. _____

2. You (singular) prepare. _____

3. She was hoping for. _____

4. You (plural) were beginning. _____

5. They were taking up. _____

6. to live _____

7. Believe! (plural) _____

8. You (singular) were choosing. _____

9. We were commanding. _____

10. He accepts. _____

8G. Translate the following sentences into coherent English.

1. Fēminae ergō nocte ārās parābant.

_____

2. Tunc iter altā ex urbe incipiēbāmus.

_____

3. Studium verbōrum modo sūmēbas.

_____

4. Māter mentem doctam nōn sōlum fīliae dulcī sed etiam amīcō fīliō optābat.

_____

5. Imperātōrēs magnī regnī saepe certī erant.

_____

6. Imperium generis Rōmānī līberīs nostrīs decorī constituēbam.

_____

7. Dux enim mīlitēs carmina alia cantāre docēbat.

_____

8. Populī Rōmānī hostīs vestrōs amīcōs appellābant.

_____

9. Vōbīscum quoque montibus sub altīs vīvēbāmus.

_____

10. Fratrēs nostrōs sceleris malī annō mediō condemnābātis.

_____

8J. Translate the following sentences into Latin. Use the rubric below each sentence as a guide.

After the war, we were preparing the public altar and new roads.

Preposition meaning "after" + case taken _____

Dictionary entry of "war" _____

Declension _____

Latin translation of "after the war" _____

Person, number, and tense of "we were preparing" _____

Dictionary entry _____

Conjugation _____

Latin translation of "we were preparing" _____

Syntactic function and case of "public altar and new roads" _____

_____

Dictionary entry of "altar" _____

Dictionary entry of "public" _____

Latin translation of "public altar" _____

Dictionary entry of "road" _____

Dictionary entry of "new" _____

Latin translation of "new roads" _____

Latin translation of entire sentence _____

_____

You (feminine plural) were by nature miserable.

Latin translation of "you were" (plural) _____

Syntactic function of "miserable" _____

Case, number, and gender of "miserable" _____

Dictionary entry of "miserable" _____

Latin adjective with correct ending _____

(Latin) syntactic function of "by nature" _____

Dictionary entry of "nature" _____

Latin translation of "by nature" _____

Latin translation of entire sentence _____

_____

8I. Fill in the blanks with correctly formed Latin words from *NLP* 1–8 required vocabulary. You may use each word only once. There is no "right" answer.

Caesar cum *(singular noun)* _____

ad *(singular noun)* _____ *(imperfect tense verb)* _____,

sed *(nominative plural noun)* _____ malī *(imperfect tense verb)* _____.

Populī Rōmānī *(accusative noun)* _____ *(genitive noun)* _____

condemnābant. Omnēs ex urbe fugiēbant.

Deinde līberī *(imperfect tense verb)* _____.

Future Tense

9A. Decline the following noun-adjective pairs.

Case	glōria, -iae, f + familiāris, -e	fīnis, -is (-ium), m + magnus, -a, -um
Singular		
Nominative		
Genitive		
Dative		
Accusative		
Ablative		
Vocative		
Plural		
Nominative		
Genitive		
Dative		
Accusative		
Ablative		
Vocative		

9B. For each of the following nouns, select the adjective that agrees in case, number, and gender. Then translate the resulting phrases. You may use each adjective only once.

Adjective bank: **altus, pūblicōrum, cārae, familiārium, omne, similī, ūnō, amīcum**

Noun	Case, No., Gender	Adjective	Translation
epistulārum			
mentium			
fīnis			
nēminī			
glōriā			
servō			
cīvem			
templum			

9C. Conjugate the following verbs. Translate each form.

verb: **respondeō, -ēre, respondī, responsus**
conjugation _____

PRESENT	Latin	Translation
Singular		
1st		
2nd		
3rd		
Imperative		
Plural		
1st		
2nd		
3rd		
Imperative		

respondeō, -ēre, respondī, responsus

IMPERFECT	Latin	Translation
Singular		
1st		
2nd		
3rd		
Plural		
1st		
2nd		
3rd		

FUTURE	Latin	Translation
Singular		
1st		
2nd		
3rd		
Imperative		
Plural		
1st		
2nd		
3rd		
Imperative		

verb: **trādō, -ere, trādidī, trāditus**

conjugation _____

PRESENT	Latin	Translation
Singular		
1st		
2nd		
3rd		
Imperative		
Plural		
1st		
2nd		
3rd		
Imperative		

IMPERFECT	Latin	Translation
Singular		
1st		
2nd		
3rd		
Plural		
1st		
2nd		
3rd		

FUTURE	Latin	Translation
Singular		
1st		
2nd		
3rd		
Imperative		
Plural		
1st		
2nd		
3rd		
Imperative		

verb: **sentiō, -īre, sensī, sensus**

conjugation _____

PRESENT	Latin	Translation
Singular		
1st		
2nd		
3rd		
Imperative		
Plural		
1st		
2nd		
3rd		
Imperative		

IMPERFECT	Latin	Translation
Singular		
1st		
2nd		
3rd		
Plural		
1st		
2nd		
3rd		

FUTURE	Latin	Translation
Singular		
1st		
2nd		
3rd		
Imperative		
Plural		
1st		
2nd		
3rd		
Imperative		

9D. Give the person, number, and mood of the following verbs. Translate each form. (N.B. Infinitives do not have person and number—just translate those forms. Imperatives are second person, but be sure to give the number and translation for those forms.)

Form	Conj.	Person	No.	Tense	Mood	Translation
cōgitābis						
incipitō						
sentiēbat						
adsumus						
trādēs						
legitōte						
respondētis						
aderās						
crēdent						
mittere						
cognoscam						
aderunt						
efficiēbam						
appellāre						
dīcitis						
gerēbāmus						
cole						
fugite						
optant						
vīvere						
faciētis						
premet						
agit						
habēbunt						
putābimus						

9E. Give the requested forms of the following verbs. Translate each form.

Verb	Requested Form	Latin Form	Translation
sentiō	1st person singular Future		
adsum	3rd person plural Present		
cognoscō	3rd person singular Future		
adsum	1st person plural Future		
legō	1st person singular Imperfect		
dīcō	Future Imperative plural		
incipiō	Infinitive		
cōgitō	2nd person plural Future		
respondeō	2nd person singular Future		
efficiō	3rd person plural Future		
trādō	1st person plural Future		
sūmō	Future Imperative singular		
adsum	3rd person singular Imperfect		

9F. Translate the following English phrases into Latin.

1. They will hand over. _____

2. We shall learn. _____

3. You (plural) will think. _____

4. You (singular) will bring about. _____

5. He will be at hand. _____

6. I shall feel. _____

7. Respond! (Future singular) _____

8. I was listening. _____

9. She was making. _____

10. They manage. _____

9G. Translate the following sentences into coherent English.

1. Opera nostra brevī tempore incipiēmus.

   _____

2. Inde pecūniam prō līberīs trādētis.

   _____

3. Vim deōrum maximē sentiēmus.

   _____

4. Vel fīliī meī vel fīliae tuae aderunt.

   _____

5. Lēgēs bonī novās ducis cōlam.

   _____

6. Tunc regnī fīnīs nostrī cognoscēbās.

   _____

7. Nēmō rursum dē sententiā levī servī novī cōgitābit.

   _____

8. Cīvēs autem magnā cum piētāte respondēbunt.

   _____

9. Nōn sōlum puerī sed etiam puellae cīvitātem magnam efficient.

   _____

10. Poētae magnī annōs multōs Rōmae aderant.

   _____

9H. Translate the following sentences into Latin. Use the rubric below each sentence as a guide.

I was entrusting the children to my wife.

Person, number, and tense of "I was entrusting" _____

Dictionary entry _____

Conjugation _____

Latin translation of "I was entrusting" _____

Syntactic function and case of "children" _____

Dictionary entry of "children" _____

Latin noun with correct ending _____

Syntactic function and case of "wife" _____

Dictionary entry of "wife" _____

Latin noun with correct ending _____

Latin translation of entire sentence _____

_____

We live here, we perceive no danger (lit: nothing of danger), and we will hand over the glory of the city to our children.

Person, number, and tense of "we live" _____

Dictionary entry _____

Conjugation _____

Latin translation of "we live" _____

Dictionary entry of "here" _____

Person, number, and tense of "we perceive" _____

Dictionary entry _____

Conjugation _____

Latin translation of "we perceive" _____

Dictionary entry of "no"/"nothing" _____

Case that renders "of" _____

Dictionary entry of "danger" _____

Latin noun with correct ending _____

Person, number, and tense of "we will hand over" _____

Dictionary entry _____

Conjugation _____

Latin translation of "we will hand over" _____

Syntactic function and case of "glory" _____

Dictionary entry of "glory" _____

Latin noun with correct ending _____

Case that renders "of" _____

Dictionary entry of "city" _____

Latin noun with correct ending _____

Syntactic function and case of "children" _____

Dictionary entry of "children" _____

Latin noun with correct ending _____

Latin translation of entire sentence _____

_____

9I. Find the Latin for the following phrases. The forms may appear horizontally, vertically, or diagonally in either direction.

C	O	P	I	A	B	L	T	E	M	E	S	S	U	N	T
Z	N	P	H	V	X	K	A	U	T	E	M	O	G	F	T
X	Z	C	I	V	U	A	B	C	A	U	N	H	O	O	U
T	K	X	Q	U	I	O	S	E	R	V	U	S	T	I	D
F	H	S	O	Q	M	R	M	A	J	I	E	H	S	F	S
K	L	E	Q	B	A	M	I	Q	C	N	M	L	E	Z	W
E	C	J	W	B	E	P	I	S	T	U	L	A	E	H	P
K	C	U	S	M	O	D	R	E	V	D	E	U	H	L	I
S	U	M	E	C	S	O	N	G	O	C	S	G	T	E	U
P	I	O	N	A	C	T	Y	O	U	H	A	P	F	M	M
G	Z	N	T	L	I	D	B	C	P	P	N	W	C	J	B
Q	T	G	I	A	V	S	K	I	F	S	N	Y	V	A	K
R	G	M	E	F	I	L	M	P	U	H	E	T	I	X	T
V	O	R	T	N	T	N	A	B	E	D	A	R	T	C	L
J	D	S	I	B	A	T	I	G	O	C	O	I	A	O	C
W	R	M	S	J	T	G	C	C	Q	L	U	R	T	C	D
V	E	P	E	O	E	Z	I	H	G	Q	Z	N	E	X	W
N	Q	K	V	L	M	I	F	Q	N	Q	Q	R	I	D	O
O	M	P	X	K	F	S	F	I	T	K	Y	P	P	A	A
H	S	X	U	U	D	V	E	L	R	F	M	B	M	F	M

I shall be present	I shall respond	letters
he said	moreover	a slave
you (plural) will perceive	state (Accusative)	of force
they were handing over	of no one	a tear
we shall understand	money (Accusative)	opinions
you shall think	with the laws	for duty
I shall bring about	glory (Nominative)	end

Fourth and Fifth Declension Nouns

10A. Decline the following noun-adjective pairs.

Case	lacus, -ūs, m + fertilis, -e	temperiēs, -iēī, f + aprīcus, -a, -um
Singular		
Nominative		
Genitive		
Dative		
Accusative		
Ablative		
Vocative		
Plural		
Nominative		
Genitive		
Dative		
Accusative		
Ablative		
Vocative		

10B. Give the requested forms of the following nouns.

Noun	Requested Form	Latin Form
adflātus	Genitive plural	
cornū	Accusative plural	
amnis	Genitive singular	
lacus	Nominative singular	
ōceanus	Dative plural	
passus	Nominative plural	
diēs	Ablative singular	
rēs	Ablative plural	
temperiēs	Dative singular	
insula	Accusative singular	

10C. Give the correct form of the specified adjective to modify each of the
following nouns. Translate the resulting phrases.

Noun	Case, No., Gender	Adjective	Latin Form	Translation
diērum		**alter**		
ortibus		**parvus**		
rem		**nōbilis**		
lacum		**aprīcus**		
adflātuum		**noxius**		
temperiēbus		**fertilis**		
cornūs		**amoenus**		
manūs (singular)		**gravis**		
passū		**longus**		

10D. Identify the following noun forms as directed. For ambiguous forms,
give all possibilities. Give the correct form of **amoenus, -a, -um** and
nōbilis, -e to modify each form.

Latin Form	Decl.	Gender	Case	No.	amoenus, -a, -um	nōbilis, -e
silvā						
ōceanō (2)						

Latin Form	Decl.	Gender	Case	No.	amoenus, -a, -um	nōbilis, -e
collibus (2)						
montium						
sōlī						
adflātum						
ortū						
sinuī						
rē						
passuum						
passibus (2)						
rem						
rēbus (2)						
lacūs (4)						
temperiēs (5)						
diēī (2)						
rēs (5)						

10E. Translate the following English phrases into Latin.

  1. sunny days (Nominative) _____

  2. of sea breezes _____

  3. with a hand _____

  4. another matter (Accusative) _____

  5. to/for a small bay _____

  6. harmful lakes (Accusative) _____

  7. of a distinguished origin _____

  8. with the other wing _____

  9. to/for large bands _____

  10. sweet mildness (Nominative) _____

10F. Translate the following sentences into coherent English.

  1. Regiōnēs aprīcae amoenam temperiem habent.

     _____

  2. Adflātūs et ōceanī et flūminum sentiēmus.

     _____

  3. Ortum sōlis collem post parvum vidēbātis.

     _____

  4. Sinus dulcis terrās fertilīs efficit.

     _____

  5. Inde insulās omnēs lacūs magnī vidēre optābās.

     _____

  6. Imperātor hostium nostrōrum cornū cum parvō ad urbem
     Rōmānam veniet.

     _____

  7. Ibi puella iter parvum passuum mille nocte facit.

     _____

  8. Rex populōs montēs trans altōs Rōmam diēs multōs dūcēbat.

     _____

9. Iuvenēs epistulās multās manū nōbilī scrībent.

_____

10. Vir bonus labōrēs pūblicōs Reī pūblicae praesidiō saepe agit.

_____

10G. Translate the following sentences into Latin. Use the rubric below each sentence as a guide.

We now shall watch the rising of the sun in front of the Roman temples.

Person, number, and tense of "we shall watch" _____

Dictionary entry _____

Latin translation _____

Dictionary entry of "now" _____

Syntactic function and case of "rising" _____

Dictionary entry _____

Latin translation _____

Syntactic function of "sun" _____

Dictionary entry _____

Latin translation _____

Latin preposition that means "in front of" + case _____

Latin translation of "in front of the Roman temples" _____

_____

Latin translation of entire sentence _____

_____

For the gods were dwelling in sunny regions between the ocean and the rivers.

Person, number, and tense of "they were dwelling" _____

_____

Dictionary entry _____

Conjugation _____

Latin translation _____

Case of "gods" _____

Dictionary entry of "gods" _____

Latin noun with correct ending _____

Latin preposition that means "in" + case _____

Latin translation of "in sunny regions" _____

Latin preposition that means "between" + case _____

Latin translation of "between the ocean and the rivers" _____

_____

Latin translation of entire sentence _____

_____

10H. Give the Latin forms for the following English phrases. Then recombine the **double-underlined** letters to spell a Greek navigational text.

(in a) sunny region: __ __ __ __ __ __ __

__ __ __ __ __ __

we hope to see: __ __ __ __ __ __

__ __ __ __ __ __ __

bays and lakes (Accusative): __ __ __ __ __

__ __ __ __ __ __ __ __

for many days: __ __ __ __ __ __   __ __ __ __

ANSWER: __ __ __ __ __ __ __ __

Irregular Verbs

11A. Decline the following noun-adjective pairs.

Case	gelū, -ūs, n: frost + bellus, -a, -um	speciēs, -iēī, f: aspect, appearance + dīves (dīvitis)
Singular		
Nominative		
Genitive		
Dative		
Accusative		
Ablative		
Vocative		
Plural		
Nominative		
Genitive		
Dative		
Accusative		
Ablative		
Vocative		

11B. For each of the following nouns, select the adjective that agrees in case, number, and gender. Then translate the resulting phrases. You may use each adjective only once.

Adjective bank: **bellīs, dīvitem, nōbilis, fertilium, vērī, alterō, familiārī, parvum**

Noun	Case, No, Gender	Adjective	Translation
reī			
diĕs			
temperiēbus			
lacū			
passum			
adflātuī			
cornū			
sinuum			

11C. Conjugate the following verbs. Translate each form.

verb: **laudō, -āre, -āvī, -ātus**
conjugation _____

PRESENT	Latin	Translation
Singular		
1st		
2nd		
3rd		
Imperative		
Plural		
1st		
2nd		
3rd		
Imperative		

verb: **negō, -āre, -āvī, -ātus**

conjugation _____

IMPERFECT	Latin	Translation
Singular		
1st		
2nd		
3rd		
Plural		
1st		
2nd		
3rd		

verb: **placeō, -ēre, -uī**

conjugation _____

FUTURE	Latin	Translation
Singular		
1st		
2nd		
3rd		
Imperative		
Plural		
1st		
2nd		
3rd		
Imperative		

11D. Give the dictionary entry, person, number, and mood of the following
verbs. Translate each form. (N.B. Infinitives do not have person and
number—just translate those forms. Imperatives are second person,
but be sure to give the number and translation for those forms.)

Form	Dictionary Entry	Person	No.	Tense	Mood	Translation
eunt						
poterimus						
nōlent						
ferēbat						
poteram						
mālēbant						
velle						
possunt						
fer						
it						
ferētis						
ībis						
nōlīte						
volumus						
mālētis						

11E. Give the requested forms of the following verbs. Translate each form.

Verb	Requested Form	Latin Form	Translation
possum	1st person plural Imperfect		
eō	3rd person plural Future		
ferō	3rd person plural Imperfect		
volō	2nd person plural Imperfect		
eō	singular Imperative		
mālō	1st person singular Future		
possum	3rd person singular Present		
nōlō	2nd person singular Future		
volō	1st person plural Imperfect		
nōlō	3rd person plural Imperfect		
possum	2nd person plural Future		
ferō	1st person plural Future		
eō	2nd person singular Present		
ferō	plural Imperative		
mālō	3rd person plural Present		

11F. Translate the following English phrases into Latin.

1. You (singular) are carrying. _____

2. You (singular) are able. _____

3. She wants. _____

4. I was going. _____

5. Don't! (singular) _____

6. We shall prefer. _____

7. to be able _____

8. Go! (plural) _____

9. You (singular) prefer. _____

10. She was wanting. _____

11G. Translate the following sentences into coherent English.

1. Puella frātrem bellum vidēre brevī tempore poterit.

_____

2. Ad oppidum nōbile mēcum rursum ībātis.

_____

3. Tandem cīvēs rēgēs noxiōs laudāre nōlēbant.

_____

4. Tamquam mīlitēs montēs altōs, ita amīcī collīs parvōs mālunt.

_____

5. Dīvitēs autem pecūniam līberīs praesidiō tenēre volent.

_____

6. Doctōrum iuvenum grātiā nunc decus magnum ad cīvitātem
    Rōmānam fertis.

_____

7. Ergō gravibus cum verbīs respondēre nōlīte.

_____

8. Fāma lacūs amoenī nōbīs hodiē placet.

_____

9. Quidem nēmō lēgēs urbis hostibus commendāre vult.

_____

10. Cum poēta carmina dulcia cantat, omnis cīvis audīre māvult.

_____

11H. Translate the following sentences into Latin. Use the rubric below each
      sentence as a guide.

The leader prefers to entrust the town to a good citizen.

Person, number, and tense of "(he) prefers" _____

Dictionary entry _____

Latin translation _____

Syntactic function of "to entrust" _____

Latin translation _____

Syntactic function and case of "town" _____

Dictionary entry _____

Latin translation _____

Syntactic function and case of "to a good citizen" _____

Dictionary entry of "citizen" _____

Dictionary entry of "good" _____

Latin translation _____

Latin translation of entire sentence _____

_____

Don't (plural) go to the temple at night.

Syntactic function of "don't" _____

Dictionary entry _____

Latin translation _____

Syntactic function of "go" _____

Dictionary entry _____

Latin translation _____

Latin preposition that means "to" + case _____

Latin translation of "to the temple" _____

Syntactic function of "at night" _____

Latin translation of "at night" _____

Latin translation of entire sentence _____

_____

11I. Give the Latin forms for the following English phrases. Then recombine the **<u>double-underlined</u>** letters to spell a word that is associated with Martial's later life.

you all will be able: __ __ __ __ __ <u>__</u> __ <u>__</u> __

we wanted: __ __ __ __ <u>__</u> __ __ __ __

they prefer: __ __ <u>__</u> __ __ __

I went: __ <u>__</u> __ __

they will go: <u>__</u> __ __ __ __

you were carrying: __ __ __ __ __ __ <u>__</u>

I am unwilling: __ __ <u>__</u> __

ANSWER: __ <u>__</u> __ __ __ __ __

Personal, Reflexive, and Intensive Pronouns, and Pronominal Adjectives

12A. Decline the following noun-adjective pairs.

Case	vulnus, vulneris, n: wound + is, ea, id	cūra, -ae, f: concern + ipse, ipsa, ipsum
Singular		
Nominative		
Genitive		
Dative		
Accusative		
Ablative		
Plural		
Nominative		
Genitive		
Dative		
Accusative		
Ablative		

12B. Identify each of the following pronouns and pronominal adjectives by case, number, and gender. Give the basic meaning of each one.

Pronoun/Pronominal Adj.	Case	No.	Gender(s)	Basic Meaning
tē (2 cases)				
sibi				
ipsam				
nostrī				
ipsīs (2 cases)				
nōbīs (2 cases)				
vōs (2 cases)				
meī				
eius				
eōrum				
id (2 cases)				
neutrīus				
aliud (2 cases)				
ūnī				
ullō				
tōtīus				
altera (3 answers)				
nullī (2 cases)				
sōlīs (2 cases)				
utram				

12C. Give the requested forms for the following pronouns and pronominal adjectives.

Pronoun/Pronominal Adj.	Requested Form	Latin Form
ego	Accusative singular	
ego	Dative plural	
ego	Genitive plural	
tū	Genitive plural	
tū	Dative singular	
tū	Ablative plural	
is, ea, id	Nominative plural feminine	
is, ea, id	Ablative singular neuter	
is, ea, id	Genitive plural masculine	
ipse, ipsa, ipsum	Dative singular neuter	
ipse, ipsa, ipsum	Genitive singular feminine	
ipse, ipsa, ipsum	Accusative plural masculine	
alius, alia, aliud	Accusative singular neuter	
alter, altera, alterum	Genitive singular feminine	
neuter, neutra, neutrum	Dative singular masculine	
nullus, -a, -um	Accusative singular feminine	
sōlus, -a, -um	Ablative singular neuter	
tōtus, -a, -um	Genitive plural feminine	
ullus, -a, -um	Dative plural masculine	
ūnus, -a, -um	Dative singular masculine	
uter, utra, utrum	Accusative singular neuter	

12D. Identify the following noun forms as directed. For ambiguous forms, give all possibilities. Give the correct form of **alter, altera, alterum** and **is, ea, id** to modify each form. (N.B. Because the vocatives for pronouns are not attested, do not include these forms among your responses.)

Latin Form	Decl.	Case	No.	Gender	alter, altera, alterum	is, ea, id
lux						
lūcem						
victōrī						
victōre						
rūra (2)						
lībertīs (4)						
silvae (3)						
lībertās						
posterī						
lībertārum						
flūminum						

12E. Conjugate the following verbs. Translate each form.

verb: **vincō, -ere, vīcī, victus**

conjugation _____

PRESENT	Latin	Translation
Singular		
1st		
2nd		
3rd		
Imperative		
Plural		
1st		
2nd		
3rd		
Imperative		

verb: **cupiō, -ere, -īvī, -ītus**

conjugation _____

IMPERFECT	Latin	Translation
Singular		
1st		
2nd		
3rd		
Plural		
1st		
2nd		
3rd		

verb: **dormiō, -īre, -īvī**

conjugation _____

FUTURE	Latin	Translation
Singular		
1st		
2nd		
3rd		
Imperative		
Plural		
1st		
2nd		
3rd		
Imperative		

12F. Give the person, number, and mood of the following verbs. Translate each form. (N.B. Infinitives do not have person and number—just translate those forms. Imperatives are second person, but be sure to give the number and translation for those forms.)

Form	Conj.	Person	No.	Tense	Mood	Translation
cresce						
vincam						
cupiunt						
spectās						
intrāre						
dormit						
spectābāmus						
crescēbant						
vincitōte						
dormīre						
intrāte						
cupiētis						

12G. Give the Latin for the following phrases.

    1. of those very women _____

    2. to neither one _____

    3. for those men themselves _____

    4. She sees herself. _____

    5. with you (plural) _____

    6. for any man _____

    7. with me _____

    8. to/for one law _____

    9. with us _____

    10. with you (singular) _____

12H. Translate the following sentences into coherent English.

    1. Mē videō. _____

    2. Līberōs meōs videō. _____

    3. Līberōs vestrōs videō. _____

    4. Līberōs eōrum vidēs. _____

    5. Ego eum videō. _____

    6. Nōbīs crēdimus. _____

    7. Tū tē vincēbās. _____

    8. Puella sē vidēbit. _____

    9. Puer sē spectābat. _____

    10. Līberta ipsa dē suīs līberīs cōgitat. _____

    11. Cīvēs ipsī suōs mōrēs constituunt. _____

    12. Tū eam spectābis. _____

    13. Nōs eōs laudāmus. _____

14. Ipsa dē eīs cōgitō. _____

15. Dē eīs ipsīs cōgitō. _____

16. Flūmen mihi placet. _____

17. Flūmen sibi placet. _____

18. Victor ipse pācem ipsam optat. _____

19. Vīs tua crescit. _____

20. Ipsae iter nostrum incipiēmus. _____

21. Lacūs victōrī ipsī placēbant. _____

22. Mens mīlitis ipsīus bona erat. _____

23. Legiōnēs meae tuās vincent. _____

24. Neutrum virum scīmus. _____

25. Nocte ullā dormīre cupimus. _____

26. Lībertī memōriās suās efficiunt. _____

27. Mīlitēs tōtam noctem nōn dormiunt. _____

28. Regiōnēs noxiae neutrī placent. _____

29. Rex manūs nostrās laudāre cupit. _____

30. Rex regiōnem ipsam suō fīliō trādit. _____

121. Translate the following sentences into Latin. Use the rubric below each sentence as a guide.

On behalf of the Republic itself I was preparing the knights and their horses.

Latin preposition that means "on behalf of" + case taken _____

_____

Dictionary entry of "Republic" _____

Dictionary entry of "itself" _____

Latin translation of "on behalf of the Republic itself" _____

_____

Person, number, and tense of "I was preparing" _____

Dictionary entry _____

Latin translation _____

Syntactic function and case of "the knights and their horses" _____

_____

Dictionary entry of "knight" _____

Dictionary entry of "horses" _____

Latin translation of "the knights and their horses" _____

_____

Latin translation of entire sentence _____

_____

The wife desired to absolve herself from the crime.

    Person, number, and tense of "(she) desired" _____
    Dictionary entry _____
    Latin translation _____

    Syntactic function and case of "herself" _____
    Dictionary entry of "herself" _____
    Latin translation of "herself" _____

    Case that renders "from" _____
    Dictionary entry of "crime" _____
    Latin translation of "from the crime" _____

    Latin translation of entire sentence _____

    _____

12J. A limerick for translation.

Rōmae dīves erat lībertus.

Condemnēbat ducis fīlius.

Nunc pugnat in cornū

et sōlis cum ortū

ipse surgit, pauper lībertus.

Note: **pugnō, -āre, -āvī, -ātus**: fight.

NLP Review B (Lessons 7–12)

I: CONCEPTS

IA: Latin case uses.

NOMINATIVE			
Syntax	**What It Does**	**What to Look For**	**Simple Examples**
Subject	performs the action of a verb		**Dī socolātiam amant**. The gods love chocolate.
Predicate	explains the subject	to be (=)	**Socolātia est cibus deōrum**. Chocolate is (=) the food of the gods!
GENITIVE "modifies" another noun; "of"			
Genitive of Possession	ownership		**fēles magistrae** teacher's cat/cat of the teacher
Subjective Genitive	acts on the noun it modifies	genitive **depends** on noun with implied verbal quality	**fuga Campestrium** flight of the (proto-) Valkyries (the [proto]-Valkyries **do** the flying)
Objective Genitive	receives "action" of noun it depends on	genitive **depends** on noun with implied verbal quality	**amor patriae** love of country (the country **receives** the love)
Partitive Genitive	part of the whole	genitive **depends** on a number/ quantity	**ūnus trium līberōrum** one of three children
Genitive of Value/Worth	gives value or expresses esteem	genitive **is** a number/quantity	**opīniō magnī** an opinion of great value **gemma pretiī ingentis** jewelry of inestimable value

(Continued)

GENITIVE "modifies" another noun; "of"			
Genitive of Material/ Quality	explains "stuff" things are made of	genitive is a physical material or abstract quality	**moenia hederārum** halls of ivy **homo ingeniī** person of character
Genitive of Charge	expresses an accusation or charge	genitive **depends** on a litigious verb; genitive **is** a crime	**Tē somniī condemnāmus.** We accuse you of sleeping (in class).
Genitive with Special Verbs/ Adjectives	completes special verb/adjective (e.g., remembering, forgetting …)	(+ genitive) as in vocab listing	**memor temporis fīnium** mindful of deadlines **plēnus consiliī bonī** full of good advice
DATIVE "to/for"			
Indirect Object (I.O.)	indirectly affected by the verb	verb of giving/ saying	**Dōnum parentibus dā.** Give a gift to your parent.
Dative of Reference	dative is a person, someone benefiting from or harmed by an action		**Placentam socolātiam amīcae faciō.** I make chocolate cake for my friend.
Dative of Purpose	explains purpose of an action or a point of view		**Placentam socolātiam voluptātī faciō.** I make chocolate cake for pleasure.
Double Dative	datives of reference and purpose		**Socolātia voluptātī mihi est.** Chocolate is a source of pleasure for me.
Dative of Possession	expresses ownership/ possession	some form of *esse* dative is a person	**Socolātia mihi est.** There is chocolate to/for me. (= **I** have chocolate.)
Dative with Special Adjectives	completes some adjectives (kind, friendly, dear, pleasing, hostile, near)		**Socolātia mihi est grāta.** Chocolate is pleasing to me.
Dative with Special Verbs	completes some verbs (favor, help, please, trust, believe, persuade, obey, command, serve, resist, pardon, threaten, spare)	technically an I.O. D.O. is inherent in the verb (e.g., the verb can have the sense of a noun)	**Ducibus crēdimus.** We trust (have trust in) the leaders. **Mollibus populīs favēmus.** We show favor to gentle people.
Dative with Compound Verbs	prefix (*ad-, ante-, con-, in-, inter-, ob-, post-, prae-, pro-, sub-,* or *super-*) + verb	dative is like an I.O.	**Rex mīlitibus imperat.** The king commands (gives commands to) the soldiers.

ACCUSATIVE			
Direct Object (D.O.)	receives the action of the verb		**Fēlem vocō.** I call <u>my cat.</u>
Double Accusative	renames the direct object D.O. + predicate/secondary object	verb of making or calling	**Fēlem Fionam vocō.** I <u>call</u> <u>my cat</u> Fiona. **Pater fīlium herēdem rogābat.** Dad <u>appointed</u> Junior (as) heir.
Accusative of Extent of Time	how long it takes for something to occur	unit of time, often in plural	**Noctem tōtam studēbāmus.** We studied <u>the entire night.</u>
Accusative with Some Prepositions	*ad, in, per*		**Fēles ad/in domum ambulat.** The cat walks <u>towards/into the house.</u>

ABLATIVE			
"by/with/from/because of"			
Ablative with Some Prepositions	*ā/ab, cum, dē, ē/ex,* *in, prō, sine*		**Fēles ab animālium medicō currit.** The cat runs <u>from the veterinarian.</u>
Ablative of Place Where	explains where something occurs	ablative is a place	**Turba studiī in bibliothēcā convenit.** The study group meets <u>in the library.</u>
Ablative of Time When	explains when something occurs	unit of time, usually singular	**Conventus studiī mediā nocte coepit.** The study session started <u>at midnight.</u>
Ablative of Means	by or with which something occurs	ablative is a physical object	**Fēles muscam pede ferit.** The cat swats the fly <u>with a paw.</u>
Ablative of Manner	how something occurs	ablative is abstraction *cum* + adjective no adjective, no *cum*	**Fēles studiō ferit.** The cat swats <u>with enthusiasm.</u> **Fēles magnō cum studiō ferit.** The cat swats <u>with great force.</u>
Ablative of Accompaniment	explains who attends an action	*cum* + person	**Cum caninbus ambulō.** I walk <u>with my dogs.</u>
Ablative of Cause	explains why something happens		**Fēles vexātōne ferit.** The cat swats <u>because of an irritation.</u>

(Continued)

ABLATIVE			
"by/with/from/because of"			
Ablative of Description			**placenta socolātia cum <u>gelū dulcī</u>** chocolate cake <u>with frosting</u>
Ablative of Separation		Verb of freeing/ lacking/depriving	**<u>Placentā socolātiā</u> carēmus. Eheu!** We lack <u>chocolate cake</u>. O dear!
Ablative of Origin	explains source/origin		**socolātia <u>Galliā Belgicā</u>** chocolate <u>from Belgium</u>
VOCATIVE			
"hey you! yo! on deck! O!"			
Direct Address		imperative or 2nd person verb	**<u>Ō Caesar,</u> nebulam meam relinque.** <u>Hey Caesar,</u> get off of my cloud.
LOCATIVE			
Place Where		toponym (cities, small islands, *domus, humus,* and *rūs*)	**<u>Rōmae</u> habitāmus.** We live in <u>Rome</u>.

IB: Nouns: Fourth and Fifth Declensions (*NLP* 10).

- fourth declension nouns are recognized by their distinctive genitive singular ending: -ūs
- fifth declension nouns are recognized by their distinctive genitive singular ending: -eī

NOUN ENDINGS (ALL DECLENSIONS)

Case	1st declension f/(m)		2nd declension m/(f)/[n]	
	Sing.	Pl.	Sing.	Pl.
Nominative	-a	-ae	-us/-r [-um]	-ī [-a]
Genitive	-ae	-ārum	-ī	-ōrum
Dative	-ae	-īs	-ō	-īs
Accusative	-am	-ās	-um	-ōs [-a]
Ablative	-ā	-īs	-ō	-īs
Vocative	-a	-ae	-e/-r [-um]	-ī [-a]

Case	3rd declension m/(f)/[n]		4th declension m/(f)/[n]		5th declension f/(m)	
	Sing.	Pl.	Sing.	Pl.	Sing.	Pl.
Nominative	(varies)	-ēs [-a/-ia]	-us [-ū]	-ūs [-ua]	-es	-ēs
Genitive	-is	-um/-ium	-ūs	-uum	-eī	-ērum
Dative	-ī	-ibus	-uī [-ū]	-ibus	-eī	-ēbus
Accusative	-em [varies]	-ēs/īs [-a/-ia]	-um [-ū]	-ūs [-ua]	-em	-ēs
Ablative	-e/-ī	-ibus	-ū	-ibus	-ē	-ēbus
Vocative	(varies)	-ēs [-a/-ia]	-us [-ū]	-ūs [-ua]	-ēs	-ēs

N.B.:

GENITIVE SINGULAR GIVES:

- DECLENSION GROUP
    - **puella, -ae**, f: girl (**-ae** indicates first declension)
    - **annus, -ī**, m: year (**-ī** indicates second declension)
    - **māter, mātris**, f: mother (**-is** indicates third declension)
    - **lacus, -ūs**, m: lake (**-ūs** indicates fourth declension)
    - **rēs, -eī**, f: thing (**-eī** indicates fifth declension)
- STEM (e.g., **mātr-**)

IC: Noun-Adjective agreement.

THE NOUN-ADJECTIVE AGREEMENT <u>MANTRA</u> STILL APPLIES:

- same case
- same number
- same gender
- (the endings will not necessarily match up)

SOME GENDER NOTES:

- 1st declension nouns are mostly **feminine**
  (+ some errant masculine nouns and a few common family names)
- 2nd declension **masculine** nouns end in -us
  (+ a few errant feminine plants);
  neuter nouns end in -um
- 3rd declension nouns are a grab bag
  (abstractions are usually feminine)
- 4th declension **masculine** nouns end in -us
  (+ a few errant feminine plants);
  neuter nouns end in -u
- 5th declension nouns are mostly **feminine**
  (+ a few errant masculine nouns)

ID: Verbs: Present, Imperfect, and Future tenses.

- You can determine the verb's conjugation group by looking at the second
  principal part (infinitive: *-āre, -ēre, -ere, -īre*)
- Review the personal endings:

Person	Singular	Plural
1st	-ō/-m	-mus
2nd	-s	-tis
3rd	-t	-nt
Imperative	-e	-te

- **PRESENT TENSE** indicates actions occurring now (I read, you are sleeping, they continue to watch).
- **IMPERFECT TENSE** indicates actions that were ongoing in the past (I was reading, you slept, they used to watch) (*NLP* 8).
- **FUTURE TENSE** indicates actions that have yet to occur (I shall read, you will sleep, they will watch) (*NLP* 9).
- The **IMPERFECT TENSE** is formed by inserting the imperfect tense signifier **-ba-** between the verb's stem and the personal ending.

Person	Singular	Plural
1st	**-bam**	**-bāmus**
2nd	**-bās**	**-bātis**
3rd	**-bat**	**-bant**

- The **FUTURE TENSE** is formed in one of two ways:
- First and second conjugation verbs follow this pattern:

Person	Singular	Plural
1st	**-bō**	**-bimus**
2nd	**-bis**	**-bitis**
3rd	**-bit**	**-bunt**
Imperative	**-tō**	**-tōte**

- Third and fourth conjugation verbs follow this pattern:

Person	Singular	Plural
1st	**-am**	**-ēmus**
2nd	**-ēs**	**-ētis**
3rd	**-et**	**-ent**
Imperative	**-itō**	**-itōte**

- N.B. For all three tenses, the personal endings **do not** change.

IE: Irregular verbs (*NLP* 11).

- Some verbs are irregular in **present tense** only.
- The only verbs that are irregular in the imperfect tense are **SUM** and **POSSUM** (and their compounds).
- The only verbs that are irregular in the future tense are **SUM** and **POSSUM** (and their compounds).
- **VOLŌ, MĀLŌ, NŌLŌ,** and **FERŌ** behave like regular third conjugation verbs in the future tense.
- **EŌ** behaves like a regular first conjugation verb in the future tense.
- Review the charts in *NLP* 11.
- N.B. The personal endings **do not** change.

Present	Imperfect Base	Future Base	Definition
sum	era-	eri-	be
possum = pot/pos + sum	potera-	poteri-	be able
volō	volēba-	vole-	want
mālō = mā + volō	mālēba-	māle-	prefer
nōlō = nō + volō	nōlēba-	nōle-	be unwilling
eō	ība-	ībi-	go
ferō	ferēba-	fere-	carry

IF: Pronouns.

- Pronouns take the place of nouns.
- Pronouns agree with their referents in **number** and **gender** but take their cases according to how they function in their own phrases.
- **PERSONAL PRONOUNS** refer to specific people (see *NLP* 4).
- **IS, EA, ID** often functions as a 3rd person pronoun.
- **REFLEXIVE PRONOUNS** "reflect" back to the subject.
  - They have no nominative form.
  - 1st person forms (myself/ourselves) are the same as first person personal pronouns (*ego, nōs*).

- ○ 2nd person forms (yourself/yourselves) are the same as second person personal pronouns (*tū, vōs*).
  - ○ 3rd person forms (him/her/itself, themselves) are:
    suī, sibi, sē (sēsē), sē (sēsē)
- **IPSE, IPSA, IPSUM** (-self, "very self") is an intensive pronoun that adds extra emphasis (in English translation, these can easily be confused with reflexive pronouns).
- **PRONOMINAL ADJECTIVES** can take the place of pronouns and decline like pronouns. These include nine adjectives (that can be remembered by the mnemonic UNUS NAUTA):
  - ○ **ūnus, -a, -um:** one
  - ○ **nullus, -a, -um:** not any
  - ○ **ullus, -a, -um:** any
  - ○ **sōlus, -a, -um:** only, sole
  - ○ **neuter, neutra, neutrum:** neither
  - ○ **alius, -a, -ud:** one, other
  - ○ **uter, utra, utrum:** either
  - ○ **tōtus, -a, -um:** all, entire, complete
  - ○ **alter, altera**, **alterum**: one of two, second, the other
- Here are the endings for many pronouns and the nine pronominal adjectives:

Case	Masculine		Feminine		Neuter	
	Singular	Plural	Singular	Plural	Singular	Plural
Nominative	(varies)	**-ī**	(varies)	**-ae**	(varies)	**-a**
Genitive	**-īus**	**-ōrum**	**-īus**	**-ārum**	**-īus**	**-ōrum**
Dative	**-ī**	**-īs**	**-ī**	**-īs**	**-ī**	**-īs**
Accusative	**-um**	**-ōs**	**-am**	**-ās**	(varies)	**-a**
Ablative	**-ō**	**-īs**	**-ā**	**-īs**	**-ō**	**-īs**

II: VOCABULARY *NLP* 7–12

NOUNS

aqua, -ae, f: water (by extension "aqueduct")

āra, -ae, f: altar

causa, -ae, f: cause, reason, legal case

cōpia, -iae, f: abundance, (plural) troops

epistula, -ae, f: letter

fāma, -ae, f: rumor, fame, name

forma, -ae, f: shape, beauty

glōria, -iae, f: glory, fame, ambition, renown

insula, -ae, f: island, apartment block

lacrima, -ae, f: tear

līberta, -ae, f: freedwoman

memoria, -iae, f: recollection, memory

nātūra, -ae, f: nature, character, temperament

pecūnia, -iae, f: money

porta, -ae, f: gate, strait

sententia, -iae, f: opinion, judgment

silva, -ae, f: woods, forest

via, viae, f: path, road, street

castra, -ōrum, n (plural): (military) camp

equus, -ī, m: horse

līberī, -ōrum, m (plural): children

lībertus, -ī, m: freedman

locus, -ī, m: place

numerus, -ī, m: number

ōceanus, -ī, m: ocean, the sea that surrounds the earth

officium, -iī, n: service, duty

oppidum, -ī, n: town

perīculum, -ī, n: danger

posterī, -ōrum, m (plural): posterity, descendants

proelium, -iī, n: battle

servus, -ī, m: slave

signum, -ī, n: sign, standard, mark

solum, -ī, n: land, soil

spatium, -iī, n: space

studium, -iī, n: pursuit, enthusiasm, zeal

templum, -ī, n: temple

amnis, -is (-ium), m: river

animal, -ālis (-ium), n: a living being, an animal

canis, -is, m/f: dog

cīvis, -is (-ium), m/f: citizen

cīvitās, -ātis, f: citizenship, state, city-state

collis, -is (-ium), m: hill, high ground

eques, equitis, m: horseman, knight

fīnis, -is (-ium), m: boundary, end, territory

flūmen, flūminis, n: river, stream

frux, frūgis, f: crops, fruit

gens, gentis (-ium), f: family, clan, race

homo, hominis, m: human being

hostis, -is (-ium), m/f: enemy

iter, itineris, n: journey, route

labor, -ōris, m: work, toil, effort

legiō, -ōnis, f: legion

lex, lēgis, f: law

lux, lūcis, f: light

mens, mentis (-ium), f: mind, understanding, judgment, attention

mīles, mīlitis, m: soldier (referring to a group); soldiery

mons, montis (-ium), m: mountain

mōs, mōris, m: custom, habit; (plural) character

nēmō, nēminis, m/f: no one

nox, noctis (-ium), f: night

pietās, -ātis, f: responsibility, sense of duty, piety

regiō, -iōnis, f: boundary, region

rūs, rūris, n: country, countryside

sermō, -ōnis, m: conversation, discourse

sōl, sōlis, m: the sun

tempus, temporis, n: time (brevī tempore: soon); (plural) temples (of head)

victor, -ōris, m: conqueror, winner

vīs, vīris (-ium), f: force, strength, power

adflātus, -ūs, m: blowing, breathing, sea breeze

cornū, -ūs, n: horn, wing

lacus, -ūs, m: lake

manus, -ūs, f: hand, band or force (of men)

passus, -ūs, m: step, pace, "foot" (mille passūs: a thousand paces, mile; the English mile is 5,280 feet; the Roman mile was about 4,851 feet)

ortus, -ūs, m: rising, origin

sinus, -ūs, m: bend, curve, fold, bay; lap, bosom, embrace

diēs, diēī, m: day

rēs, reī, f: thing, object, matter, affair, circumstance

temperiēs, -iēī, f: proper mixture, mildness

PRONOUNS

ipse, ipsa, ipsum: himself, herself, itself, themselves

is, ea, id: he, she, it; this, that

ADJECTIVES

alius, -a, -ud: one, other

alter, altera, alterum: one of two, second, the other (alter ... alter: the one ... the other)

altus, -a, -um: high, lofty

amoenus, -a, -um: beautiful, pleasant, charming

aprīcus, -a, -um: sunny

bellus, -a, -um: pretty, handsome

cārus, -a, -um (+ dative): dear (to)

hūmānus, -a, -um: human

medius, -a, -um: middle, mid-

neuter, neutra, neutrum: neither

noxius, -ia, -ium: hurtful, injurious

nullus, -a, -um: not any

parvus, -a, -um: small

pūblicus, -a, -um: public, at public expense

sōlus, -a, -um: alone, only

suus, sua, suum: his/her/its/their own (translation depends on context)

tōtus, -a, -um: all, entire, complete

ullus, -a, -um: any

ūnus, -a, -um: one, only (ūnā: at the same time)

uter, utra, utrum: either

vērus, -a, um: true

dīves (dīvitis): rich

familiāris, -e: belonging to the household (used substantively to mean
"servant, slave, friend, or intimate")

fertilis, -e: abundant, fruitful

grandis, -e: large

nōbilis, -e: distinguished, noble, famous

VERBS

appellō, -āre, -āvī, -ātus: call, name

cōgitō, -āre, -āvī, -ātus: think, reflect

intrō, -āre, -āvī, -ātus: enter

laudo, -āre, -āvī, -ātus: praise,
commend

negō, -āre, -āvī, -ātus: deny, refuse

optō, -āre, -āvī, -ātus: wish for, desire

parō, -āre, -āvī, -ātus: prepare

spectō, -āre, -āvī, -ātus: observe, watch

placeō, -ēre, -uī (+ dative): please

respondeō, -ēre, -spondī, -sponsus:
answer, reply

accipiō, -ere, -cēpī, -ceptus: receive,
accept

cognoscō, -ere, -nōvī, -nitus: learn,
understand, perceive

constituō, -ere, -stituī, -stitūtus: place,
establish, decide

crescō, -ere, crēvī, crētus: grow

cupiō, -ere, -īvī, -ītus: wish, long for,
desire

efficiō, -ere, -fēcī, -fectus: bring about,
render, complete

incipiō, -ere, -cēpī, -ceptus: begin

sūmō, -ere, sumpsī, sumptus: take up,
put on

trādō, -ere, trādidī, trāditus: hand over,
yield

vincō, -ere, vīcī, victus: conquer

dormiō, -īre, -īvī: sleep

sentiō, -īre, sensī, sensus: perceive, feel

inquit (defective verb): he/she said

adsum, adesse, adfuī: be present, be at
hand

eō, īre, īvī or iī, itus: go

ferō, ferre, tulī, lātus: bring, carry, bear,
endure, say

mālō, malle, māluī: prefer, choose

nōlō, nolle, nōluī: be unwilling, not want

possum, posse, potuī: be able, can

volō, velle, voluī: wish

PREPOSITIONS

ante (+ accusative): before, in front of;
beforehand (as an adverb)

dē (+ ablative): down from, about,
concerning

inter (+ accusative): between, among,
during

post (+ accusative): after, behind

propter (+ accusative): because of

sub (+ ablative): under

trans (+ accusative): across

CONJUNCTIONS AND ADVERBS

an: or

at: but

autem: however, moreover, but

circiter: about, approximately

cum: when, since, although

ecce: behold!

hodiē: today

ibi: there

inde: from there, from then

ita: thus, so

itaque: and so, therefore

maximē: most especially, certainly

multō: by far, by much

nisi: if not, unless, except

nōn sōlum … sed etiam: not only … but also

nōn sōlum … vērum etiam: not only … but also

plānē: clearly

quia: because

quidem: certainly, at least, indeed

rursus or **rursum**: back, again

saepe: often

tamquam: just as, so as, as it were, so to speak

tandem: finally

tot: so many

tunc: then, at that time

undique: from all sides, on all sides

vel: or, for instance

vel … vel: either … or

vērō: in fact, certainly, without doubt

vix: scarcely, hardly

III: ADDITIONAL DRILLS

IIIA. Decline the following noun-adjective pairs. Consult the glossary above for the dictionary entries.

Case	habitus + patiens	quercus + amoenus	animal + is, ea, id
Singular			
Nominative			
Genitive			
Dative			
Accusative			
Ablative			
Plural			
Nominative			
Genitive			
Dative			
Accusative			
Ablative			

IIIB. Give the requested forms of the following nouns.

Noun	Requested Form	Latin Form
sermō	Accusative singular	
temperiēs	Dative plural	
signum	Genitive plural	
iter	Nominative plural	
equus	Vocative singular	
lacus	Dative singular	
epistula	Accusative plural	
diēs	Ablative singular	
via	Genitive singular	
sinus	Ablative plural	

IIIC. Give the correct form of the specified adjective to modify each of the following nouns.

Noun	Case, No., Gender	Adjective	Latin Form
vīris		**tōtus**	
ortibus (2)		**altus**	
		altus	
mente		**suus**	
locī (plural)		**familiāris**	
rūs (2)		**medius**	
		medius	
templō (2)		**dīves**	
		dīves	
labōrēs (2)		**noxius**	
		noxius	
manuum		**hūmānus**	
legiō		**parvus**	

IIID. For each of the following nouns, select the adjective that agrees in case, number, and gender. Then translate the resulting phrases. You may use each adjective only once.

Adjective bank: **ipsīus, alterārum, grandium, ūnī, mediō, parvam, altae, familiāris**

Noun	Case, No., Gender	Adjective	Translation
passuum			
reī			
vim			
adflātū			
diēs			
lībertō			
portārum			
sōlis			

IIIE. Identify the following noun forms as directed. For ambiguous forms, give all possibilities. Give the correct form of **ipse, ipsa, ipsum** and **dīves (dīvitis)** to modify each form.

Latin Form	Case	No.	Gender	ipse, ipsa, ipsum	dīves (dīvitis)
cornuī					
adflātum					
sinibus (2)					
temperiēī (2)					
equitum					
castra (2)					
copiā					

IIIF. Give the Latin for each of the following English phrases.

    1. of sunny lakes _____

    2. in harmful water _____

    3. of the other mind _____

    4. the proper mixtures themselves (Nominative) _____

    _____

    5. a pleasant bay (Accusative) _____

    6. to/for familiar opinions _____

    7. O small stream! _____

    8. pretty lights (Accusative) _____

    9. with lofty conversations _____

    10. the winner himself (Nominative) _____

IIIG. Conjugate the following verbs. Translate each form. Consult the glossary above for the dictionary entries.

    verb: **crescō**

    conjugation _____

PRESENT	Latin	Translation
Singular		
1st		
2nd		
3rd		
Imperative		
Plural		
1st		
2nd		
3rd		
Imperative		

verb: **sentiō**

conjugation_____

IMPERFECT	Latin	Translation
Singular		
1st		
2nd		
3rd		
Plural		
1st		
2nd		
3rd		

verb: **respondeō**

conjugation _____

FUTURE	Latin	Translation
Singular		
1st		
2nd		
3rd		
Imperative		
Plural		
1st		
2nd		
3rd		
Imperative		

IIIH. Give the person, number, tense, and mood of the following verbs. Translate each form. (N.B. Infinitives do not have person and number—just translate those forms. Imperatives are second person, but be sure to give the number and translation for those forms.)

Form	Person	No.	Tense	Mood	Translation
potes					
volam					
mālēbātis					
nōlent					
ītis					
fer					
īre					
cōgitant					
cupiēmus					
respondētis					
parātōte					
accipiō					
placēmus					
incipiēbās					
sumētis					
trāditō					
aderat					
posse					
estō					
laudābāmus					

III-I. Give the requested forms of the following verbs. Translate each form.

Verb	Requested Form	Latin Form	Translation
possum	Infinitive		
eō	plural Imperative		
ferō	3rd person singular Present		
volō	2nd person plural Present		
nōlō	3rd person plural Present		
mālō	2nd person singular Present		
absum	3rd person plural Imperfect		
possum	1st person singular Future		
dormiō	1st person plural Future		
spectō	2nd person singular Future		
incipiō	1st person plural Imperfect		
cupiō	3rd person singular Imperfect		
placeō	2nd person plural Future		
trādō	1st person singular Imperfect		
vincō	plural Future Imperative		

Crossword Puzzle.

Across

3. Where a monumental scale map of the city of Rome was displayed
5. Where the Trojans must go to found their new homeland
8. He was forbidden burial in Artema's family plot
12. Cicero's affectionate nickname for his daughter
13. He professionalized the Roman army
15. The site of Caesar's elaborate siege works
18. Beloved of Vibius
20. The region that produces the bravest soldiers
24. Martial's over-vain addressee
28. The prerogative of higher office that includes the right to lead an army
30. Where Caesar encounters strange beasts
34. He orchestrated Cicero's exile from Rome
35. He conspired against the consuls in 63
36. The god against whom Gaius declares war
38. A pleasant city in central Syria
39. He completed Caesar's map of the world
43. Allied troops
44. The most beautiful island
45. Tiberius's heir
46. A beloved cithara player
47. The first man in a family to hold the consulship
48. She felt no affection for her imperial son
49. Caesar's foe at Alesia
50. The highest priesthood that an ex-slave could hold
52. Martial's "Colossal" collection
53. He ordered Cicero's assassination
54. The emperor's wife

Down

1. One of Claudius's powerful freedmen
2. A famous fictional freedman
4. "First among equals"
6. A magistrate with the authority to free a slave
7. Pallas' mourning warhorse
9. Convicted of murdering one of Cicero's outspoken rivals
10. He was over-fond of pumpkins
11. Nero's praetorian prefect
14. Cicero's devoted libertus
16. A distant land from which Claudius receives delegates
17. An ancient handbook about the Roman army
19. Cicero's philhellenic epistolary addressee
21. The Greek unit of length
22. "Little Boots"
23. Pamphilius's wife?
25. Nero's beloved liberta
26. Where Caesar defeats Pompey
27. Pyrrhic war-animals
29. A little tip
31. A collection of "gift-tags"
32. An emperor over-fond of treason trials
33. Whom Septimius prefers to the exotic beauties of Britain and Syria
37. Cicero's wife
39. Rome's first emperor
40. A collection of "gift-tags"
41. The father of Latin literature
42. Vitriolic anti-triumvirate speeches
51. The author of a handbook about the Roman army

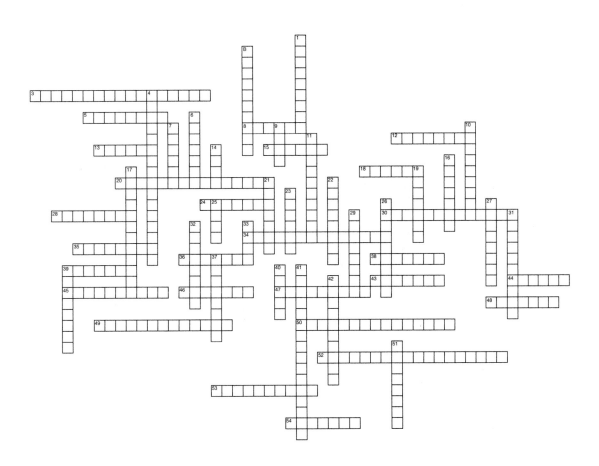

IV: ADDITIONAL PASSAGES

1. Vegetius, *de Re Militari* 1.10. Roman troops trained constantly in a variety of skills, including swimming, which could prove to be life-saving.

   Saepe repentīnīs imbribus vel nivibus solent exundāre torrentēs, et ignōrantia nōn sōlum ab hoste, sed etiam ab ipsīs aquīs discrīmen incurrit.

   Notes: **repentīnus, -a, -um**: sudden, unexpected; **imber, imbris**, m: storm, pelting rain; **nix, nivis (-ium)**, f: snow; **soleō, -ēre, solitus sum**: be accustomed (to); **exundō, -āre, -āvī**: overflow, abound; **torrens, -entis**, m: torrent, current; **ignōrantia, -iae**, f: ignorance (of swimming); **ipsīs** (*aquīs*); **discrīmen, discrīminis**, n: hazard, danger; **incurrō, -ere, -currī, -cursus**: meet with.

2. Sallust, *Bellum Jugurthinum* 17.4–5. The Numidian prince Jugurtha inherited the throne jointly with his two cousins Adherbal and Hiempsal (killed by Jugurtha), but he sought full control. The local war between Jugurtha and Adherbal was settled by Rome in a Solomon-like judgment: the province was divided in two. Jugurtha, who obtained the less-populated, less-developed western half, was not content and resumed his war, threatening Roman interests and killing Roman citizens at Cirta in 112 BCE. Senatorial armies were unsuccessful in securing a decisive defeat until Marius, as consul in 107 BCE, took charge of the war. Before proceeding to describe the campaigns, Sallust provides the expected geographical excursus, here delineating the general characteristics of Jugurtha's ancestral territory.

   Mare saevum, importuōsum; ager frūgum fertilis, bonus pecorī, arborī infēcundus; caelō terrāque pēnūria aquārum.

   Notes: supply *est* as the governing verb; **saevus, -a, -um**: fierce, raging, wrathful; **importuōsus, -a, -um**; without harbors (this adjective comes from *portus, -ūs*, m: port, harbor); **pecus, pecoris**, n: cattle, herd, flock; **arbor, -oris**, f: tree; **infēcundus, -a, -um**: barren, sterile; **pēnūria, -iae**, f: lack, scarcity, need.

3. Caesar, *de Bello Gallico* 5.13.1–2. Greek and Roman historians customarily provided geographic and ethnographic surveys to give cultural context to foreign affairs. Caesar had already seen the island of Britain firsthand in 55 BCE, and, before launching into his campaigns of 54, he provides his readers back in Rome with the anticipated excursus.

> Insula nātūrā triquetra, cuius ūnum latus est contrā Galliam. Huius lateris alter angulus, quī est ad Cantium, quō ferē omnēs ex Galliā nāvēs appelluntur, ad orientem sōlem, inferior ad merīdiem spectat. Hoc pertinet circiter mīlia passuum quingenta. Alterum vergit ad Hispāniam atque occidentem sōlem.

Notes: **triquetrus, -a, -um**: three-cornered, triangular; **cuius**: of which (genitive singular); **latus, lateris**, n: side, flank; **contrā** (+ accusative): facing, opposite; **Gallia, -iae**, f: Gaul; **huius**: "this" (genitive singular); **angulus, -ī**, m: angle, apex, corner; **quī**: which (nominative singular, construe with *angulus*); **ad Cantium**: "toward Kent"; **quō**: where; **ferē**: nearly; **nāvis, -is (-ium)**, f: ship; **appelluntur**: "(the ships) are steered"; **oriens (-ientis)**: rising; **inferior** (*angulus*): "the lower (corner)"; **merīdiēs, -diēī**, m: south; **spectō, -āre, -āvī, -ātus**: look towards; **hoc**: "this (side)" (nominative singular); **pertineō, -ēre, -uī**: reach, extend; **mīlia passuum quingenta**: five hundred miles; **vergō, -ere**: bend, incline; **Hispānia, -iae**, f: Spain; **occidens (-entis)**: falling, setting.

4. Vergil, *Aeneid* 6.860–62. In the underworld, Aeneas notices the shade of Marcellus, Augustus's nephew and intended heir, whose untimely death devastated the emperor. (See also *NLP* 6.3.) Meter: dactylic hexameter.

> Ūnā namque īre vidēbat
> ēgregium formā iuvenem et fulgentibus armīs,
> sed frons laeta parum et dēiectō lūmina vultū.

Notes: **ūnā**: at the same time; **īre vidēbat**: "he saw (that a young man) went" (indirect statement); **ēgregius, -a, -um**: distinguished, extraordinary; **fulgens (-entis)**: shining, gleaming; **laetus, -a, -um**: glad, joyful; **parum**: too little; **dēiectō vultū**: "with a cast-down expression" (ablative singular); **lūmen, lūminis**, n: light, eye.

5. Horace, *Saturae* 2.6.90–92. Horace recounts the beloved tale of the Country Mouse who generously entertained his good friend the Town Mouse at his humble country home. The persnickety Town Mouse quickly becomes bored at the rustic fare—complaining about it here—and invites the Country Mouse to experience the luxury and excitement of life in the city. The Country Mouse will quickly return to his modest estate after learning first-hand how dangerous city living can be. Meter: dactylic hexameter.

Tandem Urbānus ad hunc "Quid tē iuvat" inquit, "amīce,
praeruptī nemoris patientem vīvere dorsō?
Vīs tū hominēs urbemque ferīs praepōnere silvīs?

Notes: **urbānus, -a, -um**: of the city, courteous, witty, urbane (here, the City Mouse); **hunc**: this one (accusative singular; here, the Country Mouse); **quid**: why; **iuvō, -āre, iūvī, iūtus**: help, assist, please, delight ("it is pleasing to"); **praeruptus, -a, -um**: steep; **nemus, nemoris**, n: grove, forest; **patiens (patientis)** (+ dative): suffering, enduring (construe with *tē*); **dorsum -ī**, n: ridge, slope; **ferus, -a, -um**: wild; **praepōnō, -ere, posuī, positus**: place before, prefer.

6. Juvenal, *Saturae* 5.26–29. Juvenal describes a contentious, crowded, and inhospitable dinner party where the guests receive unappetizing, inedible fare while the host feasts on the daintiest tidbits from the finest dishes. Juvenal imagines a hostile food fight between the clients (*lībertī*) and freeborn guests who expect more dignified treatment according to the conventions of Roman society. Meter: dactylic hexameter.

Iurgia prōlūdunt, sed mox et pōcula torquēs
saucius et rubrā dētergēs vulnera mappā,
inter vōs quotiens lībertōrumque cohortem
pugna Saguntīnā fervet commissa lagōnā.

Notes: **iurgium, -iī**, n: quarrel, insult; **prōlūdō, -ere, -lūsī, -lūsus**: ensue, begin; **mox**: soon; **pōculum, -ī**, n: cup; **torqueō, -ēre, torsī, tortus**: twist, hurl, whirl (e.g., as one might brandish a spear. Juvenal is comparing this food fight to a military battle); **saucius, -a, -um**: wounded; **ruber, rubra, rubrum**: red, "bloody"; **dētergeō, -ēre, -tersī, -tersus**: wipe away; **mappa, -ae**, f: napkin; **quotiens**: how many times; **cohors, cohortis**, f: band, troop, military unit of 480 men; **pugna, -ae**, f: fist fight, battle; **Saguntīnus, -a, -um**: of Saguntum, Spain, famous for cheap earthenware (Hannibal's siege of Saguntum in 218 BCE precipitated the Second Punic War); **ferveō, -ēre, ferbuī**: seethe, boil, rage; **commissus, -a, -um**: undertaken with, incurred with, "fought with"; **lagōna, -ae**, f: pitcher, jug.

Perfect, Pluperfect, and Future Perfect Tenses

13A. Decline the following noun-adjective pair.

Case	canis, -is, m + laetus, -a, -um
Singular	
Nominative	
Genitive	
Dative	
Accusative	
Ablative	
Plural	
Nominative	
Genitive	
Dative	
Accusative	
Ablative	

13B. Identify the following noun forms as directed. For ambiguous forms, give all possibilities. Give the correct form of **vetus (veteris)** to modify each form. (N.B. Since the vocative forms are usually identical to the nominative forms, do not include these forms among your responses.)

Latin Form	Decl.	Case	No.	Gender	vetus (veteris): old
fīliī (2)					
villam					
domuum					
lectīs (2)					
canis (4)					
arte					
umbrae (3)					
penātēs (2)					
honōribus (2)					
oculō (2)					
xystum					

13C. Conjugate the following verbs. Translate each form.

verb: **dūcō, -ere, duxī, ductus**

conjugation _____

PERFECT	Latin	Translation
Singular		
1st		
2nd		
3rd		
Plural		
1st		
2nd		
3rd		
Infinitive		

verb: **cēnō, -āre, -āvī, -ātus**

conjugation _____

PLUPERFECT	Latin	Translation
Singular		
1st		
2nd		
3rd		
Plural		
1st		
2nd		
3rd		

verb: **iubeō, -ēre, iussī, iussus**

conjugation _____

FUTURE PERFECT	Latin	Translation
Singular		
1st		
2nd		
3rd		
Plural		
1st		
2nd		
3rd		

13D. For the following verbs, give the dictionary entry, person, number, tense, and mood. Underline the principal part from which the Latin form derives. Translate each form. (N.B. Infinitives do not have person and number—just translate those forms. Imperatives are second person, but be sure to give the number and translation for those forms.)

Form	Dictionary Entry	Person	No.	Tense	Mood	Translation
cāverat						
respondēs						
placuērunt						
spectāvistis						
ceciderāmus						
crēvimus						
effēcit						
cēnābās						
optat						
cēnāverās						
trādiderint						
sumpsī						
cupiet						
clauserant						
vīcēre						
contigerimus						

Form	Dictionary Entry	Person	No.	Tense	Mood	Translation
docueris						
habent						
dūcam						
duxerātis						
ēgerit						
colueritis						
iubēbāmus						
gerētis						
mīseram						
presserō						
scīvistī						

13E. Identify each of the following forms by tense. Translate the given forms. Then, keeping the same person and number, convert them as follows: present ←→ perfect; imperfect ←→ pluperfect; future ←→ future perfect. Translate the converted form.

Form	Tense	Translation of Given Form	Conversion	Translation of Converted Form
duxisse				
iusserat				
cēnāre				
clausēre				
ceciderint				
contigistī				
tenent				
cantāveram				
legēs				
audīvisse				
scīverāmus				
mōvēre				
fūgerō				
vēnerātis				
gesserit				

13F. Give the requested Latin forms.

1. huge houses (Nominative) _____

2. of a spacious country estate _____

3. household gods (Accusative) _____

4. on the bed _____

5. with no skill _____

6. for the sake of honor _____

7. You (singular) have fallen. _____

8. She has dined. _____

9. They have ordered. _____

10. I had touched. _____

11. You (plural) had fallen. _____

12. They will have been on guard. _____

13. He will have considered. _____

14. We shall have closed. _____

15. to have fallen _____

13G. Translate into coherent, idiomatic English.

1. Umbrae tecta atque xystōs contigērunt.

_____

2. Penātēs nōs domum īre iusserint.

_____

3. Fīliī nostrī multa scelera ingentī in bellō vīderant.

_____

4. Ipsī apud amīcōs super xystum cēnāverimus.

_____

5. Laetī multa carmina apud victōrem cantāverātis.

_____

6. Artemne virtūtem hominibus sacram dūcere voluistis?

_____

7. Sorōrēsne patrem miserum ducī malō trādere nōluerant?

_____

8. Dum iuvenēs bellum gerēbant, urbs cecidit.

_____

9. Villae amplae regiōnibus in aprīcīs vōs laetōs fēcerint.

_____

10. Fīlia rēgis doctī bona sententiās lībertārum suārum audīre māluit.

_____

13H. Translate the following sentences into Latin. Use the rubric below each sentence as a guide.

We shall have sent sweet letters to the freedmen.

Person, number, and tense of "we shall have sent" _____
Dictionary entry _____
Latin translation _____

Syntactic function and case of "sweet letters" _____
Dictionary entry of "letters" _____
Dictionary entry of "sweet" _____
Latin translation of "sweet letters" _____

Syntactic function and case of "to the freedmen and freedwomen" ___

_____

Dictionary entry of "freedman" _____
Latin translation of "to the freedmen" _____

Latin translation of entire sentence _____

_____

Had the kings conquered great cities?

Person, number, and tense of "(they) had conquered" _____
Dictionary entry _____
Latin translation _____

Syntactic function and case of "kings" _____

Latin translation _____

Syntactic function and case of "great cities" _____

Dictionary entry of "cities" _____

Dictionary entry of "great" _____

Latin translation of "great cities" _____

Latin translation of entire sentence _____

_____

13I. Give the Latin forms for the following English phrases. Then recombine the **double-underlined** letters to spell the Latin word for "dining room" (in the singular).

the closest estates: __ __ __ __ __ __ __ __

__ __ __ __ __ __

a huge dog: __ __ __ __ __ __   __ __ __ __ __

happy homes: __ __ __ __ __   __ __ __ __ __

we shall have dined: __ __ __ __ __ __ __ __ __

I had considered: __ __ __ __ __ __ __

to have ordered: __ __ __ __ __ __ __ __

ANSWER: __ __ __ __ __ __ __ __

Numbers

14A. Decline the following noun-adjective pair.

Case	factiō, -iōnis, f + prasinus, -a, -um
Singular	
Nominative	
Genitive	
Dative	
Accusative	
Ablative	
Plural	
Nominative	
Genitive	
Dative	
Accusative	
Ablative	

14B. Identify the following noun forms as directed. For ambiguous forms, give all possibilities. Give the correct form of **extrēmus, -a, -um** and **pār (paris)** to modify each form. (N.B. Since the vocative forms are usually identical to the nominative forms, do not include these forms among your responses.)

Latin Form	Decl.	Case	No.	Gender	extrēmus, -a, -um	pār (paris)
nepōtī						
gladiātōrum						
praemia (2)						
bestiā						
palmārum						
spectāculī						
amphitheātrīs (2)						
mūneribus (2)						
principe						
vēnātiōnis						
agitātor						

14C. Give a synopsis of the following verbs. Translate each form.

verb: **vincō, -ere, vīcī, victus**
conjugation _____
synopsis: 3rd person singular

INDICATIVES	3rd Person Singular	Translation
Present		
Imperfect		
Future		
Perfect		
Pluperfect		
Future Perfect		

vincō, -ere, vīcī, victus

IMPERATIVES	Singular	Translation
Present		
Future		

INFINITIVES	Latin Form	Translation
Present		
Perfect		

verb: **pugnō, -āre, -āvī, -ātus**
conjugation _____
synopsis: 3rd person plural

INDICATIVES	3rd Person Plural	Translation
Present		
Imperfect		
Future		
Perfect		
Pluperfect		
Future Perfect		

IMPERATIVES	Plural	Translation
Present		
Future		

INFINITIVES	Latin Form	Translation
Present		
Perfect		

14D. For the following verbs, give the dictionary entry, person, number, tense, and mood. Underline the principal part from which the Latin form derives. Translate each form. (N.B. Infinitives do not have person and number—just translate those forms. Imperatives are second person, but be sure to give the number and translation for those forms.)

Form	Dictionary Entry	Person	No.	Tense	Mood	Translation
fuēre						
dedimus						
habueram						
vīxī						
cēperat						
fēceris						
ēgerint						
dixerō						
gessērunt						
mīserās						
pressistī						
scripserit						
fūgistis						
scīvisse						
crēdidit						
sumpserant						
incēperimus						
īverāmus						
tuleritis						
māluimus						
potuerātis						
voluerint						

14E. Give the requested Latin forms.

1. both wounds (Accusative) _____

2. of joyful spectacles _____

3. for equally matched charioteers _____

   4. on account of the green faction _____

   5. with a white victory palm _____

   6. well-matched gladiators (Nominative) _____

   7. They have fought twice. _____

   8. A wild beast has conquered. _____

   9. The emperor's grandson will have ordered the soldiers. _____

      _____

  10. A red faction had touched the blue fleet. _____

14F. Translate into coherent, idiomatic English.

   1. In regiōnibus noxiīs mīles vulnera ter accēpit.

      _____

   2. Hodiē montēs albōs trīs vidēre voluistis.

      _____

   3. Victor palmās octō sumpserit.

      _____

   4. Nepōs mēcum ad septem domūs iit.

      _____

   5. Gladiātor sōlus quinque et vīgintī bestiās pugnāverat.

      _____

   6. Princeps factiōnem prasinam venetae agitātōrēs cavēre iussit.

      _____

   7. Cīvēs Rōmānī amphitheātrō in novō vēnātiōnem sexāgēsimam
      quartam spectābant.

      _____

   8. Dux factiōnibus praemia ambōbus aequa dabit.

      _____

   9. Populīs nōn sōlum animalia sed etiam classēs placent.

      _____

  10. Sī penātēs cīvitātis hostēs vīcerint, mīlia labōrum ferre volam.

      _____

14G. Translate the following sentences into Latin. Use the rubric below each sentence as a guide.

The horses had lived for twenty years.

Person, number, and tense of "(they) had lived" _____

Dictionary entry _____

Latin translation _____

Syntactic function and case of "for twenty years" _____

Latin translation _____

Latin translation of entire sentence _____

_____

Approximately one thousand gladiators will fight.

Person, number, and tense of "(they) will fight" _____

Dictionary entry _____

Latin translation _____

Latin translation of entire sentence _____

_____

14H. Fill in the blanks with correctly formed Latin words from the required lesson vocabulary (*NLP* 13–14). You may use any word only once. There is no "right" answer.

Nocte *(noun)*_____ aequī ad *(noun)*_____

magnam vēnēre, ubi spectacula *(number)*_____

vidēre incipiēbant. *(noun)*_____ dē nāvalibus

metuēbant. Tandem prō *(noun)*_____

princeps *(noun)*_____ *(infinitive)*_____

iussit. Autem cīvēs *(adjective)*_____ *(verb)*_____.

Itaque urbs *(verb)*_____.

Demonstrative and Indefinite Pronouns

15A. Decline the following noun-adjective pair.

Case	geminus, -ī, m + hic, haec, hoc
Singular	
Nominative	
Genitive	
Dative	
Accusative	
Ablative	
Plural	
Nominative	
Genitive	
Dative	
Accusative	
Ablative	

15B. Identify each of the following pronouns and pronominal adjectives by case, number, and gender. Give the basic meaning of each one.

Pronoun	Case	No.	Gender	Basic Meaning
huic (3 genders)				
eōrundem (2 genders)				
illī (3 genders; 2 cases)				
aliquibus (3 genders; 2 cases)				
hoc (2 cases)				
illās				
aliqua (3 answers)				
quendam				
haec (4 answers)				
quiddam (2 answers)				
hunc				
īsdem (3 genders; 2 cases)				
illud (2 answers)				
eandem				
alicuius (3 genders)				
quaedam (4 answers)				

15C. Give the requested forms for the following pronouns and pronominal adjectives.

Pronoun/Pron. Adj.	Requested Form	Latin Form
hic, haec, hoc	Accusative singular masculine	
hic, haec, hoc	Dative singular feminine	
hic, haec, hoc	Nominative plural masculine	
ille, illa, illud	Genitive singular neuter	
ille, illa, illud	Accusative singular neuter	
ille, illa, illud	Ablative plural feminine	
īdem, eadem, idem	Dative singular neuter	
īdem, eadem, idem	Genitive plural feminine	
īdem, eadem, idem	Accusative singular masculine	
aliquis, aliqua, aliquid	Dative singular masculine	
aliquis, aliqua, aliquid	Genitive singular feminine	
aliquis, aliqua, aliquid	Ablative plural feminine	
quīdam, quaedam, quiddam	Genitive plural neuter	
quīdam, quaedam, quiddam	Nominative singular neuter	
quīdam, quaedam, quiddam	Dative plural masculine	

15D. Identify the following noun forms as directed. For ambiguous forms, give all possibilities. Give the correct form of **īdem, eadem, idem** and **ille, illa, illud** to modify each form. (N.B. Since the vocative forms are usually identical to the nominative forms, do not include these forms among your responses.)

Latin Form	Decl.	Case	No.	Gender	īdem, eadem, idem	ille, illa, illud
familiae (3)						
dominī (2)						
castra (2)						
geminō (2)						
nāvium						
familiīs (2)						
nāvīs						

15E. Give the Latin for the following phrases.

1. these men (Nominative) _____

2. those women (Accusative) _____

3. a certain girl (Nominative) _____

4. some youth (Accusative) _____

5. of those children of yours _____

6. to/for a certain spouse _____

7. the same wild beast (Accusative) _____

8. with any freedman _____

9. these ships (Accusative) _____

10. for some gladiator _____

15F. Give a synopsis of the following verbs. Translate each form.

verb: **dīligō, -ere, dīlexī, dīlectus**
conjugation_____
synopsis: 2nd person singular

INDICATIVES	2nd Person Singular	Translation
Present		
Imperfect		
Future		
Perfect		
Pluperfect		
Future Perfect		

IMPERATIVES	Singular	Translation
Present		
Future		

INFINITIVES	Latin Form	Translation
Present		
Perfect		

verb: **abeō, -īre, -īvī, -ītus**
conjugation _____
synopsis: 2nd person plural

INDICATIVES	2nd Person Plural	Translation
Present		
Imperfect		
Future		
Perfect		
Pluperfect		
Future Perfect		

IMPERATIVES	Plural	Translation
Present		

INFINITIVES	Latin Form	Translation
Present		
Perfect		

15G. For the following verbs, give the dictionary entry, person, number, tense, and mood. Underline the principal part from which the Latin form derives. Translate each form. (N.B. Infinitives do not have person and number—just translate those forms. Imperatives are second person, but be sure to give the number and translation for those forms.)

Form	Dictionary Entry	Person	No.	Tense	Mood	Translation
fert						
poterimus						
potuerimus						
volam						
māluisse						
iēre						
tulerās						
dīligēbātis						
putābunt						
vincēs						
crēverit						
contigeram						
reddunt						
claudēbātis						
fueritis						
intellegēbam						
trādidisse						
adfuistī						
respondit						
posuerāmus						
relīquit						
esse						

15H. Translate the following sentences.

1. Nātōs illōs dīlexī.

_____

2. Hās puellās amāverātis.

_____

3. Istī libellōs reddēbant.

_____

4. Aliquī geminī castra pōnunt.

_____

5. Quīdam dominī uxōrēs suās intellegent.

_____

6. Princeps hic illōs nāvēs accēpit.

_____

7. Aliquis mātre cum hāc cēnāverit.

_____

8. Quaedam factiōnēs vincent.

_____

9. Pater cuiusdam nātī vēnātiōnēs spectābat.

_____

10. Familiae istae abeunt.

_____

15I. Translate the following sentences into Latin. Use the rubric below each sentence as a guide.

Whether slave or free, all citizens cherish the same things.

Person, number, and tense of "(they) cherish" _____
Dictionary entry _____
Latin translation _____

Syntactic function and case of "citizens" _____
Dictionary entry _____
Latin translation _____

Syntactic function and case of "slave or free" _____

Dictionary entry of "slave" _____

Dictionary entry of "free" _____

Latin translation _____

Syntactic function and case of "same things" _____

Dictionary entry _____

Latin translation _____

Latin translation of entire sentence _____

_____

Those freedmen no longer trusted these freedwomen.

Person, number, and tense of "(they) trusted" _____

_____

Dictionary entry _____

Latin translation _____

Syntactic function and case of "freedmen" _____

Latin adjective meaning "that/those" _____

Latin translation _____

Syntactic function and case of "freedwomen" _____

Latin adjective meaning "this/these" _____

Latin translation _____

Latin translation of entire sentence _____

_____

15J. Give the Latin forms for the following English phrases. Then recombine the **double-underlined** letters to spell the Latin word for a place where slaves worked (in the singular).

You have esteemed:

‗ — — — — — — ‗ —

those household slaves (Accusative):

‗ — — ‗ — — —

‗ — — — —

(who) have pitched camp:

— ‗ — — — —

— — — ‗ — — ‗ — —

for these twins of yours:

— — ‗ — ‗ — —

— — ‗ — —

ANSWER: __ __ __ __ __ __ __ __ __ __

Relative Pronouns, Relative Clauses, and Interrogative Pronouns

16A. Decline the following noun-pronoun pair.

Case	**sīdus, sīderis**, n + **quī, quae, quod**
Singular	
Nominative	
Genitive	
Dative	
Accusative	
Ablative	
Plural	
Nominative	
Genitive	
Dative	
Accusative	
Ablative	

16B. Identify each of the following forms of the relative pronoun by case, number, and gender.

Pronoun	Case	No.	Gender
quōs			
cuius (3 genders)			
quī (2 answers)			
quam			
quibus (3 genders; 2 cases)			
quae (4 answers)			
cui (3 genders)			
quō (2 genders)			
quārum			
quod (2 cases)			
quem			
quōrum (2 genders)			
quās			

16C. Give the requested forms for the interrogative pronoun **quis, quid**.

Requested Form	Latin Form
Accusative singular feminine	
Dative plural masculine	
Nominative plural neuter	
Nominative singular feminine	
Ablative singular neuter	
Ablative plural feminine	
Accusative plural masculine	
Genitive singular neuter	
Genitive plural feminine	
Dative singular masculine	

16D. Give the Latin for the following phrases (use the relative pronoun as a relative adjective).

1. which wrath (Nominative) _____

2. for which clouds _____

3. on which rock _____

4. of which blood _____

5. which groves (Nominative) _____

6. which season (Accusative) _____

7. of which moons _____

8. for which star _____

9. which winds (Nominative) _____

10. which storms (Accusative) _____

16E. Identify the following noun forms as directed. For ambiguous forms, give all possibilities. Give the correct form of **quī, quae, quod** to modify each form. Translate the resulting phrases.

Latin Form	Decl.	Case	No.	Gender	quī, quae, quod	Translation
stellam						
saxa (2)						
superōrum						
nemorī						
orbī (2)						
sanguinum						
tempestātis						
sīderibus (2)						
īrā						
lūnae (3)						
ventī (2)						

16F. Give a synopsis of the following verbs. Translate each form.

verb: **metuō, -ere, -uī**
conjugation _____
synopsis: 1st person singular

INDICATIVES	1st Person Singular	Translation
Present		
Imperfect		
Future		
Perfect		
Pluperfect		
Future Perfect		

IMPERATIVES	Singular	Translation
Present		
Future		

INFINITIVES	Latin Form	Translation
Present		
Perfect		

verb: **iaceō, -ēre, -uī**
conjugation _____
synopsis: 1st person plural

INDICATIVES	1st Person Plural	Translation
Present		
Imperfect		
Future		
Perfect		
Pluperfect		
Future Perfect		

iaceō, -ēre, -uī

IMPERATIVES	Plural	Translation
Present		
Future		

INFINITIVES	Latin Form	Translation
Present		
Perfect		

16G. For the following verbs, give the dictionary entry, person, number, tense, and mood. Underline the principal part from which the Latin form derives. Translate each form. (N.B. Infinitives do not have person and number—just translate those forms. Imperatives are second person, but be sure to give the number and translation for those forms.)

Verb	Dictionary Entry	Person	No.	Tense	Mood	Translation
nōvī						
iacuistī						
tulerint						
rediī						
recipere						
metuēre						
recipiēbāmus						
fefellerās						
iacēs						
tuleram						
nōvisse						
metuitō						

16H. Translate the following sentences into coherent English.

1. Poētae carmina quae cīvibus adhūc placent scripsēre.

_____

2. Equus quem eques spectābit iter longum fēcerit.

_____

3. Ducem in cuius manūs animōs commendāverimus dīligēmus.

_____

4. Illōs quī prō patriā suā pugnant imperātor laudat.

_____

5. Hominem cuius agrōs cēperātis fugiēbātis.

_____

6. Fēmina autem cui crēdidimus bona dux erat.

_____

7. Trans mare altōsque montēs urbēs in quibus habitābātis iacent.

_____

8. Cīvēs vīrtūtem, sine quā dormīre nōn possunt, bonam putant.

_____

9. Superī magnī lūnam stellāsque sacrās quās nocte vidēmus in caelō posuērunt.

_____

10. Populī quibus mūnera Augustus dedit laetī erant.

_____

16I. Translate the following sentences into Latin. Use the rubric below each sentence as a guide.

The stars which fall from the sky still please me.

Antecedent of "which" _____

Gender and number of the antecedent _____

Syntactic function of "which" in its own clause _____

Case, number, and gender of "which" _____

Latin translation _____

Person, number, and tense of "(they) fall" _____

Dictionary entry _____

Latin translation _____

Person, number, and tense of "(they) please" _____

Dictionary entry _____

Latin translation _____

Case of "me" _____

Latin translation _____

Latin translation of entire sentence _____

_____

The soldiers pitched camp near the rocks on which the king was lying.

Person, number, and tense of "(they) pitched camp" _____

_____

Dictionary entry _____

Latin translation _____

Antecedent of "which" _____

Gender and number of the antecedent _____

Syntactic function of "which" in its own clause _____

Case, number, and gender of "which" _____

Latin translation _____

Person, number, and tense of "(he) was lying" _____

Dictionary entry _____

Latin translation _____

Latin translation of entire sentence _____

_____

That man whose city is great is able to wage war on his neighbors.

Antecedent of "whose" _____

Gender and number of the antecedent _____

Syntactic function of "whose" in its own clause _____

Case, number, and gender of "whose" _____

Latin translation _____

Case, number, and gender of "city" _____

Latin translation _____

Person, number, and tense of "(he) is able" _____

Dictionary entry _____

Latin translation _____

Latin translation of entire sentence _____

_____

We saw the light of the moon in the grove through which few men went.

Person, number, and tense of "we saw" _____

Dictionary entry _____

Latin translation _____

Antecedent of "which" _____

Gender and number of the antecedent _____

Syntactic function of "which" in its own clause _____

Case, number, and gender of "which" _____

Latin translation _____

Person, number, and tense of "(they) went" _____

Dictionary entry _____

Latin translation _____

Latin translation of entire sentence _____

_____

16J. Give the Latin forms for the following English phrases. Then recombine the **double-underlined** letters to spell the title of a Latin work that treats meteorology.

It was raining: __ __ __ __ __ __ __ __ __

Bad storms: __ __ __ __ __ __   __ __ __ __

Of each globe: __ __ __ __ __

__ __ __ __ __ __ __ __ __

They will return: __ __ __ __ __ __ __ __

Deceive! (Future): __ __ __ __ __ __ __ __ __

A few clouds: __ __ __ __ __ __   __ __ __ __ __

Which star: __ __ __ __   __ __ __ __ __ __

ANSWER: __ __ __ __ __ __ __ __

__ __ __ __ __ __ __ __ __

Passive Verbs: Present, Imperfect, and Future Tenses

17A. Conjugate the following verbs. Translate each form.

verb: **dēbeō, -ēre, -uī, -itus**

conjugation _____

PRESENT	Active	Translation	Passive	Translation
Singular				
1st				
2nd				
3rd				
Imperative				
Plural				
1st				
2nd				
3rd				
Imperative				
Infinitive				

IMPERFECT	Active	Translation	Passive	Translation
Singular				
1st				
2nd				
3rd				

(*Continued*)

dēbeō, -ēre, -uī, -itus

IMPERFECT	Active	Translation	Passive	Translation
Plural				
1st				
2nd				
3rd				

FUTURE	Active	Translation	Passive	Translation
Singular				
1st				
2nd				
3rd				
Imperative				
Plural				
1st				
2nd				
3rd				
Imperative			XXX	XXX

verb: **petō, -ere, -īvī, -ītus**

conjugation _____

PRESENT	Active	Translation	Passive	Translation
Singular				
1st				
2nd				
3rd				
Imperative				
Plural				
1st				
2nd				
3rd				
Imperative				
Infinitive				

petō, -ere, -īvī, -ītus

IMPERFECT	Active	Translation	Passive	Translation
Singular				
1st				
2nd				
3rd				
Plural				
1st				
2nd				
3rd				

FUTURE	Active	Translation	Passive	Translation
Singular				
1st				
2nd				
3rd				
Imperative				
Plural				
1st				
2nd				
3rd				
Imperative				

verb: **inveniō, -īre, -vēnī, -ventus**

conjugation_____

PRESENT	Active	Translation	Passive	Translation
Singular				
1st				
2nd				
3rd				
Imperative				

(Continued)

inveniō, -īre, -vēnī, -ventus

PRESENT	Active	Translation	Passive	Translation
Plural				
1st				
2nd				
3rd				
Imperative				
Infinitive				

IMPERFECT	Active	Translation	Passive	Translation
Singular				
1st				
2nd				
3rd				
Plural				
1st				
2nd				
3rd				

FUTURE	Active	Translation	Passive	Translation
Singular				
1st				
2nd				
3rd				
Imperative				
Plural				
1st				
2nd				
3rd				
Imperative			XXX	XXX

17B. For the following verbs, give the 1st principal part, conjugation, person, number, and tense. Translate each form. (N.B. Infinitives do not have person and number—just translate those forms. Imperatives are second person, but be sure to give the number and translation for those forms.)

Form	Dictionary Entry and Conjugation	Person and Number	Tense and Voice (Active/Passive)	Mood	Translation
noscor					
exigō					
solvimur					
metuimus (2)					
recipere (3)					
dīdūcis					
metuēbāre					
dīdūcēbāminī					
ferris					
recipī					
dēbētur					
petēbar					
timēbās					
exigentur					
petētur					
solvēminī					
dēbēbitur					
petar					
nocēbunt					
timēbitis					
noscī					
iacēbō					
invenīrī					
fer					

17C. Give the requested forms of the following verbs. Translate each form.

Latin Verb	Requested Form	Latin Form	Translation
pugnō	1st person singular Present passive		
noceō	Present passive Infinitive		
ferō	3rd person singular Future passive		
respondeō	2nd person plural Imperfect passive		
recipiō	3rd person singular Present passive		
laudō	2nd person singular Future passive		
parō	1st person plural Imperfect passive		
ferō	2nd person plural Present passive		
petō	Present passive Infinitive		
exigō	1st person singular Future passive		
ferō	1st person plural Imperfect passive		
sciō	Present passive Infinitive		
solvō	2nd person singular Future passive		
āmittō	3rd person plural Imperfect passive		
sentiō	3rd person plural Present passive		

17D. Identify the following verbs by person, number, tense, and voice. Translate the given forms. Then, keeping the same person, number, and tense, convert the following passive forms to active and active forms to passive. Translate each converted form.

Latin Form	Person, Number, Tense, Voice, and Mood	Translation of Given Form	Conversion	Translation
trādō				
cupiēbāminī				
sūment				
appellāmus				
vincēre				
cēnāre (2)				
dūcēbātur				
claudet				
iubēbis				
pugnābāmur				
dīligēris				
intelleguntur				
pōnēbar				
recipī				
āmittēbat				

17E. Give the Latin for the following phrases.

1. I was feared. _____

2. She is discovered. _____

3. to be arrived at _____

4. We shall be sought. _____

5. It was come upon. _____

6. You (plural) are sent away. _____

7. to be harmed _____

8. They will be drawn apart. _____

9. It will be weakened. _____

10. (Money) was owed. _____

17F. Translate the following sentences into coherent English.

1. Librī populīs Rōmānīs ab imperātore hōc dēbentur.

_____

2. Ipsae illās piscīnās fontīsque invenīrī volumus.

_____

3. Lībertī ā dominīs suīs veteribus appellābuntur.

_____

4. Auxilium virōrum iustōrum quōrundam ā cīvibus īsdem exigēbātur.

_____

5. Speciēs fēminae dignae solvētur.

_____

6. Cīvitāte in vīcīnā aliquā vestrīs ā līberīs petiminī.

_____

7. Princeps bonus meīs in temporibus dūcēbar.

_____

8. Dī quīdam inter rīvōs colī nōlēbant.

_____

9. Nocte vincī poteritis.

_____

10. Mōrēs bonī puellīs aliquibus puerīsque trādentur.

_____

17G. Translate the following sentences into Latin. Use the rubric below each sentence as a guide.

Water was (being) demanded by the mothers on behalf of the children.

Person, number, tense, and, voice of "(it) was (being) demanded" _____

_____

Dictionary entry _____

Latin translation _____

Subject of "was demanded" _____

Case that renders the subject _____

Syntactic function and case of "by the mothers" _____

Latin translation _____

Latin translation of entire sentence _____

_____

The horns of the animals will not be feared by the Roman legions.

Person, number, tense, and voice of "(they) will be feared" _____

_____

Dictionary entry _____

Latin translation _____

Subject of "will be feared" _____

Case that renders the subject _____

Syntactic function and case of "of the animals" _____

_____

Latin translation _____

Syntactic function and case of "by the Roman legions" _____

_____

Latin translation _____

Latin translation of entire sentence _____

_____

O temple, you ought to be cherished.

Person, number, tense, and voice of "you ought" _____

_____

Dictionary entry _____

Latin translation _____

Tense and voice of "to be cherished" _____

Verbal construction of "to be cherished" _____

Dictionary entry of "cherish" _____

Latin translation _____

Latin translation of entire sentence _____

_____

In the neighboring grove, our horses were injured by rocks.

Person, number, tense, and voice of "(they) were injured" _____

_____

Dictionary entry _____

Latin translation _____

Subject of "were injured" _____

Case that renders the subject _____

Syntactic function and case of "by rocks" _____

Latin translation _____

Latin translation of entire sentence _____

_____

17H. A haiku to translate.

Per Aquās Rōmae
ad omnia sīdera
glōria fertur.

Haiku is a traditional form of Japanese poetry consisting of 17 syllables in three lines (5, 7, 5 syllables respectively). Using at least one passive verb form, construct your own haiku about the Roman aqueduct system in grammatically correct Latin.

_____

_____

_____

Passive Verbs: Perfect, Pluperfect, and Future Perfect Tenses

18A. Decline the following noun-adjective pairs.

Case	currus, -ūs, m + dīvus, -a, -um	aciēs, -iēī, f + cadens (-entis)
Singular		
Nominative		
Genitive		
Dative		
Accusative		
Ablative		
Plural		
Nominative		
Genitive		
Dative		
Accusative		
Ablative		

18B. Conjugate the following verb. Translate each form.

verb: **caedō, -ere, cecīdī, caesus**
conjugation _____

PRESENT	Active	Translation	Passive	Translation
Singular				
1st				
2nd				
3rd				
Imperative				
Plural				
1st				
2nd				
3rd				
Imperative				
Infinitive				

IMPERFECT	Active	Translation	Passive	Translation
Singular				
1st				
2nd				
3rd				
Plural				
1st				
2nd				
3rd				

FUTURE	Active	Translation	Passive	Translation
Singular				
1st				
2nd				
3rd				
Imperative				

caedō, -ere, cecīdī, caesus

Plural				
1st				
2nd				
3rd				
Imperative			XXX	XXX

PERFECT	Active	Translation	Passive	Translation
Singular				
1st				
2nd				
3rd				
Plural				
1st				
2nd				
3rd				
Infinitive				

PLUPERFECT	Active	Translation	Passive	Translation
Singular				
1st				
2nd				
3rd				
Plural				
1st				
2nd				
3rd				

(Continued)

caedō, -ere, cecīdī, caesus

FUTURE PERFECT	Active	Translation	Passive	Translation
Singular				
1st				
2nd				
3rd				
Plural				
1st				
2nd				
3rd				

18C. For the following verbs, give the dictionary entry, conjugation, person, number, and tense. Translate each form. (N.B. Infinitives do not have person and number—just translate those forms. Imperatives are second person, but be sure to give the number and translation for those forms.)

Form	Dictionary Entry and Conjugation	Person and No.	Tense and Voice (A/P)	Mood	Translation
mūtāris					
caedēbant					
dēfertur					
indictī erātis					
contemnēminī					
iaciam					
contempserimus					
iacta eris					
cecīderit					
dēlātae erāmus					
indīcitur					
iēcērunt					
situs eram					
caesī sunt					
contemptum esse					
mūtāveram					
sīvisse					
dētulerātis					

18D. Identify the following verbs by person, number, tense, and voice. Translate the given forms. Then, keeping the same person, number, and tense, convert the following passive forms to active and active forms to passive. Translate each converted form.

Latin Form	Person, Number, Tense, and Voice	Translation of Given Form	Conversion	Translation
mūtāvere				
caesa erat				
sīveris				
indictae erimus				
dētulisse				
iēcit				
contempserātis				
āmissum esse				
solūta erunt				
perventum erās				
petītī erātis				
exēgī				

18E. Give the requested forms of the following verbs. Translate each form.

Latin Verb	Requested Form	Latin Form	Translation
ferō	3rd person singular Perfect passive		
inveniō	Perfect passive Infinitive		
iaciō	3rd person singular Pluperfect passive		
contemnō	1st person plural Future Perfect passive		
parō	2nd person singular Pluperfect passive		
indīcō	1st person plural Perfect passive		
mūtō	2nd person plural Perfect passive		
caedō	Perfect passive Infinitive		
sinō	3rd person plural Future passive		
dēbeō	1st person singular Perfect passive		
exigō	2nd person plural Future Perfect passive		
solvō	3rd person singular Future Perfect passive		
dēferō	2nd person singular Pluperfect passive		
dīdūcō	Perfect passive Infinitive		
āmittō	1st person singular Pluperfect passive		

18F. Complete each of the following phrases with the correct form of the verb in parentheses. Translate the complete phrase.

Example: sīdus **dīlectum est** _____ (dīligō) **the star has been esteemed**

Hint: Identify the number and gender of each noun to arrive at the correct form of the fourth principal part.

PERFECT PASSIVE

auctor _____ (noscō) _____

auxilium _____ (dēbeō) _____

cornua _____ (recipiō) _____

castra _____ (pōnō) _____

exercitūs _____ (metuō) _____

imāginēs _____ (dēferō) _____

potestās _____ (capiō) _____

PLUPERFECT PASSIVE

fons _____ (indīcō) _____

imāgō _____ (mūtō) _____

milliārium _____ (sinō) _____

imbrēs _____ (contemnō) _____

nemora _____ (claudō) _____

piscīnae _____ (putō) _____

FUTURE PERFECT PASSIVE

aciēs _____ (trādō) _____

carmen _____ (cupiō) _____

dominus _____ (laudō) _____

familiae _____ (spectō) _____

senātūs _____ (respondeō) _____

opera _____ (faciō) _____

18G. Give the Latin for the following phrases.

1. I (masculine) have been despised. _____

   _____

2. She had been pointed out. _____

   _____

3. They (neuter) will have been handed over. _____

   _____

4. You (feminine plural) have been changed. _____

   _____

5. It had been said. _____

   _____

6. You (feminine singular) will have been thrown. _____

   _____

7. to have been killed _____

   _____

8. We (masculine) had been deceived. _____

   _____

9. You (masculine plural) will have been esteemed. _____

   _____

10. You (masculine singular) had been seized. _____

    _____

11. They (feminine plural) will have been received. _____

    _____

12. We (feminine) have been led. _____

    _____

18H. Translate the following sentences into coherent English.

1. Senātus litterās quae ā hostibus aliquibus missae sunt contempsit.

   _____

2. Templum quoddam metū cum magnō indictum erat.

   _____

3. Imaginēs alicuius principis cuius potestās solūta erat caesae erunt.

   _____

4. Nocte rex ipse currū in aureō urbem ad antīquam ductus est.

   _____

5. Aciēs vel cīvēs illōs vel hōs lībertōs caedere nōn sita erit.

_____

6. Populī pax Rōmānī, dum Caesar vixit, dīva vīsa est.

_____

7. Agitātōrēs factiōnis venetae mūneribus spectāculīsque suīs dīlectī erant.

_____

8. Īdem auctor in nemore extrā rīvōs istōs inventus erit.

_____

9. Sīdera atque stellae atque lūna apud dominum ā quibusdam līberīs vīsa erant.

_____

10. Quī cīvitātis penātēs Rōmānō senātuī dētulerās imperātor bonus positus erās.

_____

18I. Translate the following sentences into Latin. Use the rubric below each sentence as a guide.

The command of the cities had been sought by the fierce kings.

Subject of "had been sought" _____

Case, number, and gender of the subject _____

Latin translation _____

Case, number, and gender of "of the cities" _____

Latin translation _____

Person, number, tense, and voice of "(it) had been sought" _____

_____

Dictionary entry _____

Latin translation _____

Syntactic function and case of "by the fierce kings" _____

Latin translation _____

Latin translation of entire sentence _____

_____

The emperor has been killed by rocks, and we have been separated into three camps.

Subject of "has been killed" _____

Case, number, and gender of the subject _____

Latin translation _____

Person, number, tense, and voice of "(he) has been killed" _____

_____

Dictionary entry _____

Latin translation _____

Syntactic function and case of "by rocks" _____

Latin translation _____

Person, number, tense, and voice of "we have been separated" _____

_____

Dictionary entry _____

Latin translation _____

Latin translation of entire sentence _____

_____

18J. Fill in the blanks with correctly formed Latin words from the required lesson vocabulary (*NLP* 13–18). You may use any word only once. There is no "right" answer.

Imperātor in currū *(adjective)*_____ ad urbem *(adjective)*_____

īverat. Ipse ob *(noun)*_____ a(b) *(noun)*_____ metūtus

sed a(b) *(noun)*_____ dīlectus est. Spectāculum

prope *(noun)*_____omnibus ā populīs Rōmānīs, quī

principem *(adjective)*_____ suum *(verb)*_____,

vīsum est. Imperātor *(perfect passive verb)*_____ est.

NLP Review C (Lessons 13–18)

I: CONCEPTS

IA: Latin Verbs: Perfect System: Perfect, Pluperfect, and Future Perfect Active.

- The **PERFECT TENSE** indicates completed actions (I have read, you slept, they watched) (*NLP* 13).
- The **PLUPERFECT TENSE** indicates actions that have been completed before another past action (Before coming to class, I had read, you had slept, they had watched) (*NLP* 13).
- The **FUTURE PERFECT TENSE** indicates actions that will be completed before other actions can/will occur (By class time tomorrow, I shall have read, you will have slept, they will have watched) (*NLP* 13).

- The **PERFECT ACTIVE TENSE** is formed by adding a special set of perfect active endings to the stem of the third principal part (drop the final -ī):

Person	Singular	Plural
1st	**-ī**	**-imus**
2nd	**-istī**	**-istis**
3rd	**-it**	**-ērunt/-ēre**

- The **PLUPERFECT ACTIVE TENSE** is formed by adding *-era-* + the regular personal endings directly to the stem of the third principal part (drop the final -ī):

Person	Singular	Plural
1st	-eram	-erāmus
2nd	-erās	-erātis
3rd	-erat	-erant

- The **FUTURE PERFECT ACTIVE TENSE** is formed by adding *-eri-* + the regular personal endings directly to the stem of the third principal part (drop the final -ī):

Person	Singular	Plural
1st	-erō	-erimus
2nd	-eris	-eritis
3rd	-erit	-erint

IB: Latin Verbs: Passive Voice.

- In sentences with active voice verbs, the subject performs an action (*I read a book*). If the verb is passive, the subject receives the action (*the book is being read by me*).
- Passive verbs in the **present**, **imperfect**, and **future tenses** take a new set of personal endings (*NLP* 17):

Person	Singular	Plural
1st	-r	-mur
2nd	-ris/-re	-minī
3rd	-tur	-ntur

- The **PRESENT PASSIVE** is formed in exactly the same way as the present active. Only the endings differ (but note that **2nd person singular** in

3RD and 3RD -IO CONJUGATION VERBS takes -*e*- instead of -*i*- between the stem and ending).

Librum legō. *I read a book.* (active)
Liber legitur. *The book is (being) read.* (passive)

- The **IMPERFECT PASSIVE** is formed in exactly the same way as the imperfect active. Only the personal endings differ.

  Librum legēbam. *I was reading a book.* (active)
  Liber legebātur. *The book was (being) read.* (passive)

- The **FUTURE PASSIVE** is formed in exactly the same way as the present active. Only the endings differ (but note that **2nd person singular** in 2ND CONJUGATION VERBS will take –*be*– instead of –*bi*– between the stem and the ending).

  Librum legam. *I will read a book.* (active)
  Liber legētur. *The book will be read.* (passive)

- Passive verbs in the **perfect, pluperfect,** and **future perfect** tenses are formed from the fourth principal part and the verb *esse* (*NLP* 18).

- The **PERFECT PASSIVE** is formed from the fourth principal part— declined to agree with the subject in case, number, and gender—and the **PRESENT** tense of *esse*.

  Librum lēgī. *I have read a book.* (active)
  Liber lectus est. *The book has been read.* (passive)

- The **PLUPERFECT PASSIVE** is formed from the fourth principal part— declined to agree with the subject in case, number, and gender—and the **IMPERFECT** tense of *esse*.

  Librum lēgeram. *I had read a book.* (active)
  Liber lectus erat. *The book had been read.* (passive)

- The **FUTURE PERFECT PASSIVE** is formed from the fourth principal part—declined to agree with the subject in case, number, and gender— and the **FUTURE** tense of *esse*.

  Librum lēgerō. *I shall have read a book.* (active)
  Liber lectus erit. *The book will have been read.* (passive)

IC: More Pronouns.

- Pronouns take the place of nouns.
- Pronouns agree with their referents in **number** and **gender**.
- Pronouns take their case according to how they function in their own phrases.
- Translating pronouns is largely an issue of vocabulary (be sure to memorize the basic meanings of these common pronouns!):
  - **aliquis, aliqua, aliquid**: someone, something (*NLP* 15)
  - **hic, haec, hoc**: this, these, the former (*NLP* 15)
  - **īdem, eadem, idem**: the same (*NLP* 15)
  - **ille, illa, illud**: that, those, the latter (*NLP* 15)
  - **ipse, ipsa, ipsum**: him-/her-/it-/themselves; the very—(*NLP* 12)
  - **is, ea, id**: he, she it (*NLP* 12)
  - **iste, ista, istud**: that (of yours) (*NLP* 15)
  - **quī, quae, quod**: who, what (*NLP* 16: introduces a relative clause)
  - **quīdam, quaedam, quiddam**: a certain person(s)/things(s) (*NLP* 15)
  - **quis, quid**: who, what (*NLP* 16: introduces a question)

ID: Numbers (*NLP* 14).

- Most cardinal numbers in Latin are indeclinable, with the exceptions of *ūnus, -a, -um*; *duo, duae, duo*; *trēs, tria*; *quingentī, -ae, -a*.
- Ordinal numbers are 1st/2nd declension adjectives.
- See the tables in *NLP* 14.

II: VOCABULARY *NLP* 13–18

NOUNS

bestia, -iae, f: wild beast

culpa, -ae, f: blame, fault

familia, -iae, f: household slave, band of household slaves, family, household

īra, -ae, f: wrath, anger

littera, -ae, f: letter of the alphabet; in plural: dispatch, epistle

lūna, -ae, f: moon

palma, -ae, f: palm, hand; palm branch, palm tree, victory wreath

piscīna, -ae, f: fishpond

stella, -ae, f: star

umbra, -ae, f: shade, shadow

villa, -ae, f: country house, estate

amphitheātrum, -ī, n: amphitheater

auxilium, -iī, n: aid, help

dominus, -ī, m: household master, lord

domus, -ī or -ūs, f: house, home

fīlius, -iī, m: son

geminus, -ī, m: twin

initium, -iī, n: beginning

lectus, -ī, m: bed, couch, sofa

liber, librī, m: book

milliārium, -iī, n: milestone

nātus, -ī, m: son

nūbila, -ōrum, n (plural): clouds

oculus, -ī, m: eye

praemium, -iī, n: prize, reward

rīvus, -ī, m: stream

saxum, -ī, n: rock, cliff

spectāculum, -ī, n: spectacle, performance, show

superī, -ōrum, m (plural): gods

tectum, -ī, n: roof, building, house

ventus, -ī, m: wind

vitium, -iī, n: fault, vice

xystus, -ī, m: open colonnade, walk
planted with trees, promenade

aedēs, -is (-ium), f: temple, shrine;
room, house, home

āēr, āeris, m: air, atmosphere

agitātor, -ōris, m: driver, charioteer

ars, artis (-ium), f: skill

auctor, -ōris, m: originator, proposer,
founder

auctōritās, -ātis, f: responsibility,
authority

canis, -is, m/f: dog

classis, -is (-ium), f: fleet

factiō, -iōnis, f: band, group, team

fons, fontis (-ium), m: spring, fountain

gladiātor, -ōris, m: gladiator

honor, -ōris, m: honor, glory, mark of
respect or distinction

imāgō, imāginis, f: image, likeness,
copy

imber, imbris (-ium), m: shower, storm

imperātor, -ōris, m:
commander-in-chief, emperor,
victorious general

mūnus, mūneris, n: duty, gift, show,
performance, spectacle, function

nāvis, -is (-ium), f: ship

nemus, nemoris, n: grove, forest

nepōs, -ōtis, m: grandson,
descendent

orbis, -is (-ium) m: circle, disk; globe,
earth, world

pax, pācis, f: peace, harmony

penātēs, -ium, m (plural): the gods of
the home, hearth, or family line

potestās, -ātis, f: power, control,
authority

princeps, principis, m: leader, chief,
emperor

sanguis, sanguinis, m: blood

sīdus, sīderis, n: star, constellation,
planet

tempestās, -ātis, f: period of time,
season; bad weather, storm

vēnātiō, -iōnis, f: staged hunt

vulnus, -eris, n: wound

arcus, -ūs, m: arch, vault, bow

currus, -ūs, m: chariot

exercitus, -ūs, m: army

metus, -ūs, m: fear, dread

senātus, -ūs, m: senate

aciēs, -iēī, f: edge, battleline, battle

speciēs, -iēī, f: appearance, kind, type

PRONOUNS

aliquī, aliqua, aliquod: some, any (adjective)

aliquis, aliqua, aliquid: someone, something; anyone, anything (pronoun)

hīc, haec, hoc: this, these

īdem, eadem, idem: the same

ille, illa, illud: that, those

iste, ista, istud: that (of yours), those (of yours)

quī, quae, quod: who, what

quīdam, quaedam, quiddam: a certain one; a certain thing (pronoun)

quīdam, quaedam, quoddam: a certain (adjective)

quis, quid: who? what?

quisquam, quicquam/quidquam: any (single) person, anyone at all

ADJECTIVES

aequus, -a, -um: equal, fair, evenly matched (*in aequō*: on level ground)

albus, -a, -um: white

ambō, ambae, ambō: both, two

amplus, -a, -um: large, spacious

antīquus, -a, -um: ancient, old

aureus, -a, -um: golden

cēterus, -a, -um: other, the rest

dignus, -a, -um (+ ablative): worthy

dīvus, -a, -um: divine, deified

extrēmus, -a, -um: last, uttermost, lengthy, furthest

iustus, -a, -um: just

laetus, -a, -um: glad, joyful, happy

nullus, -a, -um: not any, no

paucī, -ae, -a (plural): few

prasinus, -a, -um: green

proximus, -a, -um: closest

russātus, -a, -um: red

ullus, -a, -um: any

uterque, utraque, utrumque: each (of two), both

venetus, -a, -um: blue

vīcīnus, -a, -um: neighboring, near

ingens (-entis): huge, enormous

nāvālis, -e: naval

pār (paris): equal, pair

plūs (plūris): more

turpis, -e: disgraceful, shameful, ugly

vetus (-eris): old, ancient

VERBS

cēnō, -āre, -āvī, -ātus: dine, eat

mūtō, -āre, -āvī, -ātus: change, alter, shift

pugnō, -āre, -āvī, -ātus: fight

caveō, -ēre, cāvī, cautus: be on guard, beware

dēbeō, -ēre, -uī, -itus: owe, ought to

iaceō, -ēre, iacuī: lie

iubeō, -ēre, iussī, iussus: order, command

noceō, -ēre, -uī: hurt, harm, injure

rīdeō, -ēre, rīsī, rīsus: laugh, laugh at

timeō, -ēre, -uī: fear, dread

āmittō, -ere, -mīsī, -missus: send away, let go, lose

cadō, -ere, cecidī, cāsus: fall, be killed, abate

caedō, -ere, cecīdī, caesus: cut down, strike, beat, kill

claudō, -ere, clausī, clausus: close, shut

contemnō, -ere, -tempsī, -temptus: despise

contingō, -ere, -tigī, -tactus: touch

dīdūcō, -ere, -duxī, -ductus: draw apart, separate

dīligō, -ere, -lexī, -lectus: cherish, esteem

dūcō, -ere, duxī, ductus: lead; think, consider

exigō, -ere, -ēgī, -actus: demand, discover

fallō, -ere, fefellī, falsus: deceive, cheat, be mistaken

iaciō, -ere, iēcī, iactus: throw, hurl

indīcō, -ere, -dixī, -dictus: declare, point out

inpluō, -ere, -uī: rain

intellegō, -ere, -lexī, -lectus: understand

metuō, -ere, -uī, -ūtus: to fear, to dread

noscō, -ere, nōvī, nōtus: learn, know

petō, -ere, -īvī/iī, -ītus: seek, demand, ask, beg

pōnō, -ere, posuī, positus: put, place, put aside, consider (castra pōnere: to pitch camp)

recipiō, -ere, -cēpi, -ceptus: take back, receive

reddō, -ere, -didī, -ditus: return, give back

sinō, -ere, sīvī, situs: allow, leave; place, lay down, bury

solvō, -ere, solvī, solūtus: break, weaken, loosen, relax

inveniō, -īre, -vēnī, -ventus: come upon, find, meet, discover

perveniō, -īre, -vēnī, -ventus: come to, reach, arrive at

abeō, -īre, -īvī or -iī, -itus: go away

dēferō, -ferre, -tulī, -lātus: bring down, hand over

redeō, -īre, -iī or īvī, -itus: go back, return

PREPOSITIONS

apud (+ accusative): at, among, in the case of, at the house of

circā (+ accusative): around, about (*circā* can also be used alone as an adverb)

extrā (+ accusative): beyond, outside

ob (+ accusative): against, on account of

super (+ accusative): above

CONJUNCTIONS AND ADVERBS

adhūc: thus far, to this point, still

bis: two times

cēterum: in addition, however

dum: while, as long as, provided that

em: here; often followed by the dative case (*em tibi* = "here you are!")

ferē: nearly, almost

hinc: from here

ideō: therefore, for this reason

interim: meanwhile

item: likewise

magis: more, to a greater extent

mox: soon

-ne: introduces a question that expects a positive answer

numquam: never

posteā: afterward

prīmum or **prīmō**: at first, for the first time

quasi: as if

quondam: once, formerly

sīcut: as, just as

tam: so

ter: three times

tum: then

ubi: where, when

utrum … an: whether … or

viciens: twenty times

III: ADDITIONAL DRILLS

IIIA. Decline the following noun-adjective pairs. Consult the glossary above for the dictionary entries.

Case	nemus + antīquus	speciēs + aureus	metus + aliquī
Singular			
Nominative			
Genitive			
Dative			
Accusative			
Ablative			
Plural			
Nominative			
Genitive			
Dative			
Accusative			
Ablative			

IIIB. Identify the following noun forms as directed. For ambiguous forms, give all possibilities. Give the correct form of **hic, haec, hoc** and **ille, illa, illud** to modify each form.

Latin Form	Decl.	Case	No.	Gender	hic, haec, hoc	ille, illa, illud
culpārum						
stellīs (2)						
mūnera (2)						
saxī						
auctōre						
fīliō (2)						

IIIC. Give the Latin for each of the following English phrases.

1. of worthy books _____

2. because of a shameful estate _____

3. a green season (Accusative) _____

4. to/for the other gladiators _____

5. these showers (Accusative) _____

6. those worlds (Nominative) _____

7. the same twin (Nominative) _____

8. with a certain general _____

9. to/for some household gods _____

10. of that army of yours _____

IIID. Give the requested forms of the pronouns to agree with the antecedents (in **number** and **gender**).

Antecedent	No. and Gender of the Antecedent	Pronoun	Requested Case	Latin Form
nātīs		ille	Nominative	
auctōrī		aliquis	Ablative	
familiārum		īdem	Accusative	
mūneribus		iste	Genitive	
librōs		quis	Dative	
agitātor		quisquam	Ablative	
lūnam		quīdam	Ablative	
sīdus		hic	Nominative	
superōrum		iste	Accusative	
vitia		quis	Dative	
aciēbus		īdem	Nominative	
senātuum		quī	Genitive	
nemore		ille	Accusative	
speciem		quī	Genitive	
vulnerum		iste	Accusative	
dominō		īdem	Dative	
tectum		quī	Nominative	
tempestātēs		ille	Genitive	
bestiā		hic	Dative	

IIIE. Give a synopsis of the following verb. Translate each form.

verb: **pōnō, -ere, posuī, positus**
conjugation _____
synopsis: 3rd person singular

INDICATIVES	Active	Translation	Passive	Translation
Present				
Imperfect				
Future				
Perfect				
Pluperfect				
Future Perfect				

IMPERATIVES	Active	Translation	Passive	Translation
Present				
Future				

INFINITIVES	Active	Translation	Passive	Translation
Present				
Perfect				

IIIF. For the following verbs, give the dictionary entry, person, number, tense, and mood. Underline the principal part from which the Latin form derives. Translate each form. (N.B. Infinitives do not have person and number—just translate those forms. Imperatives are second person, but be sure to give the number and translation for those forms.)

Form	Dictionary Entry and Conjugation	Person and No.	Tense and Voice (Active/Passive)	Mood	Translation
iacueram					
noscēs					
contigimus					
inveniminī					
abībātis					

(*Continued*)

Form	Dictionary Entry and Conjugation	Person and No.	Tense and Voice (Active / Passive)	Mood	Translation
reddēmus					
contempserit					
receptus esse					
rīdētō					
iussa erunt					
solvēris					
ductī estis					

IIIG. Give the requested forms of the following verbs. Translate each form.

Latin Verb	Requested Form	Latin Form	Translation
cēnō	1st person plural Perfect active		
rīdeō	Future plural Imperative		
dūcō	2nd person singular Pluperfect passive		
petō	3rd person plural Future Perfect passive		
redeō	3rd person singular Imperfect active		
dēferō	2nd person plural Perfect active		
iubeō	1st person singular Present passive		
mūtō	2nd person singular Future passive		
perveniō	1st person plural Imperfect active		
fallō	Perfect passive Infinitive		
āmittō	3rd person singular Pluperfect active		
recipiō	Present passive Infinitive		

IIIH. Identify the following verbs by person, number, tense, and voice. Then, keeping the same person, number, and tense, convert the following passive forms to active and active forms to passive. Translate each converted form.

Latin Form	Person, No., Tense, and Voice	Conversion	Translation
intellegēbāmus			
fefellisse			
sinētur			
posuerimus			
dīlecta erat			
noscet			
contigimus			
caedēbar			
petī			
mūtās			
iēcistis			
exigite			

III-I. Translate the following sentences into coherent English.

1. Virī quōrum uxōrēs prō rē pūblicā pugnāverant ab principibus bonīs dīligēbantur.

_____

_____

2. Hōs factiōnēs metuimus sed nōbīs illae placuērunt.

_____

3. Sī montibus in vīcīnīs inpluēbat, apud suōs dominōs lībertī quīdam lībertaeque cēnāverunt.

_____

_____

4. Aliquis ab quō laudābāmur vēnātiōnēs plūrēs contempsit.

_____

5. Agitātor factiōnis venetae cuius vox ad sīdera audiēbātur equīs cum suīs hodiē vincet.

_____

_____

6. Nātus īdem quem māter maximē timuit penātēs hostibus trādidit.

_____

7. Quis ingentem nāvem quae ob pācem Rōmam redīt vidēbat?

_____

8. Ubi aciēs cecidit, illī mīlitēs ab hōc imperātōre victī sunt.

_____

9. Lūna caelō in bellō hominibus omnibus spectāculō posita est.

_____

10. Ambō geminī utrumque canem rīdent.

_____

IV: ADDITIONAL PASSAGES

1. Horace, *Saturae* 2.6.110–12. The Country Mouse has agreed to accept the hospitality of his fastidious Town Mouse friend. Although at first seduced by the allures of urbanity, the Country Mouse quickly discovers the dangers of city living when the guard dogs throw the charming dinner party into an uproar (see *NLP* Review B, passage 5). Meter: dactylic hexameter.

Ille cubans gaudet mūtātā sorte bonīsque
rēbus agit laetum convīvam, cum subitō ingens
valvārum strepitus lectīs excussit utrumque.

Notes: **ille**: the Country Mouse; **cubans (-antis)**: reclining; **gaudeō, -ēre, gāvīsus sum**: rejoice (at); **mūtātus, -a, -um**: changed, altered; **sors, sortis (-ium)**, f: lot, fate, destiny; **agit**: "he plays, he acts"; **convīva, -ae**, m/f: guest, dining companion; **subitō**: suddenly, unexpectedly; **valva, -ae**, f: folding door; **strepitus, -ūs**, m: noise, din, racket; **excutiō, -ere, -cussī, -cussus**: shake off (from), cast off.

2. Vergil, *Aeneid* 2.310–12. As Troy is destroyed by fire, so too do the houses of Aeneas' friends burn down. Meter: dactylic hexameter.

Iam Dēiphobī dedit ampla ruīnam,
Vōlcānō superante, domus; iam proximus ardet
Ūcalegōn; Sīgēa ignī freta lāta relūcent.

Notes: **Dēiphobus, -ī**, m: the son of Priam and Hecuba, prince of Troy, who married Helen after the death of Paris; **ruīna, -ae**, f: catastrophe, collapse, destruction (*ruīnam dare*: fall to ruin); **Vōlcānō superante**: "Vulcan prevailing" (ablative absolute; Vulcan was the Roman god of fire, the forge, and technology); **proximus, -a, -um**: nearest, neighboring; **ardeo, -ēre, arsī, arsus**: blaze, glow; **Ūcalegōn, -ontis**, m: an elder Trojan leader (here *Ūcalegōn = Ūcalegontis domus*; in English, the obscure noun Ucalegon refers to a neighbor whose house has burned down); **Sīgēus, -a, -um**: of Sigeum, a promontory near Troy; **fretum, -ī**, n: strait, water; **lātus, -a, -um**: broad, wide; **relūceō, -ēre, -luxī**: shine out, glow.

3. Augustus, *Res Gestae* 22.1. Augustus sponsored many athletic events.

Bis āthlētārum undique accītōrum spectāculum populō praebuī meō nōmine et tertium nepōtis meī nōmine. Lūdōs fēcī meō nōmine quater, aliōrum autem magistrātuum vicem ter et viciens.

Notes: **āthlēta, -ae**, m: athlete; **accītus, -a, -um**: invited, summoned; **praebeō, -ēre, -uī**: offer, present, produce; **lūdus, -ī**, m: game, contest; **quater**: four times; **magistrātus, -ūs**, m: magistrate; **vicem** (+ genitive): on behalf of.

4. *CIL* VI 10047. Rome. A tombstone from the Via Flaminia details this famous charioteer's win record and the horses that helped him achieve his victories. (This passage is excerpted from a much longer list of 1,127 prizes!)

P. Aelius Marī Rogātī fīl(ius) Gutta Calpurniānus equīs hīs vīcī in factiōne venetā:

Germinātōre n(igrō) Āf(ricānō) LXXXXII
Silvānō r(ussātō) Āf(ricānō) CV
Nitid(iō) gil(vō) Āf(ricānō) LII
Saxōne n(igrō) Āf(ricānō) LX
Et vīcī praemia M L̄ I X̄L̄ IX X̄X̄X̄ XVII

Notes: **P(ūblius) Aelius Gutta Calpurniānus, Pūbliī Aeliī Guttae Calpurniānī**, m: a charioteer (*Gutta*: from *gutta, -ae*, f: spot, speck); **Marius Rogātus, Mariī Rogātī**, m: a man's name (*Rogātus*: from *rogātus, -ūs*, m: request); **Germinātor, -ōris**, m: a horse's name (from *germinō, -āre, -āvī, -ātus*: sprout); **niger, nigra, nigrum**: black; **Āfricānus, -a, -um**: African; **Silvānus, -ī**, m: a horse's name calling to mind the "god of the woods"; **Nitidius, -ī**, m: a horse's name (from *nitidus, -a, -um*: shining, bright, "glowing"); **gilvus, -a, -um**: pale yellow; **Saxō, -ōnis**, m: a horse's name ("the Rock"); **M L̄ I X̄L̄ IX X̄X̄X̄ XVII**: "50,000 sesterces once, 40,000 sesterces nine times, and 30,000 sesterces seventeen times" (the overbar [*vinculum*] above a numeral indicates × 1,000).

5. Ovid, *Metamorphoses* 1.568–73. Ovid describes Tempe, Apollo's beautiful abode, nestled in a valley in the mountains of northern Greece. Meter: dactylic hexameter.

Est nemus Haemoniae, praerupta quod undique claudit
silva: vocant Tempē; per quae Pēnēos ab īmō
effūsus Pindō spūmōsīs volvitur undīs
dēiectūque gravī tenuēs agitantia fūmōs
nūbila condūcit summīsque adspergine silvīs
inpluit et sonitū plūs quam vīcīna fatīgat.

Notes: **Haemonia, -iae**, f: Haemonia, an archaic name for Thessaly; **praeruptus, -a, -um**: steep; **Tempē**, n (plural, indeclinable): a beautiful valley in northern Greece; **Pēnēos, -eī**, m: the Peneus river; **īmus, -a, -um**: lowest, deepest; **effūsus, -a, -um**: poured out, drained, vast, sprawling; **Pindus, -ī**, m: a mountain range in northern Greece between Thessaly and Epirus; **spūmōsus, -a, -um**: foaming, frothy; **volvitur**: "(the Peneus river) rolls"; **dēiectus, -ūs**, m: steep slope; **tenuis, -e**: thin, fine, delicate; **agitans (-antis)** (+ accusative): stirring, shaking, agitating; **fūmus, -ī**, m: smoke, steam, vapor; **condūcō, -ere, -dūxī, -ductus**: collect, unite; **summus, -a, -um**: highest, furthest; **adspergō, -inis**, f: sprinkling, spray; **inpluō, -ere, -uī**: rain upon; **sonitus, -ūs**, m: sound, noise; **plūs ... quam**: more ... than; **fatīgō, -āre, -āvī, -ātus**: tire, wear out.

6. Martial 4.44. Martial here contrasts Vesuvius's former lushness with its current bleakness. This epigram was written in 88 CE, a mere ten years after the eruption. Meter: elegiac couplets.

Hīc est pampineīs viridis modo Vesbius umbrīs,

   presserat hīc madidōs nōbilis ūva lacūs:

haec iuga quam Nȳsae collēs plūs Bacchus amāvit;

   hōc nūper Satyrī monte dedēre chorōs;

haec Veneris sēdēs, Lacedaemone grātior īllī;

   hīc locus Herculeō nōmine clārus erat.

Cuncta iacent flammīs et tristī mersa favillā:

   nec superī vellent hoc licuisse sibi.

Notes: **pampineus, -a, -um**: garlanded with vine-tendrils; **viridis, -e**: green (all shades), rich in olive-trees; **Vesbius, -ī, m**: Vesuvius; **madidus, -a, -um**: moist, wet; **ūva, -ae, f**: cluster of grapes; **iugum, -ī, n**: yoke, ridge; **quam ... plūs**: more than; **Nȳsa, -ae, f**: a mountain in some indeterminate place (Ethiopia, Libya, India) where baby Bacchus was raised; **Bacchus, -ī, m**: Greek god of wine and revelry; **nūper**: recently, not long ago; **Satyrus, -ī, m**: satyr, a goat-footed, horse-tailed follower of Bacchus; **chorus, -ī, m**: choral dance in a circle, troop, crowd; **sēdēs, -is (-ium), m**: seat, abode; **Lacedaemon, -onis, f**: Sparta (Helen, favored by Venus, hailed from Sparta, and the goddess was robustly worshipped there); **grātior**: "more pleasing (than)" (+ ablative); **Herculeus, -a, -um**: Herculean (while Hercules was completing his twelve labors, he passed through southern Italy, finding there a "plain of fire" [the volcano], and he subdued Giants engaging in banditry there. The nearby town of Herculaneum was named for the hero); **clārus, -a, -um**: clear, distinct, renowned; **cunctus, -a, -um**: all, entire; **flamma, -ae, f**: flame, fire; **tristis, -e**: sad, gloomy; **mersus, -a, -um**: immersed, overwhelmed; **favilla, -ae, f**: glowing ash; **vellent licuisse**: "[nor] would [the gods] have wanted to have allowed this."

Crossword Puzzle.

Across

5. A pool
7. Where rainwater in Roman houses collects
11. Baucis and Philemon's heavenly visitors
14. Decimus Laelius Balbus served as this kind of magistrate
17. A play featuring a clever slave
19. He wrote biographies of the early Roman emperors
23. He was the only Roman who refused to become emperor
26. An office in a Roman house
27. The third emperor in the "year of the four emperors"
28. A lightly protected gladiator
29. The second of the four emperors in the year 69 CE
33. A victorious general
35. Augustus's heir
38. The south wind
41. A bedroom in a Roman house
43. A boxer in the *Aeneid*
45. A gladiator trainer
46. A famous charioteer of the red faction
47. He provided many athletic shows for the Roman people
48. Large plantations where thousands of slaves labored
50. The color that indicates rainy weather

Down

1. Because of an amphitheater riot, this town was barred from holding athletic events for ten years
2. An ex-slave
3. This threatens Pliny and his mother as they try to escape from the erupting volcano
4. The aqueduct at Rome with the purest water

6. A gladiator who led a slave revolt
8. A Vestal Virgin who was not allowed to free her slaves
9. A Gallic chieftain vanquished by Verginius Rufus
10. The king of the winds
11. A victorious general under Nero
12. Catullus's friend who will dine well if
13. A Roman author who wrote on meteorology
15. Caligula's father
16. What might be branded on the forehead of a runaway slave
17. A Roman who wrote comedies
18. The central barrier in the Circus
20. A dining room in a Roman house
21. The site of a celebrated temple of Venus
22. A Roman author whose novel features a prominent freedman
23. Of all the Roman emperors, he alone changed for the better
24. Augustus received envoys from this distant land
25. He wrote a handbook about the water supply at Rome
30. The Roman name for the constellations Ursa Major and Minor
31. A Roman who gave advice on how to maintain slaves
32. Gladiators who fight with nets
34. The east wind
36. An apartment block
37. He gathered seashells as "proof" of his victory over Neptune
39. A Roman writer on architecture
40. Another Roman author who wrote on meteorology
42. The turning posts in the Circus
44. The Roman Games
49. His troops overthrew Nero

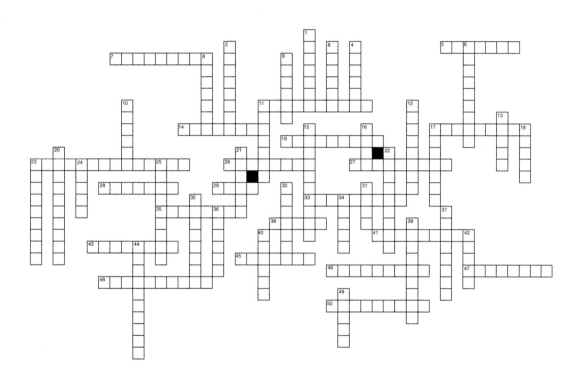

LESSON 19

Comparatives and Superlatives of Adjectives and Adverbs

19A. Decline the following noun-adjective pairs.

Case	fluctus, -ūs, m + Comparative of **grātus, -a, -um**	avis, -is (-ium), f + Superlative of **fortis, -e**
Singular		
Nominative		
Genitive		
Dative		
Accusative		
Ablative		
Plural		
Nominative		
Genitive		
Dative		
Accusative		
Ablative		

19B. Give the requested forms of the following adjectives.

Adjective	Requested Form	Latin Form
grātus	Accusative singular feminine Comparative	
tūtus	Nominative plural neuter Comparative	
facilis	Ablative singular masculine Comparative	
dulcis	Dative plural feminine Superlative	
similis	Accusative singular neuter Superlative	
miser	Ablative singular feminine Superlative	
pius	Genitive plural masculine Comparative	
dīves	Nominative plural feminine Comparative	
ingens	Dative singular neuter Superlative	
fertilis	Genitive plural neuter Superlative	
tener	Accusative singular masculine Superlative	
nōbilis	Nominative plural neuter Superlative	
bonus	Dative singular feminine Comparative	
malus	Ablative plural feminine Comparative	
multus	Genitive singular masculine Superlative	

19C. Identify the following adjectives by case, number, gender, and degree. Keeping the same case, number, and gender, convert the positive adjectives to comparative, comparatives to superlative, and superlatives to positive.

Adjective	Case, No., Gender	Degree	Convert to	Requested Latin Form
tūtiōre (feminine)				
pulcherrimōs				
fortem				
dissimillimīs				
bonum (neuter)				
minimās				
superī (masc.; 2)				
pēiōrum				
iustior (2)				
turpissimōs				
dignae (Dative)				
graviōribus				

19D. Give a synopsis of the following verb. Translate each form.

suscipiō, -ere, -cēpī, -ceptus
conjugation _____
synopsis: 2nd person plural

INDICATIVES	Active	Translation	Passive	Translation
Present				
Imperfect				
Future				
Perfect				
Pluperfect				
Future Perfect				

suscipiō, -ere, -cēpī, -ceptus

IMPERATIVES	Active	Translation	Passive	Translation
Present				
Future			XXX	XXX

INFINITIVES	Active	Translation	Passive	Translation
Present				
Perfect				

19E. Translate the following English phrases into Latin.

1. the greatest injuries (Nominative) _____

2. a worse practice (Nominative) _____

3. O most graceful beast! _____

4. for the worst beaches _____

5. by the sharpest waves _____

6. the prettiest spouse (Accusative) _____

7. of better practices _____

8. of a rather similar bird _____

9. with the most rapid weapon _____

10. for the smallest heart _____

11. the safest bulk (Accusative) _____

12. with a rather clever bird _____

19F. Translate the following sentences into coherent English.

1. Avēs celerrimē discunt.

_____

2. Hae bēluae fertiliōrēs illīs fuērunt.

_____

3. Victor cuius equī saepius vīcēre gracillimus omnium erat.

_____

4. Canēs, animālium piissimī, omne officium implēbunt.

_____

5. Itaque exercitus noster vestrō fortius pugnābat.

_____

6. Puella tamen pulchrior imāginem suam rīsit.

_____

7. Agitātōrēs plūs gladiātōribus dīligēbantur.

_____

8. Librī auctōris cuiusdam digniōrēs quam dulcia carmina
   aliquōrum principum ductī sunt.

_____

9. Iuvenēs bellissimī tunc meliōris praemia labōris cognōscent.

_____

10. Diēs noctēsque rūrī quam dulcissimē agēbātis.

_____

19G. Translate the following sentences into Latin. Use the rubric below each
sentence as a guide.

Dogs are more clever than certain types of birds.

Degree of "more clever" _____

What noun does "more clever" modify? _____

Case, number, gender, and syntactic function of that noun _____

_____

Latin translation of "more clever" _____

"Than certain types" can be translated in two ways. Give both versions.
Latin translation of "than certain types" (1) _____

_____

Latin translation of "than certain types" (2) _____

_____

Latin translation of entire sentence _____

_____

Soon the soldiers will not be harmed since they will soon have the best weapons of all.

Person, number, tense, and voice of "(they) will be harmed" _____

_____

Dictionary entry _____

Latin translation of "(they) will be harmed" _____

"They" = Dative of possession

Person, number, tense, and voice of "they will have" _____

_____

Latin translation of "they will have" _____

Degree of "best" _____

What noun does "best" modify? _____

Case, number, gender, and syntactic function of that noun _____

_____

Latin translation of "best weapons" _____

Syntactic function and case of "all" _____

Latin translation of "all" _____

Latin translation of entire sentence _____

_____

19H. A limerick about dogs for translation, with apologies to Ogden Nash.

Canis est optimus amīcus

virō. Sunt dentēs in ōribus

ac in tergō cauda,

quattuor pedēs infrā.

Baubānt saepissimē noctibus.

Notes: **ōs, ōris**, n: mouth; **dens, dentis (-ium)**, m: tooth; **tergum, -ī**, n: back; **cauda, -ae**, f: tail; **pēs, pedis**, m: foot; **infrā**: underneath; **baubō, -āre, -āvī, -ātus**: bark.

Impersonal Verbs and Fiō

20A. Decline the following noun-adjective pair.

Case	spīritus, -ūs, m + audax (audācis)
Singular	
Nominative	
Genitive	
Dative	
Accusative	
Ablative	
Plural	
Nominative	
Genitive	
Dative	
Accusative	
Ablative	

20B. Give the requested forms of the following nouns.

Noun	Requested Form	Latin Form
praetor	Accusative singular	
crīmen	Dative singular	
dīvitiae	Accusative plural	
sacerdōtium	Genitive plural	
spīritus	Ablative plural	
parens	Nominative plural	
fidēs	Ablative singular	
māior	Genitive singular	

20C. Give the correct form of the specified adjective to modify each of the following nouns. Translate the resulting phrases.

Noun	Case, No., Gender	Adjective	Latin Form	Translation
dōnīs (2)		quisque		
spīrituum		audax (Comparative)		
vestigiō (2)		tālis		
rēī (2)		audax (Superlative)		
moenibus (2)		tūtus (Comparative)		
praetōre		humilis (Superlative)		
grātiae (3)		pius (Positive)		

20D. For each of the following nouns, select the adjective that agrees in case, number, and gender. Then translate the resulting phrases. You may use each adjective only once.

Adjective bank: **tālem, quamque, audāciōra, cuiusque, fortissimā, tūtiōre, quīque**

Noun	Case, No., Gender	Adjective	Translation
flammā			
vestigiō			
parentis			
spīritum			
fidem			
praetor			
crīmina			

20E. Give a synopsis of the following verb. Translate each form.

sustineō, -ēre, -uī, -tentus
conjugation _____
synopsis: 3rd person singular

INDICATIVES	Active	Translation	Passive	Translation
Present				
Imperfect				
Future				
Perfect				
Pluperfect				
Future Perfect				

IMPERATIVES	Active	Translation	Passive	Translation
Present				
Future			XXX	XXX

INFINITIVES	Active	Translation	Passive	Translation
Present				
Perfect				

20F. Give the Latin for each of the following English phrases.

1. It will be proper. _____

2. It was causing regret. _____

3. to have been pleasing _____

4. It mattered. _____

5. It will distress. _____

6. It will have benefited. _____

7. It was happening. _____

8. They will become. _____

9. They (feminine) will have become. _____

10. You (masculine, plural) have become. _____

20G. Translate the following Latin sentences into English.

   1. Extrā moenia pergere nōn licuit.

   _____

   2. Sacerdōtium sustinēre necesse erit.

   _____

   3. Praetōrem valuisse oportēbat.

   _____

   4. Vōs crīminum māiōrum piget taedetque.

   _____

   5. Nōbīs dē parentibus poscere prōdest.

   _____

   6. Nēminem urbem servāre pudet.

   _____

   7. Grātiās nōn agere quemque paenitēbat.

   _____

   8. Dōnum tāle tangere nōn decet.

   _____

   9. Nostrīs līberīs mōrum antiquōrum meminisse refert.

   _____

  10. Dīs templa colere placitum est.

   _____

  11. Tē castrōrum miserēbit.

   _____

  12. Coepisse libitum est.

   _____

  13. Bellum gerī omnem annum constat.

   _____

  14. In cīvitātem veterem venitur.

   _____

15. Multitūdō mātrum in templō fit.

_____

16. Melior fīēbās.

_____

17. Equī nostrī celerrimī factī sunt.

_____

18. Imperātōrēs bonī pēiōrēs fient.

_____

19. In silvīs vestigia fiunt.

_____

20. Spīritus audācior factus erit.

_____

20H. Translate the following sentences into Latin. Use the rubric below each sentence as a guide.

It displeases me to see very bold children.

Latin translation of "it displeases"_____

Degree of "very bold"_____

What noun does "very bold" modify?_____

Case, number, gender, and syntactic function of that noun_____

_____

Latin translation of "very bold"_____

Latin translation of entire sentence_____

_____

It is in accord with divine law to worship the gods here in the temples.

       Latin translation of "it is in accord with divine law"_____

       _____

       Subject of "it is in accord with divine law"_____

       Syntactic function of "the gods"_____
       Latin translation of "the gods"_____

       Latin translation of entire sentence_____

       _____

I pity these city walls.

       "I pity" = "it pities me"
       Latin translation of "I pity"_____

       Case of "walls"_____
       Case of "city"_____
       Correct translation of "city walls"_____

       Latin translation of entire sentence_____

       _____

20I. Find the Latin for the following phrases. The forms may appear horizontally, vertically, or diagonally in either direction.

S	V	K	F	W	T	Q	H	N	Z	R	B	O	O	U
M	G	T	F	A	C	T	A	E	E	R	A	T	I	S
Y	R	F	E	A	E	U	S	C	Q	P	L	P	Q	W
T	I	D	I	C	C	A	D	E	C	E	B	A	T	A
J	E	P	A	E	I	T	I	S	D	T	T	Q	E	O
T	W	L	R	G	B	L	I	S	S	A	A	B	R	T
M	P	G	Q	O	Q	A	Q	E	B	J	P	Z	E	N
W	M	S	Q	H	F	C	M	E	R	T	A	R	B	U
R	N	U	J	X	M	U	T	R	Y	U	E	V	I	I
M	X	M	K	M	T	R	I	A	P	S	N	D	L	F
S	G	E	O	C	O	N	S	T	I	T	I	T	U	T
A	Y	I	A	P	S	X	X	M	G	L	T	Z	Z	P
I	P	F	O	K	E	R	T	R	E	F	E	R	E	J
O	S	L	K	A	C	M	A	E	T	T	T	F	Z	B
W	Z	V	N	U	I	K	G	Q	B	X	X	M	K	D

it was proper

it has been agreed

it displeases

it is permitted

it disgusts

they become

it has become

to be pleasing

it causes regret

it is agreeable

it distresses

it shames

we shall become

you (feminine, plural) had become

it was fitting

it has benefited

it happens

it matters

it was necessary

I became

they (masculine) will have become

Deponent Verbs

21A. Decline the following noun-adjective pairs.

Case	vulgus, -ī, n + Comparative of malus, -a, -um (singular only)	sēdēs, -is (-ium), f + Superlative of bonus, -a, -um
Singular		
Nominative		
Genitive		
Dative		
Accusative		
Ablative		
Plural		
Nominative	XXX	
Genitive	XXX	
Dative	XXX	
Accusative	XXX	
Ablative	XXX	

21B. Give the requested forms of the following nouns.

Noun	Requested Form	Latin Form
sēdēs	Nominative plural	
prōvincia	Ablative plural	
ardor	Dative singular	
vulgus	Accusative singular	
grātia	Ablative singular	
sacerdōtium	Genitive plural	
crīmen	Accusative plural	
parens	Genitive singular	

21C. Give the correct form of the specified adjective to modify each of the following nouns. Translate the resulting phrases.

Noun	Case, No., Gender	Adjective	Latin Form	Translation
prōvinciam		līber		
sēdis		reliquus		
ardōre		fessus		
lītoribus (2)		singulus		
tēlō (2)		tālis		
ūsuum		ācer		
dīvitiae		grātus		
vulgus (2)		audax		

21D. Identify the following noun forms as directed. For ambiguous forms, give all possibilities. Give the correct form of **fessus, -a, -um** (Comparative) and **audax (audācis)** (Superlative) to modify each form.

Latin Form	Decl.	Case	No.	Gender	fessus, -a, -um (Comparative)	audax (audācis) (Superlative)
prōvinciae (3)						
vulgus (2)						
ardōribus (2)						
sēdēs (3)						

21E. Conjugate the following verbs. Translate each form.

verb: **mīror, -ārī, mīrātus sum**

conjugation _____

PRESENT	Latin	Translation
Singular		
1st		
2nd		
3rd		
Imperative		
Plural		
1st		
2nd		
3rd		
Imperative		
Infinitive		

verb: **ūtor, -ī, ūsus sum**

conjugation _____

IMPERFECT	Latin	Translation
Singular		
1st		
2nd		
3rd		
Plural		
1st		
2nd		
3rd		

verb: **sequor, sequī, secūtus sum**

conjugation _____

FUTURE	Latin	Translation
Singular		
1st		
2nd		
3rd		
Plural		
1st		
2nd		
3rd		

verb: **gaudeō, -ēre, gāvīsus sum**

conjugation _____

PERFECT	Latin	Translation
Singular		
1st		
2nd		
3rd		

gaudeō, -ēre, gāvīsus sum

Plural		
1st		
2nd		
3rd		
Infinitive		

verb: **reor, rērī, ratus sum**

conjugation _____

PLUPERFECT	Latin	Translation
Singular		
1st		
2nd		
3rd		
Plural		
1st		
2nd		
3rd		

verb: **regredior, -gredī, regressus sum**

conjugation _____

FUTURE PERFECT	Latin	Translation
Singular		
1st		
2nd		
3rd		
Plural		
1st		
2nd		
3rd		

21F. Give the person, number, tense, voice, and mood of the following verbs.
Translate each form.

Form	Conj.	Person and No.	Tense	Voice (A/P/D)	Mood	Translation
regēbantur						
rapiēminī						
rectus sum						
raptum eris						
suscepta sunt						
mīrāre (2)						
adloquī						
loquētur						
oblīviscar						
proficiscēbāris						
prōsequimur						
secūta sum						
ultī erant						
dēgressa erunt						
ingressus es						
regrediētur						
transgredī						

21G. Give the requested forms of the following verbs. Translate each form.

Verb	Requested Form	Latin Form	Translation
reor	2nd person singular Future		
transgredior	1st person plural Imperfect		
proficiscor	3rd person singular Present		
ulciscor	1st person singular Pluperfect		
audeō	2nd person plural Perfect		
polliceor	3rd person plural Future Perfect		
ūtor	Present singular Imperative		
oblīviscor	Present Infinitive		
soleō	Perfect Infinitive		

21H. Identify the following verbs by person, number, tense, and voice. Then, keeping the same person, number, and tense, convert the following singular forms to plural and plural forms to singular. (For verbs in the perfect system, keep the same gender!) Translate each converted form.

Latin Form	Person, No., Tense, and Voice	Conversion	Translation
rēbitur			
ūtēbāmur			
consequiminī			
proficiscor			
adloquēbāris			
oblīviscentur			
ratī estis			
gāvīsa erās			
adlocūta erō			
ausum erit			
orta sunt			
solitus sum			

21I. Using the required deponent and semi-deponent vocabulary, give the Latin for the following phrases.

1. We were thinking. _____

2. She will step down. _____

3. You (singular) are avenging. _____

4. I (feminine) had followed. _____

5. You (masculine, plural) will have promised. _____

6. They (masculine) have retreated. _____

7. We (feminine) have rejoiced. _____

8. It has dared. _____

9. You (feminine, plural) had been accustomed. _____

10. to have departed _____

21J. Translate the following sentences into coherent English.

1. Igitur sōl hōdiē oritur.

  _____

2. Vulgus fessum dominum aliquem sequētur.

  _____

3. Lūnam amplissimam illā nocte mīrābāminī.

  _____

4. Fēminae istae reī pūblicae patriaeque suae oblītae erant.

  _____

5. Dux bona regnō in pulcherrimō hostēs suās ulta est.

  _____

6. Līberōrum grātiā parentēs consiliō optimō ūtuntur.

  _____

7. Gladiātōrēs bestiās ingentiōrēs consecūtī sunt.

  _____

8. Imperātor exercitum fortem ante proelium longum adloquitur.

  _____

9. Ad prōvinciam hanc cuius nōs miseret dēgredī ausī sumus.

  _____

10. Ardōrem cīvibus malō reor.

  _____

21K. Translate the following sentences into Latin. Use the rubric below each sentence as a guide.

Today we will set out to the greatest temples.

Person, tense, number, and voice of "we will set out" _____

_____

Dictionary entry _____

Latin translation of "we will set out" _____

Degree of "greatest" _____

What noun does "greatest" modify? _____

Case, number, gender, and syntactic function of that noun _____

_____

Latin translation of "to the greatest temples" _____

Latin translation of entire sentence _____

_____

On account of his oration, the soldiers had followed their general.

Person, number, tense, and voice of "(they) had followed" _____

_____

Dictionary entry _____

Gender of the subject _____

Latin translation of "(they) had followed" _____

Syntactic function and case of "general" _____

Latin translation of "general" _____

Latin translation of entire sentence _____

_____

Caesar will have addressed the legions in the provinces.

Person, number, tense, and voice of "(he) will have addressed" _____

_____

Dictionary entry _____

Gender of the subject _____

Latin translation of "(he) will have addressed" _____

Syntactic function and case of "legions" _____

Latin translation of "legions" _____

Syntactic function and case of "provinces" _____

Latin translation of "in the provinces" _____

Latin translation of entire sentence _____

_____

Certain kings were being killed in front of the ancient city.

Person, number, tense, and voice of "(they) were being killed" _____

_____

Dictionary entry _____

Latin translation of "(they) were being killed" _____

_____

Syntactic function and case of "certain kings" _____

Latin translation of "certain kings" _____

Syntactic function and case of "ancient city" _____

_____

Latin translation of "in front of the ancient city" _____

_____

Latin translation of entire sentence _____

_____

21L. A haiku to translate.

Germānicum tunc

sequī vulgus est ausum,

ducem audācem.

Haiku is a traditional form of Japanese poetry consisting of 17 syllables in three lines (5, 7, 5 syllables respectively). Using at least one of the required deponent verbs, construct your own haiku about Germanicus, Corbulo, or Agrippa in grammatically correct Latin.

_____

_____

_____

Participles

22A. Decline the following participles.

Case	misceō, -ēre, -uī, mixtus (Present active: neuter)	cingō, -ere, cinxī, cinctus (Perfect passive: masculine)	hortor, -ārī, hortātus sum (Future deponent: feminine)
Singular			
Nominative			
Genitive			
Dative			
Accusative			
Ablative			
Plural			
Nominative			
Genitive			
Dative			
Accusative			
Ablative			

22B. Give the requested forms of the following participles.

Noun	Requested Form	Latin Form
misceō	Accusative plural masculine Present active	
arō	Genitive plural neuter Perfect passive	
cernō	Genitive singular feminine Future passive	
disiiciō	Nominative singular feminine Future active	
hortor	Accusative singular feminine Present active	
patior	Nominative plural neuter Future active	
sequor	Ablative singular masculine Future passive	
reor	Ablative plural masculine Perfect deponent	

22C. Give the correct form of the specified participle to modify each of the
following nouns. Translate the resulting phrases.

Noun	Case, No., Gender	Participle	Latin Form	Translation
aequor		cernō Future passive		
pontō (2)		hortor Present active		
aurium		patior Perfect deponent		
ratiōnem		tegō Future active		
voluptāte		disiiciō Perfect passive		

Noun	Case, No., Gender	Participle	Latin Form	Translation
faciēbus (2)		**cingō** Future passive		
cursū		**arō** Future passive		
murmura		**errō** Present active		
vultuī		**condō** Future active		

22D. For each of the following nouns, select the participle that agrees in case, number, and gender. Then translate the resulting phrases. You may use each participle only once.

Participle bank: **cessūrum, tectās, hortantium, condendō, currentis, disiectae, passam, erratūrīs**

Noun	Case, No., Gender	Participle	Translation
vultuum			
cursibus			
arvō			
ratiōnī			
murmur			
faciem			
aequoris			
voluptātēs			

22E. Identify the following noun forms as directed. For ambiguous forms, give all possibilities. Give the correct form of the requested participles to modify each form.

Latin Form	Case	No.	Gender	patior: Present deponent	cernō: Perfect passive	tegō: Future active
murmur (2)						
pontī (2)						
pretiō (2)						
aequorī						
ratiōnem						
voluptātibus						
cursuum						
vultūs (3)						

22F. Identify the following participles as directed. Translate each form.

Form	Tense	Voice (A/P/D)	Case(s)	No.	Gender(s)	Translation
intrans (2 cases)						
arandō (2 cases)						
cessum (3)						
errantum						
hortantibus						
transgressīs						
crētūrus						
patientis						
condendīs						

Form	Tense	Voice (A/P/D)	Case(s)	No.	Gender(s)	Translation
miscendae (3)						
mīrātūram						
cingendōrum						
disiectōs						
ūsā						
cursūra (3)						
tectūrās						

22G. Give a synopsis of the following verb. Translate each form.

cernō, -ere, crēvī, crētus
conjugation _____
synopsis: 2nd person singular

INDICATIVES	Active	Translation	Passive	Translation
Present				
Imperfect				
Future				
Perfect				
Pluperfect				
Future Perfect				

IMPERATIVES	Active Singular	Translation	Passive Singular	Translation
Present				
Future			XXX	XXX

cernō, -ere, crēvī, crētus

INFINITIVES	Active	Translation	Passive	Translation
Present				
Perfect				

PARTICIPLES	Active	Translation	Passive	Translation
Present			XXX	XXX
Perfect	XXX	XXX		
Future				

22H. Translate the following English phrases into Latin.

1. men encouraging children (Nominative) _____

2. of crimes having been hidden _____

3. for birds about to be scattered _____

4. (a woman) girding her head (Nominative) _____

5. the shore having been seen (Accusative) _____

6. of boats about to be seized _____

7. for parents about to guide the boys _____

8. of a suffering ear _____

9. with eagerness having been concealed _____

10. murmurs about to wander (Accusative) _____

22I. Translate the following sentences into coherent English.

1. Vulgus rēgem scelera tegentem condemnāvit.

_____

2. Puellae per lītora currentēs murmura ē marī missa audient.

_____

3. Lībertās libellōs puerīs puellīsque dōnantēs cernitis.

_____

4. Errātūrī trans arva, nocte degrediēbāmur.

_____

5. Mīlitibus regnum servantibus equōs fessōs hortārī licet.

_____

6. Aequor gracillimīs nāvibus arandum spectāre placet.

_____

7. Cum hostēs cecidērunt, gaudēre ā dūce regressūrō iubēbāmur.

_____

8. Praetor audax sacerdōtium poscens patriam victam ingreditur.

_____

9. Iuvenēs parentum oblītī caesī erunt.

_____

10. Imperātor vulgō dōna trādenda iam pollicitus erat.

_____

22J. Translate the following sentences into Latin. Use the rubric below each sentence as a guide.

Yielding to the crowd, the poets wrote about the pleasures of the soul.

Which noun does "yielding" modify? _____

Dictionary entry of "yielding" _____

Case, number, and gender _____

Tense and voice _____

Latin translation _____

Syntactic function and case of "to the crowd" _____

Latin translation _____

Latin preposition that means "about" + case taken _____

Latin translation of "about the pleasures" _____

Case of "of the soul" _____

Dictionary entry _____

Latin translation _____

Latin translation of entire sentence _____

_____

I saw the mothers teaching the children.

Syntactic function and case of "mothers" _____

Dictionary entry _____

Latin translation _____

Which noun does "teaching" modify? _____

Dictionary entry of "teaching" _____

Case, number, and gender _____

Tense and voice _____

Latin translation _____

Syntactic function and case of "children" _____

Dictionary entry _____

Latin translation _____

Latin translation of entire sentence _____

_____

22K. Give the Latin forms for the following English phrases. Then recombine the **double-underlined** letters to spell the title of a rich source for Roman mythology.

we encourage: __ __ __ __ __ __ __ __

(men) of reason: __ __ __ __ __ __ __ __

to found: __ __ __ __ __ __ __

powerful kingdoms (Accusative):

__ __ __   __ __ __ __ __ __ __

ANSWER: __ __ __ __ __ __ __

Ablatives Absolute

23A. Decline the following noun-participle pairs.

Case	lēgātus, -ī, m + Future active participle of maneō, -ēre, mansī, mansus	rūs, rūris, n + Future passive participle of celebrō, -āre, -āvī, -ātus
Singular		
Nominative		
Genitive		
Dative		
Accusative		
Ablative		
Plural		
Nominative		
Genitive		
Dative		
Accusative		
Ablative		

23B. Give the correct form of the specified participle to modify each of the following nouns. Translate the resulting phrases.

Noun	Case, No., Gender	Participle	Latin Form	Translation
impetūs (Nom.)		**celebrō** Perfect passive		
precēs (Acc.)		**pereō** Future active		
cūrārum		**vertō** Perfect passive		
pretiī		**prohibeō** Future passive		
turbam		**laetor** Present active		
somnō (Abl.)		**immineō** Present active		
consule		**maneō** Future active		
iugō (Dat.)		**vertō** Future passive		

23C. For each of the following nouns, select the participle that agrees in case, number, and gender. Then translate the resulting phrases. You may use each participle only once.

Participle bank: **laetum, oblīviscendōrum, prohibentem, celebrātōs, patiendā, imminentī, versīs, mansūrī**

Noun	Case, No., Gender	Participle	Translation
dominae			
fenestram			
lēgātī			
ōs			
impetibus			
prece			
campōrum			
somnōs			

23D. Identify the following participles as directed. Translate each form.

Form	Tense	Voice (A/P/D)	Case(s)	No.	Gender	Translation
celebrans (n)						
imminentibus						
laetantium						
peritūrō						
prohibenda (n)						
mansūrīs						
versum (2)						
perentī						
laetandārum						
celebrāta (f)						
perendōs						
laetās						
prohibita (n)						
laetātūrae (3)						
versī (plural)						
versūrā						
imminendō						
celebrandīs						
prohibitūrōrum						
manentīs						

23E. Give a synopsis of the following verb. Translate each form.

prohibeō, -ēre, -uī, -itus
conjugation _____
synopsis: 1st person singular

INDICATIVES	Active	Translation	Passive	Translation
Present				
Imperfect				
Future				
Perfect				
Pluperfect				
Future Perfect				

IMPERATIVES	Active	Translation	Passive	Translation
Present				
Future			XXX	XXX

INFINITIVES	Active	Translation	Passive	Translation
Present				
Perfect				

PARTICIPLES	Active	Translation	Passive	Translation
Present			XXX	XXX
Perfect	XXX	XXX		
Future				

23F. Translate the following English **ABLATIVES ABSOLUTE** into Latin.

1. the crowds remaining in the city _____

   _____

2. the consul having been celebrated by the people _____

   _____

3. the mistress having rejoiced with her children _____

   _____

4. the envoy about to restrain the attack _____

_____

5. when the fields were destroyed by the enemy _____

_____

6. since the reward was about to perish _____

_____

7. although concerns were continuously threatening the public _____

_____

8. when the window had been shut _____

_____

9. since requests are to be sought from a distance _____

_____

10. although the citizens follow their general _____

_____

23G. Translate the following sentences into coherent English.

1. Caesare imperātōre, exercitus saepe vincit.

_____

2. Dominā mōrēs māiōrum celebratūrā, līberī valuērunt.

_____

3. Turbā ā lēgātō optimō prohibitā, pax in regnō manēbit.

_____

4. Fenestrā nōn clausā, noctem tōtam impluit.

_____

5. Arvīs ā lībertīs honestīs arātīs, omnia beāta rursus crescunt.

_____

6. Cicerōne consule, rēs pūblica plānē servābātur.

_____

7. Parentibus dona puellīs magna pulchriōribus pollicentibus,
Rōmam veniēbāmus.

_____

8. Spīritū iuvenum mīrandō, poētae doctī carmina potentia cantant.

_____

9. Sōle oriente, nōbīs lacum amoenum īre prōdest.

_____

10. Spectāculō vīsō, dē gladiātōribus ac agitātōribus loquiminī.

_____

23H. Translate the following sentences into Latin. Use the rubric below each sentence as a guide.

Our children rejoicing, we built a temple.

What sort of clause is "our children rejoicing"? _____

_____

Case of "children" _____

Case, number, and gender of "rejoicing" _____

Tense and voice of "rejoicing" _____

Latin translation of clause _____

Syntactic function and case of "temple" _____

Dictionary entry _____

Latin translation _____

Person, number, tense, and voice of "we built" _____

_____

Dictionary entry _____

Latin translation _____

Latin translation of entire sentence _____

_____

The horses having been hindered by their yokes, the fields were not plowed.

What sort of clause is "the horses having been hindered by their yokes"? _____

Case of "horses" _____

Case, number, and gender of "having been hindered" _____

_____

Tense and voice of "having been hindered" _____

Latin translation of the clause _____

Person, number, tense, and voice of "(they) were plowed" _____

_____

Dictionary entry _____

Latin translation _____

Latin translation of entire sentence _____

_____

23I. Fill in the blanks with correctly formed Latin words from the required vocabulary (through *NLP* 23). You may use any word only once. There is no "right" answer.

Domina ad *(noun)* _____ *(adjective)* _____

cum *(pronoun)* _____ vēnit. *(ablative noun)* _____

cantantibus, consul igitur fīliam *(ablative noun)* _____

cum saevō/saevā *(accusative participle)* _____laudāvit.

Autem *(noun)* _____ currentēs *(noun)* _____

grātiā mīrātī sunt.

Indirect Statement

24A. Decline the following noun-adjective pairs.

Case	mulier, mulieris, f + Superlative of tristis, -e	lapis, lapidis, m + Perfect passive participle of offerō, -ferre, obtulī, oblātus
Singular		
Nominative		
Genitive		
Dative		
Accusative		
Ablative		
Plural		
Nominative		
Genitive		
Dative		
Accusative		
Ablative		

24B. Give the correct form of the specified adjective or participle to modify each of the following nouns. Translate the resulting phrases.

Noun	Case, No., Gender	Adjective/Participle	Latin Form	Translation
fātō (dative)		**tristis** Comparative		
lapidēs (2)		**taceō** Future active		
		taceō Future active		
caedīs		**falsus** Positive		
mulierum		**morior** Present active		
prōdigiī		**canō** Future passive		
pede		**lātus** Superlative		
medicum		**ēdō** Present active		
bovī (Dative: 2)		**turbō** Perfect passive		
		turbō Perfect passive		
facibus		**cūrō** Perfect passive		

24C. Give a synopsis of the following verb. Translate each form.

canō, -ere, cecinī, cantus
conjugation _____
synopsis: 3rd person singular

INDICATIVES	Active	Translation	Passive	Translation
Present				
Imperfect				
Future				
Perfect				
Pluperfect				
Future Perfect				

IMPERATIVES	Active	Translation	Passive	Translation
Present				
Future			XXX	XXX

INFINITIVES	Active	Translation	Passive	Translation
Present				
Perfect				
Future				

PARTICIPLES	Active	Translation	Passive	Translation
Present			XXX	XXX
Perfect	XXX	XXX		
Future				

24D. Identify the following infinitives by tense and voice. Translate each one.

Latin Form	Tense (Pres./Perf./Fut.)	Voice (A/P/D)	Translation
cūrārī			
terruisse			
tacēre			
oblātum esse			
genitūrum esse			
morī			
ēditum īrī			
nātam esse			
laetūrum esse			

24E. Give the requested **INFINITIVES** of the following verbs.

Latin Verb	Requested Form	Latin Form	English Translation
pugnō	Present passive		
dēferō	Perfect active		
dūcō	Perfect passive		
videō	Future active		
agō	Future passive		
capiō	Present passive		
consequor	Present deponent		
mīror	Present deponent		
transgredior	Perfect deponent		
ulciscor	Future active		

24F. Translate the following sentences into grammatically correct Latin. Note carefully if the indirect statement occurs at the same time as, before, or after the main verb.

1. We say that the girl is good. _____

   _____

2. You (singular) say that the boy will be good. _____

   _____

3. The women say that the children were good. _____

   _____

4. I said that the torches were offering light. _____

   _____

5. You (plural) said that the soldiers would disturb the stones. _____

   _____

6. She said that the cattle had been silent. _____

   _____

7. I shall say that our fate is announced. _____

   _____

8. You (plural) will say that the physician was taking care of your feet.

   _____

9. He will say that the woman will explain the prodigies. _____

   _____

24G. Translate the following sentences into coherent English.

1. Nuntiō consulem tacēre.

   _____

2. Dīcis consulem tacuisse.

   _____

3. Canunt consulem tacitūrum esse.

   _____

4. Mulier scrīpsit sē dōnum medicō offerre.

   _____

5. Consul crēvit mulierem dōnum medicō obtulisse.

   _____

    6. Imperātor putāvit mulierem dōnum medicō oblātūram esse.

    _____

    7. Bōs nōn sciēbat medicum dōnum recipere.

    _____

    8. Puella cōgitābat dōnum ā medicō recipī.

    _____

    9. Fēminae locūtae sunt dōnum ā medicō recipī.

    _____

    10. Omnēs locūtī erant dōnum ā medicō receptum esse.

    _____

    11. Rēbar turbam saevam esse.

    _____

    12. Dīcitis turbam saevam fuisse.

    _____

    13. Pīratae ēdēbant turbam saevam futūram esse.

    _____

    14. Dux dixit turbam saevam futūram esse.

    _____

    15. Medicī noscunt sē dōna oblātūrōs esse.

    _____

    16. Medicī negābunt sē dōna recepisse.

    _____

24H. Translate the following sentences into Latin. Use the rubric below each sentence as a guide.

Romulus and Remus announced that two prodigies were perceived in the sky.

    Person, number, tense, and voice of "(they) announced" _____

    _____

    Dictionary entry _____

    Latin translation _____

Does the indirect statement occur at the same time as, before, or after the main verb? _____

Syntactic function and case of "prodigies" _____
Dictionary entry _____
Latin translation of "two prodigies" _____

Tense and voice of "(they) were perceived" _____
Dictionary entry _____
Latin translation _____

Latin translation of entire sentence _____
_____

Hispulla said that her spouse Corellius had died.

Person, number, tense, and voice of "(she) said" _____
_____
Dictionary entry _____
Latin translation _____

Does the indirect statement occur at the same time as, before, or after the main verb? _____

Syntactic function and case of "spouse" _____
Dictionary entry _____
Latin translation _____

Tense and voice of "(he) had died" _____
Dictionary entry _____
Latin translation _____

Latin translation of entire sentence _____
_____

24I. A haiku to translate.

Putō nātūram

rērum semper insignem

omnēs mīrārī.

Note: **insignis, -e**: notable, remarkable.

Haiku is a traditional form of Japanese poetry consisting of 17 syllables in three lines (5, 7, 5 syllables respectively). Adapt your favorite passage from *NLP* 24 into a grammatically correct Latin haiku featuring an indirect statement.

_____

_____

_____

NLP Review D (Lessons 19–24)

I: CONCEPTS

IA: Latin Adjectives (*NLP* 19).

- Like English adjectives, Latin adjectives have degree: *big, bigger, biggest.*

- **Positive adjectives** (*big*) give the basic definition and agree with their nouns in case, number, and gender. Positive adjectives can be either 1st/2nd declension (*-us/-r, -a, -um*) or 3rd declension.

  Nostrī canēs <u>celerēs</u> sunt.
  Our dogs are <u>fast</u>.

- **Comparative adjectives** (*bigger*) are always 3rd declension, and most are formed by adding *-ior-* between the adjective stem and the third declension endings.

  Nostrī canēs <u>celeriōrēs</u> quam ventus sunt.
  Nostrī canēs <u>celeriōrēs</u> ventō sunt.
  Our dogs are <u>faster</u> than the wind.

- **Superlative adjectives** (*biggest*) are always 1st/2nd declension, and most are formed by adding *-issim-* between the adjective stem and the 1st/2nd ending.

  Nostrī canēs <u>celerrimī</u> omnium sunt.
  Our dogs are the <u>fastest</u> of all (dogs).

- Adjectives in *-er* (*pulcher*) form their superlative by adding *-errim-* (*pulcherrimus, -a, -um*) between the adjective stem and the 1st/2nd ending.
- Some very common adjectives form their comparatives and superlatives irregularly, and these must be memorized (see tables in *NLP* 19).

IB: Latin Adverbs (*NLP* 19).

- Latin adverbs are indeclinable.
- Like English adverbs, Latin adverbs have degree: *quickly, more quickly, most quickly.*
- **Positive adverbs** (*quickly*), formed from corresponding adjectives, end in *-ē* or *-iter.*

  Canēs <u>celeriter</u> currunt.
  Dogs run <u>quickly</u>.

- **Comparative adverbs** (*more quickly*) are identical to the corresponding comparative adjective in the nominative singular neuter.

  Canēs <u>celerius</u> currunt.
  Dogs run <u>rather quickly</u>.

- **Superlative adverbs** (*most quickly*) are formed from the corresponding superlative adjective. The *-us* ending is replaced by *-ē.*

  Canēs <u>celerrimē</u> currunt.
  Dogs run <u>very quickly</u>.

- N.B. *quam* + the superlative translates "as _____ as possible."

  Canēs <u>quam celerrimē</u> currunt.
  Dogs run <u>as quickly as possible</u>.

- Some very common adverbs form their comparatives and superlatives irregularly, and these must be memorized (see tables in *NLP* 19).

IC: Latin Verbs: Impersonal Verbs (*NLP* 20).

- Impersonal verbs appear only in the third person singular and are usually completed by an infinitive.
- They can be tricky since they are rare in English.
- The key to success is in memorizing the list of common impersonal verbs in *NLP* 20, so you can recognize these constructions when you see them.

Canēs per domum currere <u>nōn licet</u>.
<u>It is not permitted</u> for dogs to run through the house.

Mē canium currentium <u>taedet</u>.
<u>It disgusts</u> me of the running dogs (or The running dogs disgust me).

ID: Latin Verbs: Deponent Verbs (*NLP* 21).

- Deponent verbs are passive in form but active in meaning.

Līberī canem <u>sequuntur</u>.
The children <u>follow</u> their dog.

- Deponent verbs are recognized by their distinctive principal parts. The dictionary entry gives only three principal parts (instead of the usual four):
  - **cōnor**: 1st person singular present ("I try").
  - **cōnārī**: present infinitive ("to try").
  - **cōnātus sum**: 1st person singular perfect ("I have tried").

- To determine the conjugation group to which a deponent verb belongs, look at the infinitive ending on the second principal part (i.e., the present passive infinitive): *-ārī, -ērī, -ī, -īrī*.
- Recognizing the third conjugation can be a bit tricky since the infinitive ending (-i) is so short and omits the familiar -r- (*ingredī*: to enter).

Līberī canem <u>sequī</u> volunt.
The children want <u>to follow</u> their dog.

IE: Latin Participles (*NLP* 22).

- Participles are verbal adjectives.
  - ° Like **verbs**, participles have TENSE (present, perfect, or future) and VOICE (active or passive).
  - ° Like **adjectives**, a participle agrees with the noun it modifies in CASE, NUMBER, and GENDER.

- The **Present Active Participle** is a third declension adjective formed from the second principal part, with the same connecting vowel that you use for the regular imperfect or future tense forms: *amans (-antis)*: "loving."

  Līberī canem <u>currentem</u> vident.
  The children see their <u>running</u> dog.

- The **Perfect Passive Participle** is the fourth principal part of the verb and always takes 1st/2nd declension endings: *amātus, -a, -um*: "having been loved."

  Līberī canem <u>vocātum</u> vident.
  The children see their dog <u>having been called</u>.

- The **Future Active Participle** is formed from the fourth principal part of the verb with the signifier *-ūr-* between the base and the adjective endings. The future active participle always takes 1st/2nd declension endings: *amātūrus, -a, -um*: "about to love."

  Līberī canem <u>cursūrum</u> vident.
  The children see their dog <u>about to run</u>.

- The **Future Passive Participle**, also known as the gerundive, is a 1st/2nd declension adjective formed from the second principal part, with the same connecting vowel that you use for the regular imperfect or future tense forms + the signifier *-nd-*: *amandus, -a, -um*: "to be loved."

  Līberī canem <u>amandum</u> vident.
  The children see their dog about <u>to be loved</u>.

IF: Ablatives Absolute (*NLP* 23).

- Ablatives absolute are phrases, separate or "absolute" from the grammar of the sentence, typically consisting of a noun and a participle in the ablative case and expressing many nuances of meaning including temporal (when), causal (because), and conditional (if).
- Ablatives absolute can appear anywhere in the sentence.
- Ablatives absolute can employ any of the four participles listed above.

Cane <u>currente</u>, līberī domum veniunt.
The dog <u>running</u>, the children come home.

Cane <u>vocātō</u>, līberī domum veniunt.
The dog <u>having been called</u>, the children come home.

Cane <u>cursūrō</u>, līberī domum veniunt.
The dog <u>about to run</u>, the children come home.

Cane <u>vocandō</u>, līberī domum veniunt.
The dog about <u>to be called</u>, the children come home.

- Occasionally, ablatives absolute occur without participles.

<u>Caesare consūle</u>, canēs per urbem currunt.
<u>Caesar as consul</u>, dogs run through the city.

- Ablatives absolute can feature prepositional phrases and subordinate clauses.

<u>Canibus currentibus</u>, Caesar castra pōnit.
<u>The dogs running</u>, Caesar pitches camp.

<u>Canibus in domō currentibus</u>, Caesar castra pōnit.
<u>The dogs running in the house</u>, Caesar pitches camp.

<u>Canibus in domō in quō habitāmus currentibus</u>, Caesar castra pōnit.
<u>The dogs running in the house in which we live</u>, Caesar pitches camp.

<u>Canibus in domō cum impluit currentibus</u>, Caesar castra pōnit.
<u>The dogs running in the house when it rains</u>, Caesar pitches camp.

IG: Indirect Statements (*NLP* 24).

- Indirect statements are a special type of dependent clause in Latin.
- Indirect statements are triggered by words of saying, thinking, knowing, hearing, and feeling.
- Indirect statements have accusative subjects and infinitive verbs.

Scīmus <u>canēs</u> <u>currere</u>.
We know that <u>dogs</u> <u>run</u>.

- A present tense infinitive indicates an indirect statement that occurs at the same time as the action of the main verb.

Consul <u>nuntiat</u> canēs <u>currere</u>.
The consul <u>announces</u> that dogs <u>are running</u>. (The dogs run as the consul makes the announcement.)

Consul <u>nuntiābat</u> canēs <u>currere</u>.
The consul <u>announced</u> that dogs <u>were running</u>. (The dogs ran as the consul made the announcement.)

Consul <u>nuntiābit</u> canēs <u>currere</u>.
The consul <u>will announce</u> that dogs <u>will run</u>. (The dogs will run as the consul makes the announcement.)

- A perfect tense infinitive indicates an indirect statement that occurs before the action of the main verb.

Consul <u>nuntiat</u> canēs <u>cucurrisse</u>.
The consul <u>announces</u> that dogs (already) <u>ran</u>. (The dogs ran before the consul makes the announcement.)

Consul nuntiābat canēs cucurrisse.

The consul <u>announced</u> that dogs <u>had</u> (already) <u>run</u>. (The dogs had run before the consul made the announcement.)

Consul nuntiābit canēs cucurrisse.

The consul <u>will announce</u> that dogs (already) <u>had run</u>. (The dogs ran before the consul makes the announcement.)

- A future tense infinitive indicates an indirect statement that occurs after the action of the main verb.

Consul nuntiat canēs cursūrōs esse.

The consul <u>announces</u> that dogs <u>will run</u>. (The dogs will run after the consul makes the announcement.)

Consul nuntiābat canēs cursūrōs esse.

The consul <u>announced</u> that dogs <u>would run</u>. (The dogs would start running after the consul made the announcement.)

Consul nuntiābit canēs cursūrōs esse.

The consul <u>will announce</u> that dogs <u>will run</u>. (The dogs will run after the consul makes the announcement.)

II: VOCABULARY *NLP* 19–24

NOUNS

bēlua, -ae, f: beast, large animal

cūra, -ae, f: concern, care, trouble, distress

dīvitiae, -iārum, f (plural): riches, wealth

domina, -ae, f: mistress, lady friend

fenestra, -ae, f: window

flamma, -ae, f: flame, blaze, torch

grātia, -iae, f: favor, esteem, regard (**grātiās agere**: to give thanks)

iniūria, -ae, f: injury, wrong, injustice

prōvincia, -iae, f: command, province, the backwoods

turba, -ae, f: crowd

arvum, -ī, n: region, country, field
campus, -ī, m: plain, field
dōnum, -ī, n: gift
fātum, -ī, n: fate
iugum, -ī, n: yoke, team, crossbar, ridge
lēgātus, -ī, m: envoy, delegate
medicus, -ī, m: doctor, physician
pontus, -ī, m: sea
pretium, -iī, n: price, reward
prōdigium, -iī, n: prodigy, portent
sacerdōtium, -iī, n: priesthood
somnus, -ī, m: sleep
tēlum, -ī, n: missile, dart, javelin, spear
vestīgium, -iī, n: track, trace, mark
vulgus, -ī, n: the people, the public, the crowd

aequor, -oris, n: level surface, sea
ardor, -ōris, m: passion, eagerness
auris, -is (-ium), f: ear
avis, -is (-ium), f: bird
bōs, bovis, m/f: ox, bull, cow
caedēs, -is (-ium), f: killing, slaughter
consul, consulis, m: a high political office in Rome
crīmen, crīminis, n: crime, guilt, charge
fās, n (indeclinable): in accord with divine law
fax, facis (-ium), f: torch
lapis, lapidis, m: stone
latus, lateris, n: side, flank
lītus, lītoris, n: seashore, beach

magnitūdō, magnitūdinis, f: size, bulk, greatness
māior, -ōris, m/f: ancestor (from comparative adjective of *magnus*: "the greater ones")
moenia, -ium, n (plural): walls, fortifications
mulier, mulieris, f: woman
murmur, -uris, n: murmur, roar, rumble
ōs, ōris, n: mouth, face
parens, -entis, m/f: parent
pectus, -oris, n: breast, heart, soul
pēs, pedis, m: foot, foot soldier
praetor, -ōris, m: leader, military leader, magistrate at Rome with the constitutional authority to lead an army
prex, precis, f: request, entreaty
ratiō, -iōnis, f: account, reckoning, reasoning, method
sēdēs, -is (-ium), f: seat, base, home
voluptās, -ātis, f: pleasure, enjoyment

cursus, -ūs, m: course, running, race
fluctus, -ūs, m: wave
impetus, -ūs, m: attack, assault, charge
spīritus, -ūs, m: breath, spirit, soul
ūsus, -ūs, m: practice, skill, exercise, use, need
vultus, -ūs, m: face, appearance

faciēs, -iēī, f: shape, form, appearance
fidēs, -ēī, f: faith, trust

PRONOUNS

quisque, quaeque, quidque: each

ADJECTIVES

beātus, -a, -um: happy, fortunate

dūrus, -a, -um: hard, inflexible, harsh

falsus, -a, -um: deceptive, false, fake

fessus, -a, -um: tired, weary

grātus, -a, -um (+ dative): pleasing, welcome, agreeable

honestus, -a, -um: respectable, honorable, proper, virtuous

īmus, -a, -um: lowest, deepest

lātus, -a, -um: broad, wide

līber, lībera, līberum: free

pius, pia, pium: dutiful, devoted, affectionate

pulcher, pulchra, pulchrum: pretty

reliquus, -a, -um: remaining, left

saevus, -a, -um: fierce, raging, violent

singulus, -a, -um: single, separate, one at a time

superus, -a, -um: high

tūtus, -a, -um: safe, protected, secure

ācer, acris, acre: sharp, vigorous, brave, bitter

audax (audācis): bold, daring, courageous, foolhardy

celer, celeris, celere: quick, fast, rapid, swift

dissimilis, -e: dissimilar

facilis, -e: easy

fortis, -e: brave

gracilis, -e: graceful

humilis, -e: low, humble

mollis, -e: soft, supple

potens (-entis): powerful

quālis, -e: of what sort/kind as

tālis, -e: of such a kind

tristis, -e: sad, gloomy

VERBS

arō, -āre, -āvī, -ātus: plow

celebrō, -āre, -āvī, -ātus: practice, repeat, celebrate, make known

cūrō, -āre, -āvī, -ātus: care for, attend to

errō, -āre, -āvī, -ātus: wander, stray

nuntiō, -āre, -āvī, -ātus: announce

servō, -āre, -āvī, -ātus: observe, watch over, keep, protect

turbō, -āre, -āvī, -ātus: disturb, throw into confusion

audeō, -ēre, ausus sum: dare

gaudeō, -ēre, gāvīsus sum: rejoice, delight in

immineō, -ēre: overhang, threaten

impleō, -ēre, -ēvī, -ētus: fill in/up, complete

maneō, -ēre, mansī, mansus: remain, stay

misceō, -ēre, -uī, mixtus: mix, mingle

prohibeō, -ēre, -uī, -itus: restrain, hinder

soleō, -ēre, solitus sum: be accustomed

sustineō, -ēre, -uī, -tentus: hold back, support, sustain

taceō, -ēre, -uī, -itus: be silent

terreō, -ēre, -uī: frighten, terrify

valeō, -ēre, -uī: be strong, be able, fare well, prevail

canō, -ere, cecinī, cantus: sing, prophesy

cēdō, -ere, cessī, cessus: proceed, yield

cernō, -ere, crēvī, crētus: discern, distinguish, see

cingō, -ere, cinxī, cinctus: gird, wreathe, crown

condō, -ere, -didī, -ditus: build, found;
plunge, conceal, hide, store

currō, -ere, cucurrī, cursus: run, rush

discō, -ere, didicī: learn, get to know

disiiciō, -ere, -iēcī, -iectus: scatter, rout,
destroy

ēdō, -ere, -didī, -ditus: bring forth,
explain, emit

gignō, -ere, genuī, genitus: bear, bring
forth

pariō, -ere, peperī, partus: bring forth,
bear, give birth (to)

pergō, -ere, perrexī, perrectus:
continue, proceed, go on with

poscō, -ere, poposcī: demand, inquire

rapiō, -ere, -uī, raptus: tear away, seize,
snatch

regō, -ere, rexī, rectus: rule, guide

suscipiō, -ere, -cēpī, -ceptus: accept,
receive, maintain, undertake

tangō, -ere, tetigī, tactus: touch, reach,
border on, affect

tegō, -ere, texī, tectus: cover, hide

vertō, -ere, vertī, versus: turn, destroy

coepī, -isse, coeptus (defective verb
appearing only in the perfect system):
begin

meminī, -isse (+ genitive: defective verb
appearing only in the perfect system):
remember, recall

cōnor, -ārī, cōnātus sum: try

hortor, -ārī, hortātus sum: encourage,
urge, exhort

laetor, -ārī, laetus sum: rejoice, be glad

mīror, -ārī, mīrātus sum: wonder (at),
marvel (at)

polliceor, -ērī, pollicitus sum: offer,
promise

reor, rērī, ratus sum: think, suppose,
judge, consider

adloquor, -loquī, adlocūtus sum: speak,
address

consequor, -sequī, consecūtus sum:
follow, go after

dēgredior, -gredī, dēgressus sum: step
down, depart for

ingredior, -gredī, ingressus sum:
enter

loquor, loquī, locūtus sum: speak,
mention, say, address

morior, -ī, mortuus sum: die

nascor, -ī, nātus sum: be born, come
into existence

oblīviscor, -ī, oblītus sum (+ genitive):
forget

orior, -īrī, ortus sum: rise, begin, spring
forth (from)

patior, -ī, passus sum: suffer,
endure

proficiscor, proficiscī, profectus sum:
set out, depart

prōsequor, -sequī, prōsecūtus sum:
follow, accompany, attend

regredior, -gredī, regressus sum: step
back, retreat

sequor, sequī, secūtus sum: follow,
accompany, attend, yield, aim at

transgredior, -gredī, transgressus sum:
cross over, pass over to

ulciscor, -ī, ultus sum: take vengeance,
punish

ūtor, -ī, ūsus sum (+ ablative): use

fiō, fierī, factus sum: become

offerō, -ferre, obtulī, oblātus: present, offer

pereō, -īre, -iī, -ītus: waste, be lost, perish

accidit, -ere, accidit: it happens

constat, -āre, constitit/constātum est: it is agreed, it is well-known

decet, -ēre, -uit: it is proper, it is seemly, it is fitting

libet, -ēre, libuit/libitum est: it pleases

licet, -ēre, -uit/licitum est: it is permitted

miseret, -ēre, miseruit/miseritum est: it distresses, it pities

necesse est: it is necessary

oportet, -ēre, -uit: it is fitting

paenitet, -ēre: it causes regret

piget, -ēre, -uit: it displeases

placet, -ēre, -uit/placitum est: it pleases, it is agreeable

prōdest, -esse, -fuit: it is useful, it is advantageous, it benefits

pudet, -ēre, puduit, puditum est: it shames, it disgraces

refert, -ferre, -tulit: it matters

taedet, -ēre, taeduit/taesum est: it bores, it disgusts

CONJUNCTIONS AND ADVERBS

adeō: thus far, truly

crās: tomorrow

frustrā: in vain

haud: by no means, not at all

hūc: here

igitur: therefore

iterum: again

longē: by far

ōlim: once

paulō, paulum: a little

plērumque: for the most part, commonly, generally

postquam: after, when

praeter + accusative: beyond, except, in addition to, in front of

procul: from a distance

quā: where, how

quam: than

quamvīs: although, however much

quandō: when

quoniam: since, because

semel: once

semper: always, every time

simul: at once, at the same time

sīve ... sīve: whether ... or

statim: immediately

subitō: suddenly

ultrā (+ accusative): on the other side; beyond, farther (as an adverb)

unde: from where, whence

usque: continuously, all the way

III: ADDITIONAL DRILLS

IIIA. Decline the following noun-adjective pairs. Consult the glossary above
for the dictionary entries.

Case	lapis + superlative of **pulcher**	lītus + comparative of **mollis**	mulier + perfect deponent participle of **ulciscor**
Singular			
Nominative			
Genitive			
Dative			
Accusative			
Ablative			
Plural			
Nominative			
Genitive			
Dative			
Accusative			
Ablative			

IIIB. Give the requested forms of the following nouns.

Noun	Requested Form	Latin Form
aequor	Accusative singular	
cūra	Genitive plural	
prētium	Dative singular	
fluctus	Ablative plural	
fidēs	Ablative singular	
praetor	Accusative plural	
prex	Dative plural	
prōvincia	Genitive singular	
ūsus	Nominative plural	

IIIC. Give the correct form of the specified adjective/participle to modify
each of the following nouns. Translate the resulting phrases.

Noun	Case, No, Gender	Adj./Part.	Latin Form	Translation
campō		quālis		
sēdis		impleō Perfect passive		
spīritūs (Accusative)		beātus Superlative		
medicīs		canō Future active		
voluptātem		mollis Positive		
ratiō		grātus Comparative		
avī		discō Present active		
faciēs (Nominative, plural)		saevus Comparative		
vultibus		pius Positive		
fidēī (2)		offerō Future passive		
		offerō Future passive		

IIID. Give a synopsis of the following verb. Translate each form.

cernō

conjugation_____

synopsis: 1st person plural

INDICATIVES	Active	Translation	Passive	Translation
Present				
Imperfect				
Future				
Perfect				
Pluperfect				
Future Perfect				

IMPERATIVES	Active	Translation	Passive	Translation
Present				
Future			XXX	XXX

INFINITIVES	Active	Translation	Passive	Translation
Present				
Perfect				
Future				

PARTICIPLES	Active	Translation	Passive	Translation
Present			XXX	XXX
Perfect	XXX	XXX		
Future				

IIIE. Give the person, number, tense, voice, and mood of the following
verbs. Translate each form. (N.B. Infinitives do not have person and
number—just translate those forms!)

Form	Person and No.	Tense and Voice (A/P/D)	Mood	Translation
prohibeor				
hortāre (2)				
rapiunt				
cingī				
ēdidistis				
gignam				
sustinēbuntur				
terrēs				
obtulerat				
tacitūrōrum				
perrexerimus				
turbāre				
mansūrum esse				
mixta erant				
servāvisse				
cantum īrī				
cēde				
poscitōte				
regēbātis				
consequentur				
ratus es				
mortuae erant				
oblītus erō				
vertēbāminī				

IIIF. Give the tense, voice, number, case, and gender of the following participles. Translate each form.

Form	Tense and Voice (A/P/D)	Case(s) and No.	Gender	Translation
audentis				
arātō				
conditūrīs				
nuntiandōrum				
cōnantem				
dēgredientibus				
tecta (feminine)				
implētūrae (3)				
crētūrī (2)				
suscipendārum				
loquendam				

IIIG. Give the Latin for each of the following English phrases.

1. a very graceful woman (Nominative)

   _____

2. with threatening roars

   _____

3. of a rather sad parent

   _____

4. reason having been celebrated (Ablative absolute)

   _____

5. to/for a most dutiful spirit

   _____

6. of waves about to be thrown into confusion

   _____

7. the bitterest faces (Accusative)

8. O very bold heart!

9. the praetors about to encourage (Ablative absolute)

10. the crowds having entered (Nominative)

IIIH. Translate the following sentences into coherent English.

1. Nuntiō consulem hostem disiicere.

2. Canit consulem hostem disiectūrum esse.

3. Discunt consulem hostem disiēcisse.

4. Mīrābāminī medicum valēre.

5. Mulierēs sē tacitūrās esse pollicitae sunt.

6. Adlocūtī erant moenia condita esse.

7. Carmine cantō, precēs hostis discēmus.

8. Fluctibus crescentibus, mulierēs capita sua in templō texērunt.

9. Lībertō per prōvinciam transgressūrō, imperātor exercitum adloquētur.

10. Mūnus gladiātōrum tuī spectāre paenitet.

Crossword Puzzle.

<u>**Across**</u>

6. He had a difficult birth
7. Ovid lists the names of his 35 fine hunting dogs
8. An epithet of Caesar's divine ancestress
9. A brilliant Carthaginian tactician
12. Nero's diplomatic eastern general
15. The swiftest of all animals
18. Domitian's over-successful governor in Britain
19. He suffered a humiliating defeat in the Teutoberg Forest
21. A Turkish physician
22. Germanicus's German foe
23. The Carthaginian "Father of Latin Christianity"
25. He saw a ghost in Africa
27. A quickly growing sea-snail
28. Where Faustinus goes to retreat from city life
30. An animal with an equine crest
31. Caligula's bride
32. A Roman festival in honor of the sister of Carthage's legendary founder
36. A Roman dictator who returned to his fields
37. Carthage's legendary founder
40. He is beset by a swarm of bees
42. Her hair catches fire
43. Prescribed for eye complaints
44. A werewolf
45. An alternate name for Carthage's legendary founder
47. The father of Rome's founder
48. He described a literate elephant
50. Nothing is wiser than these animals
51. He wrote a handbook on agriculture
53. Pallas' horse
54. A hero with an important cult in central Italy
55. She does not weep in solitude
56. A hybrid creature seen by Pliny

<u>**Down**</u>

1. A Turkish port
2. Propertius's literary mistress
3. A legendary bird sighted during Tiberius's reign
4. Where Pliny the Younger goes to retreat from city life
5. A rich source for Roman mythology
10. Odysseus' dog
11. She makes life miserable for everyone
13. An epithet of Vulcan
14. The deceased spouse of Carthage's legendary founder
16. The art of divination by liver-reading
17. "Serpent Lady"
20. An epithet of Jupiter and Pluto
21. He wrote a handbook on agriculture
24. Favored by Augustus to succeed Tiberius
26. An epithet of Diana
29. A Carthaginian navigator who aspired to circumnavigate Africa
30. Another rich source for Roman mythology
33. A Greek author who recounts the Punic Wars
34. He once encountered a werewolf
35. The divine king of the winds
38. An adjective that describes Atlas' summit
39. They foretold the loss of a naval battle for the Romans
41. She led a revolt in Britain
46. Marius' Numidian foe
48. The site of a decisive British battle
49. Where Martial goes to retreat from city life
52. His forces murdered Tacitus' grandmother-in-law

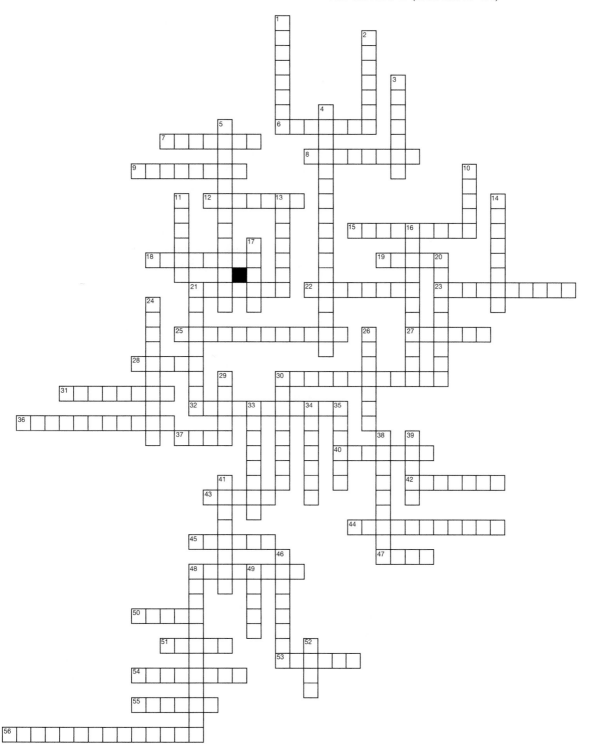

IV: ADDITIONAL PASSAGES

1. Martial 5.58.1–2. Martial's friend Postumus refuses to live his life and the epigrammatist chides Postumus for his elusive "tomorrow" which never comes. Meter: elegiac couplets.

> Crās tē victūrum, crās dīcis, Postume, semper:
> dīc mihi, crās istud, Postume, quando venit?

Notes: **Postumus, -ī**, m: the addressee of several of Martial's poems; **quando**: the final "o" scans short in order for the meter to work out correctly.

2. Tacitus, *Annālēs* 1.41.3. To protect his family from the mutinous army, Germanicus decided to send them to a tribe beyond the war zone. Agrippina, his proud and courageous wife, granddaughter of Augustus, protested, as did Germanicus's troops, who were protective of the lady and enamored with her young son, whom they nicknamed "Caligula" for the army boots he so often wore. Agrippina's retinue leaves the camp, and the soldiers come out to watch her leave (or to prevent her from leaving).

> Pars Agrippīnae occursantēs, plūrimī ad Germānicum regressī.

Notes: **Agrippīna, -ae**, f: Vipsania Agrippina, the daughter of Julia and Augustus's friend Agrippa; **occursans (-antis)** (+ dative): rushing, mobbing, obstructing; **Germānicus, -ī**, m: the agnomen (an honorary nickname) of Tiberius's nephew, awarded posthumously by the Senate to his father, Tiberius's younger brother Drusus, in honor of his own conquests in Germany (13–9 BCE); **regressī** (*sunt*).

3. Celsus, *de Materia Medica* 3.10.1. Celsus here describes a headache cure using an aromatherapeutic bandage.

> Sī capitis dolōrēs sint, rosam cum acētō miscēre oportet et in id ingerere; deinde habēre duo pittacia, quae frontis lātitūdinem longitūdinemque aequent, ex hīs invicem alterum in acētō et rosā habēre, alterum in fronte; aut intinctam iīsdem lānam sūcidam inpōnere.

Notes: **sint**: "there might be" (present subjunctive); **rosa, -ae**, f: rose (oil); **acētum, -ī**, n: vinegar; **ingerō, -ere, -gessī, -gestus**: pour in; **pittacium, -iī**, n: slip of parchment or cloth; **lātitūdō, lātitūdinis**, f: breadth; **longitūdō, longitūdinis**, f: length; **aequent**: "(which) should equal" (present subjunctive); **invicem**: in turn; **intingō, -ere, -tinxī, -tinctus**: saturate, soak; **lāna, -ae**, f: wool; **sūcidus, -a, -um**: juicy, full of sap; **inpōnō, -ere, -posuī, -positus**: place on.

4. Livy, *ab Urbe Condita* 26.37.6. In 210 BCE, both the Romans and the Carthaginians take stock of the war. Each side considers its gains equally offset by its losses. Here Livy gives the Carthaginian point of view.

Carthāginiēnsēs quoque Capuae āmissae Tarentum captum aequābant, et ut ad moenia urbis Rōmānae—nullō prohibente—sē pervēnisse in glōriā pōnēbant, ita pigēbat inritī inceptī.

Notes: **Carthāginiensis, -is**: Carthaginian; **Capua, -ae**, f: a city in southern Italy, north of Naples. After the battle of Cannae in 216 BCE, Capua defected to Carthage, becoming Hannibal's winter quarters for 215 BCE. In 212 BCE, Capua was the site of a cavalry skirmish of Capuans, Numidians, and Carthaginians against Romans. Though indecisive, Hannibal withdrew and the Romans later besieged the city. Neither side gained any strategic advantage; **Tarentum, -ī**, n: Sparta's only colony in Italy, famous for its purple dye, in the heel of Italy's boot. Hoping to shake off Roman rule, the Taurentines favored the Carthaginians who campaigned there in 212 BCE, defeating the Roman occupiers. Hannibal was careful to respect Taurentine freedom and curtailed looting after his victory; **aequō, -āre, -āvī, -ātus**: make equal, compare; **sē**: the Carthaginians; **inritus, -a, -um**: void, useless, ineffectual; **inceptum, -ī**, n: undertaking, attempt.

5. Tacitus, *Annales* 14.32.1. King Prasutagus of the Iceni in Britain, who died in 61 CE, had named Nero as co-heir with his daughters. The Roman army in Britain, however, did not honor the will but instead plundered the kingdom and raped the princesses. This incited several tribes to arms, under the leadership of Prasutagus's widow, Boudicca. At the outbreak of the war, at the colonial capital at Camulodunum (Colchester), several eerie prodigies seem to portend Roman defeat.

Et fēminae in furōre[m] turbātae adesse exitium canēbant, externōsque frēmitūs in cūriā eōrum audītōs, consonuisse ululātibus theātrum vīsamque speciem in aestuāriō Tamesae subversae colōniae.

Notes: **furor, -ōris**, m: rage, frenzy; **exitium, -iī**, n: destruction, ruin; **externus, -a, -um**: foreign; **frēmitus, -ūs**, m: roaring, growling; **cūria, -iae**, f: the Senate House; **audītōs** (*esse*); **consonō, -āre, -uī**: sound loudly, resound, echo; **ululātus, -ūs**, m: wailing, shrieking, yelling; **theātrum, ī**, n: theater; **vīsam** (*esse*); **aestuārium, -iī**, n: creek, the part of a river over which the tide flows; **Tamesa, -ae**, m: the river Thames; **subvertō, -ere, -vertī, -versum**: turn upside down, overthrow; **colōnia, -iae**, f: colony.

6. Frontinus, *de Aquaeductu Urbis Romae* 1.7. The Sibylline books were purchased by Lucius Tarquinius Superbus, Rome's last king, from Apollo's priestess, the Sibyl of Cumae. A collection of Greek hexameters, they were considered oracular proclamations from the god and as such were consulted during times of political or social crisis. The crisis for which they were consulted in 146 BCE is otherwise unknown, but is likely related to Scipio Africanus's destruction of Carthage or Corinth (both in 146 BCE). While researching this other matter, the *decemvirī* discover that it is improper to bring water into the Capitoline. After years of deliberation, the *decemvirī* were overruled, largely thanks to the influence of the city praetor Quintus Marcius, and sufficient water supplies were arranged for the Capitoline.

Eō tempore decemvirī, dum aliīs ex causīs librōs Sibyllīnōs inspiciunt, invēnisse dīcuntur, nōn esse fās Aquam Marciam seu potius Aniōnem (dē hōc enim constantius trāditur) in Capitōlium perdūcī.

Notes: **decemvir, -ī**, m: a board of ten men, serving for life, responwsible for consulting the Sibylline books under senatorial mandate; **Sibyllīnus, -a, -um**: of the Sibyl, the priestess of Apollo's cult at Cumae near Naples; **inspiciō, -ere, -spexī, -spectus**: examine, consult, inspect; **seu**: or; **potius**: rather; **constantius**: more steadfastly, more resolutely; **Capitōlium, -iī**, n: one of the seven hills of Rome, where stood the temple of Jupiter Optimus Maximus built by Tarquinius Superbus; **perdūcō, -ere, -dūxī, -ductus**: lead through, carry, construct.

Correlatives

25A. Decline the following noun-adjective pairs.

Case	nūmen, nūminis, n + Positive of exiguus, -a, -um	sapientia, -iae, f + Present active participle of prōcēdō, -ere, -cessī, -cessus
Singular		
Nominative		
Genitive		
Dative		
Accusative		
Ablative		
Plural		
Nominative		
Genitive		
Dative		
Accusative		
Ablative		

25B. Give the requested forms of the following noun-adjective pairs. Translate the resulting phrases.

Noun	Adjective	Requested Form	Latin Form	Translation
beneficium	mortālis Superlative	Dative singular		
sapientia	exiguus Comparative	Nominative plural		
laus	quantus Positive	Accusative singular		
vōtum	tollō Pres. act. part.	Genitive plural		
fūnus	dēcernō Fut. pass. part	Dative plural		
ops	creō Perf. pass. part.	Ablative singular		
ōrātiō	properō Perf. pass. part.	Genitive singular		
nūmen	existimō Fut. act. part	Accusative plural		

25C. Give the correct form of the specified adjective or participle to modify each of the following nouns.

Noun	Case, No., Gender	Adjective/Participle	Latin Form
laudēs (Nom.)		existimō Perf. pass. part.	
fūnere		prōcēdō Fut. act. part.	
sapientiīs		mortālis Comparative	
ops		exiguus Superlative	
nūminī		tollō Perf. pass. part.	
beneficiī		dēsciscō Fut. pass. part.	
ōrātiōnibus		quantus Positive	
vōta		dēficiō Pres. act. part.	

25D. Give a synopsis of the following verb. Translate each form.

tollō, -ere, sustulī, sublātus
conjugation _____
synopsis: 2nd person plural

INDICATIVES	Active	Translation	Passive	Translation
Present				
Imperfect				
Future				
Perfect				
Pluperfect				
Future Perfect				

IMPERATIVES	Active	Translation	Passive	Translation
Present				
Future			XXX	XXX

INFINITIVES	Active	Translation	Passive	Translation
Present				
Perfect				
Future				

PARTICIPLES	Active	Translation	Passive	Translation
Present			XXX	XXX
Perfect	XXX	XXX		
Future				

25E. Identify the following verbs as directed. Translate each form.

Form	Person (finite verbs)	No.	Tense	Voice (A/P/D)	Mood (finite verbs) Case/Gender (part.)	Translation
āfuerat						
tollī						
existimās						
descīvistis						
aiunt						
dēficient						
creantibus						
dēcernēbāmur						
āfutūrae (Genitive)						
prōcessisse						
dēfectō						
properātī erunt						

25F. Give the requested forms of the following verbs. Translate each form.

Latin Verb	Requested Form	Latin Form	English Translation
creō	2nd person plural Future passive indicative		
existimō	1st person plural Pluperfect passive indicative		
properō	Present active participle Genitive plural		
dēcernō	2nd person singular Imperfect passive indicative		
descīscō	3rd person singular Future perfect passive indicative	,	

Latin Verb	Requested Form	Latin Form	English Translation
prōcēdō	Present active singular Imperative		
tollō	Future active participle Dative singular feminine		
dēficiō	3rd person plural Perfect active indicative		
absum	1st person singular Future indicative		

25G. Translate the following sentences into coherent English.

1. Tam docta quam pulchra es.

_____

2. Cum equōs tum canēs amāmus.

_____

3. Quotiens Mūsam audiēs, totiens carmina scrībēs.

_____

4. Eō celerius prōcēdēbātis, quō saevius pugnābant.

_____

5. Quantum opis habēs tantum volumus.

_____

6. Quantī mīlitēs hostibus tantī nōbīs cīvēs sunt.

_____

7. Tot laudem accipimus quot trāditur.

_____

8. Spectāculum tāle quāle Caesar numquam dedit vīdimus.

_____

25H. Translate the following sentences into Latin. Use the rubric below each sentence as a guide.

Caesar was as great a general as Cincinnatus had been.

Correlative expression that translates "as great ... as"_____

_____

Syntactic function and case of "general"_____

Dictionary entry_____

Latin translation_____

Syntactic function and case of "Cincinnatus"_____

Dictionary entry_____

Latin translation_____

Person, number, tense, and voice of "(he) had been" _____

_____

Dictionary entry_____

Latin translation_____

Latin translation of entire sentence_____

_____

We wrote to our brothers and sisters as often as our mothers and fathers written to us.

Correlative expression that translates "as often ... as"_____

_____

Person, number, tense, and voice of "we wrote"_____

_____

Dictionary entry_____

Latin translation_____

Person, number, tense, and voice of "(they had) written"_____

_____

Dictionary entry_____

Latin translation_____

Latin translation of entire sentence_____

_____

We heard as many sweet songs as the poet was able to sing.

Correlative expression that translates "as many ... as"_____
_____

Person, number, tense, and voice of "we heard"_____
_____

Dictionary entry_____
Latin translation_____

Syntactic function and case of "sweet songs"_____
Dictionary entry of "sweet"_____
Dictionary entry of "songs"_____
Latin translation_____

Syntactic function and case of "poet"_____
Dictionary entry_____
Latin translation_____

Person, number, tense, and voice of "(he) was able"_____
_____

Latin translation_____

Latin translation of entire sentence_____
_____

25I. Word Find. The words may appear horizontally, vertically or diagonally in either direction.

Roman Republican Heroes and Villains

T	F	E	J	Z	H	Q	X	W	I	U	A	A	O	A	O	Q	D	J	S
C	I	K	Y	X	U	S	D	H	D	I	L	F	R	Y	O	D	C	R	K
S	N	B	M	B	U	M	C	Y	K	Y	C	A	X	A	G	I	G	U	K
C	V	V	E	C	H	O	Z	Z	A	U	E	J	W	Q	S	N	O	G	U
H	V	X	Q	R	S	O	E	J	M	T	A	P	M	P	I	E	O	Z	P
V	Z	A	V	H	I	H	R	J	A	A	J	A	M	F	F	U	A	T	L
L	I	P	T	F	S	U	N	A	C	I	R	F	A	O	I	P	I	C	S
L	C	K	H	C	H	J	S	V	T	C	V	I	I	K	P	Y	T	I	S
B	I	L	D	M	C	C	A	G	A	I	X	L	U	I	I	M	E	N	M
K	J	W	O	H	J	A	R	N	R	U	U	S	U	S	S	A	R	C	I
C	X	U	F	E	B	T	T	S	I	A	Q	S	Z	F	U	Y	C	I	R
F	L	L	O	C	L	O	D	I	U	S	C	O	C	N	Z	L	U	N	Y
Q	U	V	S	U	N	I	T	A	L	L	O	C	A	O	W	V	L	N	L
I	Z	X	N	Y	R	A	A	P	A	I	R	I	H	G	C	C	O	A	M
H	B	I	J	J	R	A	H	U	M	D	N	C	J	U	J	L	I	T	Z
F	T	Q	A	O	G	O	D	Z	Z	I	E	E	T	A	S	U	E	U	G
F	F	X	H	D	F	I	M	I	G	I	L	R	E	B	K	V	V	S	A
Z	T	G	K	S	U	T	U	R	B	E	I	O	T	D	M	Y	K	D	P
N	F	Q	Y	S	C	A	E	V	O	L	A	K	G	R	Q	D	T	D	H
C	N	I	M	L	R	V	L	U	S	P	U	U	D	J	R	O	O	E	G

Appius Claudius	Cicero	Cornelia	Lucretia	Scaevola
Brutus	Cincinnatus	Crassus	Marc Antony	Scipio Africanus
Caesar	Clodius	Fulvia	Marius	Sulla
Catiline	Cloelia	Horatii	Milo	Tiberius Gracchus
Cato	Collatinus	Horatius Cocles	Pompey	Verginia

Present and Imperfect Subjunctives

26A. Decline the following noun-adjective pairs.

Case	flōs, flōris, m + Superlative of castus, -a, -um	coma, ae, f + Present active participle of aperiō, -īre, -uī, -pertus
Singular		
Nominative		
Genitive		
Dative		
Accusative		
Ablative		
Plural		
Nominative		
Genitive		
Dative		
Accusative		
Ablative		

26B. For each of the following nouns, select the adjective that agrees in case, number, and gender. Then translate the resulting phrases. You may use each adjective only once.

Adjective bank: **inimīciōribus, difficilī, pauperēs, corruptōrum, querentis, sonantium**

Noun	Case, No., Gender	Adjective	Translation
animae			
comā			
ianuārum			
ingeniīs			
aetātis			
flōrum			

26C. Give a synopsis of the following verb. Translate each form.

dēserō, -ere, -seruī, -sertus
conjugation_____
synopsis: 1st person singular

INDICATIVES	Active	Translation	Passive	Translation
Present				
Imperfect				
Future				
Perfect				
Pluperfect				
Future Perfect				

SUBJUNCTIVES	Active	Passive
Present		
Imperfect		

IMPERATIVES	Active	Translation	Passive	Translation
Present				
Future			XXX	XXX

dēserō, -ere, -seruī, -sertus

INFINITIVES	Active	Translation	Passive	Translation
Present				
Perfect				
Future				

PARTICIPLES	Active	Translation	Passive	Translation
Present			XXX	XXX
Perfect	XXX	XXX		
Future				

26D. Identify the following verbs as directed. Translate each form. Translate
each converted form. (Translate present tense subjunctives "let/may …"
and imperfect tense subjunctives "were/would that.")

Form	Person (finite verbs)	No.	Tense	Voice (A/P/D)	Mood (finite verbs) Case/Gender (part.)	Translation
pateat						
sonentur						
aperiētis						
merēret						
superfuistis						
corrumpantur						
dēsererēs						
aperiāmur						
querāminī						
contuleram						
querēbātur						
supersint						
dēserī						
superessēs						
conferendōs						

26E. Give the requested forms of the following verbs.

Latin Verb	Requested Form	Latin Form	English Translation
aperiō	third person plural Present active indicative		
conferō	first person singular Imperfect active subjunctive		
corrumpō	second person singular Present passive subjunctive		
dēserō	first person plural Imperfect active subjunctive		
mereō	third person singular Imperfect passive indicative		
pateō	second person plural Present active subjunctive		
queror	first person singular Imperfect deponent subjunctive		
sonō	third person singular Present passive subjunctive		
supersum	second person singular Present active subjunctive		

26F. Identify the following verbs by person, number, tense, voice, and mood. And translate the given forms. Then, keeping the same person, number, tense, and voice, convert the indicative forms to subjunctive and subjunctive forms to indicative. Translate each converted form. (Translate present tense subjunctives "let/may …" and imperfect tense subjunctives "were/would that." For ambiguous forms, assume that the given form is subjunctive.)

Latin Form	Person, No., Tense, Voice, Mood	Translation of Given Form	Conversion	Translation of Converted Form
regam				
cēditur				
offerās				
gaudēbāmus				
pugnārentur				

Latin Form	Person, No., Tense, Voice, Mood	Translation of Given Form	Conversion	Translation of Converted Form
caedēbāminī				
trādit				
vincerēris				
sentior				
videāmur				
mittant				
agēbātis				

26G. Translate the following sentences into coherent English.

1. Iānua tua mihi semper pateat.

   _____

2. Nē fortasse flōrēs bovibus ā grandibus corrumpantur.

   _____

3. Utinam ingenium fīliārum doctārum populīs Rōmānīs aperiātur.

   _____

4. Imperium ducis omnibus cīvibus beneficiō supersit.

   _____

5. Quid in aetāte tālī mereāmus?

   _____

6. Utinam sapientia hās terrās nōn dēsereret.

   _____

7. Quid tandem querāmur?

   _____

8. Utinam hīc adforēs, mī amīce caste!

   _____

26H. Translate the following sentences into Latin. Use the rubric below each sentence as a guide.

Would that the Roman army wins the long war.

Person, number, tense, and mood of "would that (it) wins" _____

_____

Dictionary entry _____

Latin translation _____

Syntactic function and case of "Roman army" _____

Dictionary entry of "army" _____

Latin translation of "Roman army" _____

Syntactic function and case of "long war" _____

Dictionary entry of "long" and "war" _____

Latin translation _____

Latin translation of entire sentence _____

_____

What should I do? I have destroyed my little book of songs.

Person, number, tense, voice, and mood of "should I do" _____

_____

Dictionary entry _____

Latin translation _____

Person, number, tense, voice, and mood of "I have destroyed" _____

_____

Dictionary entry _____

Latin translation _____

Syntactic function and case of "little book" _____

Dictionary entry _____

Latin translation _____

Syntactic function and case of "of songs" _____

Dictionary entry _____

Latin translation _____

Latin translation of entire sentence _____

_____

Perhaps the difficult door may lie open for me alone.

Person, number, tense, voice, and mood of "(it) may lie open" _____

_____

Dictionary entry _____

Latin translation _____

Syntactic function and case of "difficult door" _____

_____

Dictionary entry of "difficult" and "door" _____

Latin translation _____

Syntactic function and case of "for me alone" _____

Latin translation _____

Latin translation of entire sentence _____

_____

26I. A haiku to translate.

Tēcum tam pulchrā
quam stellā laetissimus
vīvere velim.

Haiku is a traditional form of Japanese poetry consisting of 17 syllables in three lines (5, 7, 5 syllables respectively). Adapt your favorite passage from *NLP* 26 into a grammatically correct Latin haiku featuring a subjunctive verb.

_____

_____

_____

Perfect and Pluperfect Subjunctive and Cum Clauses

27A. Decline the following noun-adjective pairs.

Case	quidquid + Present active participle of redeō, -īre, -iī or īvī, -itus	dēlātor, -ōris, m + Future passive participle of prōdō, -ere, -didī, -ditus
Singular		
Nominative		
Genitive		
Dative		
Accusative		
Ablative		
Plural		
Nominative		
Genitive		
Dative		
Accusative		
Ablative		

27B. Give the requested forms of the following noun-adjective pairs. Translate the resulting phrases.

Noun	Adjective	Requested Form	Latin Form	Translation
forum	plēnus Comparative	Nominative singular		
clāmor	repetō Fut. pass. part.	Genitive plural		
odium	addō Pres. act. part.	Ablative plural		
exemplum	prōdō Perf. pass. part.	Accusative singular		
ferrum	dōnō Fut. pass. part.	Accusative plural		
dēlātor	doleō Fut. act. part.	Dative singular		
gladius	dexter Positive	Genitive singular		

27C. Give the correct form of the specified adjective or participle to modify each of the following nouns. Translate the resulting phrases.

Noun	Case, No., Gender	Adjective/Participle	Latin Form	Translation
forō		compōnō Perf. pass. part.		
clāmōrēs (Acc.)		plēnus Positive		
odiōrum		cunctus Positive		
exempla		repetō Fut. pass. part.		
ferrīs		dexter Positive		
dēlātōre		posterus Positive		
gladiī (singular)		prōdō Pres. act. part.		

27D. Give a synopsis of the following verb. Translate each form.

dōnō, -āre, -āvī, -ātus

conjugation _____

synopsis: 3rd person singular

INDICATIVES	Active	Translation	Passive	Translation
Present				
Imperfect				
Future				
Perfect				
Pluperfect				
Future Perfect				

SUBJUNCTIVES	Active	Passive
Present		
Imperfect		
Perfect		
Pluperfect		

IMPERATIVES	Active	Translation	Passive	Translation
Present				
Future			XXX	XXX

INFINITIVES	Active	Translation	Passive	Translation
Present				
Perfect				
Future				

PARTICIPLES	Active	Translation	Passive	Translation
Present			XXX	XXX
Perfect	XXX	XXX		
Future				

27E. Identify the following verbs as directed. Translate all forms. (Translate present tense subjunctives "let/may ..." and imperfect, perfect, and pluperfect tense subjunctives "were/would that." For ambiguous forms assume that the given form is subjunctive.)

Form	Person and No.	Tense	Voice	Mood	Translation
ōdissēs					
prōditus esset					
repetītae sīmus					
dolueritis (2)					
dōnāvī					
additum est					
compōsita erant					
aperueram					
questī essēmus					
conlātae erātis					
meruit					
superfuerint (2)					

27F. Give the requested forms of the following verbs. Translate all forms. (Translate present tense subjunctives "let/may ..." and imperfect, perfect, and pluperfect tense subjunctives "were/would that.")

Latin Verb	Requested Form	Latin Form	Translation
dōnō	third person plural Perfect passive subjunctive		
doleō	second person singular Perfect active indicative		
addō	third person singular Pluperfect active subjunctive		
compōnō	first person plural Pluperfect active subjunctive		
repetō	third person plural Pluperfect active indicative		
prōdō	first person singular Perfect passive indicative		
ōdī	second person plural Perfect active subjunctive		

27G. Identify the following verbs by person, number, tense, voice, and mood. Translate the given forms. Then, keeping the same person, number, tense, and voice, convert the indicative forms to subjunctive and subjunctive forms to indicative. (Translate subjunctives as: "let/may …"; "were/would that…".)

Latin Form	Person, No., Tense, Voice, Mood	Translation of Given Form	Conversion	Translation of Converted Form
tulerāmus				
ēgerint				
cēperās				
dictum sit				
dedisset				
māluerim				
missus eram				
scripsistis				
gestum est				
voluissem				
facta essent				
īvērunt				

27H. Translate the following sentences into coherent English.

1. Nē dolueris!

   _____

2. Utinam urbs tunc nōn cecidisset!

   _____

3. Cum ferrō prōditī sīmus, tamen vincēmus.

   _____

4. Cum hostēs in nōs gladiīs ūsī essent, plūrimī mīlitum mortuī sunt.

   _____

5. Cum exempla māiōrum repetāmus, imperātor mūnera nōbīs dōnat.

   _____

6. Cum hostēs ōderimus, saevissimē pugnāmus.

_____

7. Cum forum plēnum cīvium dūrōrum sit, quisque tamen tacet.

_____

8. Cum poētae pulcherrima carmina cantent, omnēs mīrantur.

_____

271. Translate the following sentences into Latin. Use the rubric below each sentence as a guide.

Although we had escaped the town, nevertheless we suffered and lived with the worst hatred.

What sort of clause is "Although we had escaped …"? _____

_____

Person, number, tense, voice, and mood of "we had escaped"_____

_____

Dictionary entry _____

Latin translation _____

Person, number, tense, voice, and mood of "we suffered and lived" ___

_____

Dictionary entry of "suffer" _____

Dictionary entry of "live" _____

Latin translation of "we suffered and lived" _____

Syntactic function and case of "with the worst hatred" _____

_____

Dictionary entry of "hatred" _____

Latin translation of "with the worst hatred" _____

Latin translation of entire sentence _____

_____

Would that the informers had broken the gates and seen the crimes.

    Person, number, tense, voice, and mood of "would that (they) had broken" _____
    Dictionary entry _____
    Latin translation _____

    Person, number, tense, voice, and mood of "would that (they) had seen" _____
    Dictionary entry _____
    Latin translation _____

    Syntactic function and case of "informers" _____
    Dictionary entry _____
    Latin translation _____

    Syntactic function and case of "gates" and "crimes" _____
    _____
    Dictionary entry of "gate" _____
    Dictionary entry of "crime" _____
    Latin translation of "gates" and "crimes" _____

    Latin translation of entire sentence _____
    _____

27J. Give the Latin forms for the following English phrases. Then recombine the **double-underlined** letters to spell the word for a constitutional prerogative of higher office at Rome.

would that : __ — __ — — —

the informer: __ — __ — __ — __

had been betrayed: __ — __ — __ — — —

__ — — — —

by a shout: __ — — __ — — —

ANSWER: __ — __ — — — —

LESSON 28

Purpose Clauses

28A. Decline the following noun-adjective pairs.

Case	lupus, -ī, m + Comparative of suāvis, -e	līmen, līminis, n + Future active participle of surgō, -ere, surrexī, surrectus
Singular		
Nominative		
Genitive		
Dative		
Accusative		
Ablative		
Plural		
Nominative		
Genitive		
Dative		
Accusative		
Ablative		

28B. Give the correct form of the adjective or participle to modify each of the following nouns. Translate the resulting phrases.

Noun	Case, No., Gender	Adjective/Participle	Latin Form	Translation
dolī (plural)		**vacuus** Comparative		
lupum		**dubitō** Pres. act. part.		
marītōrum		**suāvis** Positive		
cruōris		**sānus** Superlative		
līmina		**fingō** Fut. pass. part.		
fideī (Dative)		**impōnō** Perf. pass. part.		
exercitibus		**praeclārus** Positive		
villās		**comparō** Perf. pass. part		

28C. For each of the following nouns, select the adjective that agrees in case, number, and gender. Then translate the resulting phrases. You may use each adjective only once.

Adjective bank: **ēreptus, convenientibus, praeclāram, surgentium, vacuae, suāvīs, sāniōrem, fictī**

Noun	Case, No., Gender	Adjective	Translation
dolōrum			
lupīs			
marītum			
cruor			
līminis			
Mānēs			
gentem			
pācī			

28D. Give a synopsis of the following verb. Translate each form.

conveniō, -īre, -vēnī, -ventus
conjugation _____
synopsis: 1st person plural

INDICATIVES	Active	Translation	Passive	Translation
Present				
Imperfect				
Future				
Perfect				
Pluperfect				
Future Perfect				

SUBJUNCTIVES	Active	Passive
Present		
Imperfect		
Perfect		
Pluperfect		

IMPERATIVES	Active	Translation	Passive	Translation
Present				
Future			XXX	XXX

INFINITIVES	Active	Translation	Passive	Translation
Present				
Perfect				
Future				

PARTICIPLES	Active	Translation	Passive	Translation
Present			XXX	XXX
Perfect	XXX	XXX		
Future				

28E. Identify the following verbs as directed. Translate all forms. (Translate present tense subjunctives "let/may ..." and imperfect, perfect, and pluperfect tense subjunctives "were/would that.")

Form	Person and No.	Tense	Voice	Mood	Translation
conveniātis					
intenditur					
impōnēbam					
fingerēris					
accēdent					
ēripiam (2)					
comparāvisse					
dubitāverim					
surrexisse					
fuerās					
agī					
placuit					

28F. Give the requested forms of the following verbs. Translate all forms. (Translate present tense subjunctives "let/may ..." and imperfect, perfect, and pluperfect tense subjunctives "were/would that.")

Latin Verb	Requested Form	Latin Form	English Translation
comparō	first person singular Imperfect passive indicative		
dubitō	third person singular Imperfect active subjunctive		
accēdō	first person plural Pluperfect active indicative		
ēripiō	third person plural Present passive subjunctive		
fingō	third person singular Present passive indicative		
impōnō	second person plural Imperfect active subjunctive		
intendō	second person singular Future passive indicative		
surgō	second person singular Present active subjunctive		
conveniō	third person plural Perfect active subjunctive		

28G. Translate the following sentences into coherent English.

1. Sōl ubique surgit nē cīvēs tōtam diem dormiant.

   _____

2. Lupus accessit ut hostīs nostrōs scīlicet terrēret.

   _____

3. Marītus dōna dīvitia uxōrī pulcherrimae dat ut prōtinus gaudeat.

   _____

4. Poētae carmina alta scrībent ut patriam celebrent.

   _____

5. Coniunx dolīs malīs ūtēbātur ut rēgem suāvem falleret.

   _____

6. Utinam puella hīc manēret nē pater māterve comam venetam cerneret.

_____

7. Imperātōrēs undique convēnēre ut exercitūs suōs comparārent.

_____

8. Lībertī ā līberīs gladiōs ēripuerant nē quid perīculī accideret.

_____

9. Rex lēgēs cīvitātī impōnat ut pax omnēs per terrās sit.

_____

10. Līmina villae prōtinus claudēbantur nē equī ingrederentur.

_____

28H. Translate the following sentences into Latin. Use the rubric below each sentence as a guide.

Let the army seize the hill so that it may be able to pitch camp.

Person, number, tense, voice, and mood of "let (it) seize" _____

_____

Dictionary entry _____

Latin translation _____

What sort of clause is "so that it may be able to pitch camp"? _____

_____

Person number, tense, voice, and mood of "(it) may be able" _____

_____

Dictionary entry _____

Latin translation _____

Latin translation of entire sentence _____

_____

If only the mothers had not seen their children! They approached in order to protect them.

Person, number, tense, voice, and mood of "if only (they) had seen"

_____

Dictionary entry _____

Latin translation _____

Person, number, tense, voice, and mood of "They approached" _____

_____

Dictionary entry _____

Latin translation _____

What sort of clause is "in order to protect" [= "so that they might protect"]? _____

Person, number, tense, voice, and mood of "in order to protect"

_____

Dictionary entry _____

Latin translation _____

Latin translation of entire sentence _____

_____

281. A limerick to translate.

Amans pulchriōrem Meroë

virum mox venit ab Hecatē

ut ipse prōtinus

amet ipsam bellus,

manens semper tristis Meroë.

Result Clauses

29A. Decline the following noun-adjective pairs.

Case	necessitās, -ātis, f + Positive of clārus, -a, -um	agmen, agminis, n + Perfect passive participle of trahō, -ere, traxī, tractus
Singular		
Nominative		
Genitive		
Dative		
Accusative		
Ablative		
Plural		
Nominative		
Genitive		
Dative		
Accusative		
Ablative		

29B. Give the requested forms of the following noun-adjective or noun-participle pairs. Translate the resulting phrases.

Noun	Adjective/Participle	Requested Form	Latin Form	Translation
cor	afficiō Perf. pass. part.	Accusative singular		
hōra	clārus Comparative	Ablative plural		
comes (f)	stō Pres. act. part.	Dative singular		
testis (m)	īrātus Superlative	Genitive plural		
Britannia	inferus Positive	Genitive singular		
conditiō	damnō Fut. pass. part.	Accusative plural		
sacerdōs (m)	quaerō Pres. act. part.	Dative plural		

29C. Give the correct form of the adjective or participle to modify each of the following nouns. Translate the resulting phrases.

Noun	Case, No., Gender	Adjective/Participle	Latin Form	Translation
cordī		inferus Positive		
testīs (2)		quaerō Fut. pass. part.		
		quaerō Fut. pass. part.		
hōrae (3)		trahō Perf. pass. part.		
		trahō Perf. pass. part.		
		trahō Perf. pass. part.		

Noun	Case, No., Gender	Adjective/Participle	Latin Form	Translation
sacerdōtibus (4)		damnō Fut. pass. part.		
		damnō Fut. pass. part.		
		damnō Fut. pass. part.		
		damnō Fut. pass. part.		
comitum (2)		afficiō Fut. act. part.		
		afficiō Fut. act. part.		
Britanniā		clārus Comparative		
victoriārum		stō Pres. act. part.		
conditiōnēs (2)		quaerō Perf. pass. part.		
		quaerō Perf. pass. part.		

29D. Give a synopsis of the following verb. Translate each form.

afficiō, -ere, -fēcī, -fectus
conjugation_____
synopsis: 2nd person singular

INDICATIVES	Active	Translation	Passive	Translation
Present				
Imperfect				
Future				
Perfect				
Pluperfect				
Future Perfect				

afficiō, -ere, -fēcī, -fectus

SUBJUNCTIVES	Active	Passive
Present		
Imperfect		
Perfect		
Pluperfect		

IMPERATIVES	Active	Translation	Passive	Translation
Present				
Future			XXX	XXX

INFINITIVES	Active	Translation	Passive	Translation
Present				
Perfect				
Future				

PARTICIPLES	Active	Translation	Passive	Translation
Present			XXX	XXX
Perfect	XXX	XXX		
Future				

29E. Identify the following verbs as directed. Translate all. (Translate present tense subjunctives "let/may …" and imperfect, perfect, and pluperfect tense subjunctives "were/would that".)

Form	Person and No.	Tense	Voice (A/P/D)	Mood	Translation
stārī					
trahitōte					
damnātum īrī					
afficerētur					
damnāverint (2)					
fluēbat					
sequāminī					
coepisserat					
duxistī					
posuerint (2)					

29F. Give the requested forms of the following verbs. Translate all forms. (Translate present tense subjunctives "let/may …" and imperfect, perfect, and pluperfect tense subjunctives "were/would that.")

Latin Verb	Requested Form	Latin Form	Translation
damnō	Perfect passive Infinitive		
stō	second person singular Present active subjunctive		
fluō	third person singular Perfect active indicative		
quaerō	third person plural Imperfect passive subjunctive		
trahō	first person plural Pluperfect passive subjunctive		
afficiō	second person plural Perfect active indicative		

29G. Identify the following verbs by person, number, tense, voice, and mood. And translate the given forms. Then, keeping the same person, number, tense, and voice, convert the indicative forms to subjunctive and subjunctive forms to indicative. (Translate subjunctives as: "let/may . . ."; "were/would that. . . ." For ambiguous forms assume that the given form is subjunctive.)

Latin Form	Person, No., Tense, Voice, and Mood	Translation of Given Form	Conversion	Translation of Converted Form
absīs				
vult				
poteram				
fertur				
prōfuit				
īvistī				
mālim				
nōluissētis				

29H. Translate the following sentences into coherent English.

1. Testis tam īrātus est ut clāmōribus cum magnīs dīcat.

_____

2. Umbrae tantae cadunt ut nihil spectētis.

_____

3. Tālia mūnera ā imperātōre dantur ut populī Rōmānī laetentur.

_____

4. Equus principis tam celerrimē currit ut paene vidēre nōn possīmus.

_____

5. Labōrēs nōbilēs usque eō faciēbāmus ut etiam sacerdōtēs afficerentur.

_____

6. Mīlitēs tantam victōriam petēbant ut nēmō nōs vinceret.

_____

7. Puella orbem terrārum adeō cognoscet ut nihil sē fallat.

_____

8. Accidēbat ut puer omne perīculum propter canis suī praesidium gereret.

_____

9. Urbem ita altam Rōmulus condidit ut mīrātī sītis.

_____

10. Fidēs comitum valdē erat ut dī placērentur.

_____

29I. Translate the following sentences into Latin. Use the rubric below each sentence as a guide.

So great was the victory in Britain that all the citizens rejoiced.

What sort of clause is "that all the citizens rejoiced"? _____

_____

Person, number, tense, voice, and mood of "(they) rejoiced" _____

_____

Dictionary entry _____

Latin translation _____

Latin translation of entire sentence _____

_____

It happened that all the witnesses and informers were absent.

Person, number, tense, voice, and mood of "(it) happened" _____

_____

Dictionary entry _____

Latin translation _____

What sort of clause is "that all the witnesses and informers were absent"? _____

Person, number, tense, voice, and mood of "(they) were absent"

_____

Dictionary entry _____

Latin translation _____

Latin translation of entire sentence _____

_____

29J. A haiku to translate.

Britannia tam
est ampla vincāt ut nec
Caesar etiam.

Haiku is a traditional form of Japanese poetry consisting of 17 syllables in three lines (5, 7, 5 syllables respectively). Adapt your favorite passage from *NLP* 29 into a grammatically correct Latin haiku featuring a result clause.

_____

_____

_____

Indirect Commands

30A. Decline the following noun-adjective pairs.

Case	poena, -ae, f + Positive of commūnis, -e	ordō, ordinis, m + Perfect passive participle of cōgō, -ere, coēgī, coactus
Singular		
Nominative		
Genitive		
Dative		
Accusative		
Ablative		
Plural		
Nominative		
Genitive		
Dative		
Accusative		
Ablative		

30B. For each of the following nouns, select the adjective that agrees in case, number, and gender. Then translate the resulting phrases. You may use each adjective only once.

Adjective bank: **cohortandārum, occupātum, perpetuō, suādentī, parcentīs**

Noun	Case, No., Gender	Adjective	Translation
poenae			
socium			
tribūnōs			
coniūrātiōnum			
ordine			

30C. Give a synopsis of the following verb. Translate each form.

persuādeō, -ēre, -suāsī, -suāsus
conjugation _____
synopsis: 3rd person plural

INDICATIVES	Active	Translation	Passive	Translation
Present				
Imperfect				
Future				
Perfect				
Pluperfect				
Future Perfect				

SUBJUNCTIVES	Active	Passive
Present		
Imperfect		
Perfect		
Pluperfect		

persuādeō, -ēre, -suāsī, -suāsus

IMPERATIVES	Active	Translation	Passive	Translation
Present				
Future			XXX	XXX

INFINITIVES	Active	Translation	Passive	Translation
Present				
Perfect				
Future				

PARTICIPLES	Active	Translation	Passive	Translation
Present			XXX	XXX
Perfect	XXX	XXX		
Future				

30D. Identify the following verbs as directed. Translate all forms. (Translate present tense subjunctives "let/may ..." and imperfect, perfect, and pluperfect tense subjunctives "were/would that.")

Form	Person and No.	Tense	Voice	Mood	Translation
persuāsit					
coactī erunt					
impellēris					
adeās					
postulābunt					
cohortēminī					
dīmittī					
orāvissem					
transitum īrī					
discesserō					

30E. Give the requested forms of the following verbs. Translate all forms. (Translate present tense subjunctives "let/may ..." and imperfect, perfect, and pluperfect tense subjunctives "were/would that.")

Latin Verb	Requested Form	Latin Form	Translation
occupō	third person singular Future passive indicative		
suādeō	second person plural Present active subjunctive		
parcō	first person singular Perfect active subjunctive		
pendō	third person plural Pluperfect passive indicative		
prōnuntiō	second person singular Imperfect passive subjunctive		
exeō	first person plural Future perfect active indicative		

30F. Translate the following sentences into coherent English.

1. Līberīs suādēmus nē discēdant.

2. Malōs hortāmur nē coniūrātiōnem in rēgem bonum faciant.

3. Dēnique vōs moneō nē regiōnem hanc occupētis.

4. Eques equōs suōs cohortābātur ut quam celerrimē currerent.

5. Puer prōtinus postulāvit ut poēta carmina legeret.

6. Fortasse nōbīs imperābātis nē hostibus parcerēmus.

7. Tribūnus crās ōrābit ut sociī poenās dent.

8. Omnibus haud persuāsistis ut frātrem vestrum consulem rogent.

9. Cīvēs frustrā prōnuntiābunt nē exercitus castra hīc ponat.

_____

10. Deōs iterum rogās ut nostra cīvitās valeant per ordinem aetātum perpetuum.

_____

30G. Translate the following sentences into Latin. Use the rubric below each sentence as a guide.

The general encouraged the ranks to cross the fields and approach the city.

Person, number, tense, voice, and mood of "(he) encouraged" _____

_____

Dictionary entry _____
Latin translation _____

What sort of clause is "to cross the fields and approach the city"?

_____

Person, number, tense, voice, and mood of "(they) cross" _____

_____

Dictionary entry _____
Latin translation _____

Person, number, tense, voice, and mood of "(they) approach" _____

_____

Dictionary entry _____
Latin translation _____

Latin translation of entire sentence _____

_____

The allies persuade Caesar to spare them.

Person, number, tense, voice, and mood of "(they) persuade" _____

_____

Dictionary entry _____
Latin translation _____

Syntactic function and case of "Caesar" _____

What sort of clause is "to spare them"? _____
Person, number, tense, voice, and mood of "he spares" _____

_____

Dictionary entry _____
Latin translation _____

Latin translation of entire sentence _____

_____

30H. Fill in the blanks with correctly formed Latin words from the required
vocabulary (through *NLP* 30). You may use any word only once. There
is no "right" answer.

Mīlitēs Caesārem/Caesārī (*verb*)_____ ut prōtinus

(*verb*)_____. Sed (*plural noun*)_____

(*adjective*)_____ ubīque vīdērunt et, quoniam valdissimē

terrēbant, Caesārem (*adverb*)_____ rogābant ut

(*verb*)_____. Caesar statim in (*noun*)_____

propter (*noun*)_____ (*verb*)_____. Tandem

omnēs cīvēs (*genitive noun*)_____ (*verb*)_____ .

NLP Review E (Lessons 25–30)

I: CONCEPTS

IA: Latin Verbs: Subjunctive Mood (*NLP* 26–27).

- There are three moods in Latin:
    - Indicative (the regular verbs that present statements of fact).
    - Imperative (verbs of direct command).
    - Subjunctive (verbs that indicate the possibility or hope of action).
- Latin has four tenses of the subjunctive:
    - present
    - imperfect
    - perfect
    - pluperfect
- All four tenses take the same regular verb endings that you learned in *NLP* 1 (active) and *NLP* 17 (passive). The present and imperfect tenses are formed from the first two principal parts, and the perfect and the pluperfect from the third and fourth principal parts.
- The **PRESENT SUBJUNCTIVE** involves a special connecting vowel depending on the conjugation between the stem and the regular active/passive endings (-e-, -ea-, -a-, -ia-, -ia-).
- The **IMPERFECT SUBJUNCTIVE** is formed by adding the active/passive endings directly to the present active infinitive (second principal part).
- To form the **IMPERFECT DEPONENT SUBJUNCTIVE**, the second principal part must be made to look like a "regular" active infinitive (e.g., *ūtī* → *ūtere*) before adding the passive endings.
- The **PERFECT ACTIVE SUBJUNCTIVE** is formed from the perfect stem (remember to drop the -ī from the third principal part) + eri + regular active endings.

- The **PERFECT PASSIVE SUBJUNCTIVE** is formed from the fourth principal part, declined to agree in case, number, and gender with its subject + the present subjunctive of *esse: sim, sīs, sit, sīmus, sītis, sint.*
- The **PLUPERFECT ACTIVE SUBJUNCTIVE** is formed from the perfect stem + *isse* + regular active endings.
- The **PLUPERFECT PASSIVE SUBJUNCTIVE** is formed from the fourth principal part, declined to agree in case, number, and gender with its subject + the imperfect subjunctive of *esse: essem, essēs, esset, essēmus, essētis, essent.*

IB: Latin Verbs: Clauses with subjunctive verbs.

- Independent uses of the subjunctive (*NLP* 26)
  - **HORTATORY** (1st person) and **JUSSIVE** (2nd/3rd person) subjunctives indicate a polite command.

    Quid placentae socolātiae <u>capiāmus</u>.
    <u>Let us take</u> some chocolate cake.

  - **OPTATIVE** subjunctives (often with *utinam*) indicate a wish.

    <u>Utinam</u> quid placentae socolātiae <u>capiāmus</u>.
    O <u>would that we</u> take some chocolate cake!

  - **POTENTIAL** subjunctives indicate a possible action.

    Quid placentae socolātiae capere <u>possimus</u>.
    <u>We may be able</u> to take some chocolate cake.

  - **DELIBERATIVE** subjunctives indicate seeking advice in the form of a question.

    Quidne placentae socolātiae <u>capiēmus</u>?
    <u>Should we take</u> some chocolate cake?

- *Cum* clauses (*NLP* 27)
  - *Cum* **TEMPORAL** clauses (with indicative verbs) indicate when the action of the sentence occurs.

    <u>Cum</u> quid placentae socolātiae capimus, gaudēmus.
    <u>When we take chocolate cake</u>, we are happy.

○ *Cum* **CIRCUMSTANTIAL** clauses (with imperfect or pluperfect subjunctive verbs) indicate circumstances accompanying the main action of the verb.

<u>Cum quid placentae socolātiae caperēmus</u>, amīcī manēbant.
<u>While we were taking some chocolate cake</u>, our friends waited.

○ *Cum* **CAUSAL** clauses (with subjunctive verbs) can express why the action of the main verb occurs and is sometimes triggered by *praesertim* (especially), *quippe* (naturally), or *utpote* (inasmuch as)

<u>Cum quid placentae socolātiae cēpissēmus</u>, <u>quippe</u> vīnum bibēbāmus.
<u>Since we had taken some chocolate cake</u>, we <u>naturally</u> drank wine.

○ *Cum* **CONCESSIVE** clauses (with subjunctive verbs) indicate concession, often triggered by *tamen*.

<u>Cum quid placentae socolātiae caperēmus</u>, <u>tamen</u> infans dormiēbat.
<u>Although we were taking some chocolate cake</u>, <u>nonetheless</u> the baby slept.

- **PURPOSE** clauses (*NLP* 28) with subjunctive verbs indicate the purpose or aim of the action of the main verb. These clauses are introduced by ***ut/nē***.

Coquimus <u>ut placentam socolātiam habeāmus</u>.
We bake <u>so that we have a chocolate cake</u>.

- **RESULT** clauses (*NLP* 29) with subjunctive verbs show the effect or outcome of the action of the main verb and are triggered by a special adjective or adverb in the main clause: *adeō, ita, tālis/-e, tam, tantus/-a/-um, sīc, usque eō, valdē*. They are introduced by ***ut/ut nōn***.

Placentam socolātiam <u>tam celerē</u> <u>ut ventrī dolērēmus</u> ēdimus.
We ate our chocolate cake <u>so quickly</u> <u>that we got a stomachache</u> (literally: that we were grieving in the belly).

- **INDIRECT COMMANDS** (*NLP* 30) indicate encouragement, warnings, or advice. They are triggered by verbs of commanding, urging, and begging. Be careful here, as many of the verbs that can trigger indirect commands can also trigger indirect statements. Your clue is the subjunctive verb + *ut/nē*.

Amīcī nōs hortantur <u>ut sibi quid placentae socolātiae dēmus</u>.
Our friends urge <u>us to give them some chocolate cake</u> (that we give them some chocolate cake).

IC: Correlatives (*NLP* 25).

- Correlatives indicate a complementary relationship between two words or phrases in the same sentences (*both ... and; neither ... nor; as many ... as*).

<u>Tam partēs placentae</u> <u>quam amīcōs</u> habēmus.
We have <u>as many pieces of cake</u> <u>as (we have) friends</u>.

- Correlatives are introduced by a number of corresponding adjectives, adverbs, and conjunctions.
- Correlatives can be tricky, and it is best to focus on mastering the list of correlative expressions in the required vocabulary (and below) so that you will be able to recognize them in context.

II: VOCABULARY *NLP* 25–30

NOUNS

anima, -ae, f: soul, spirit
Britannia, -iae, f: Britain
coma, -ae, f: hair, foliage
hōra, -ae, f: hour
iānua, -ae, f: door
poena, -ae, f: punishment, penalty (*poenam dare*: to pay the penalty)
sapientia, -iae, f: wisdom, discernment, prudence
victōria, -iae, f: victory

beneficium, -iī, n: favor, kindness, service
dolus, -ī, m: deceit, trick
exemplum, -ī, n: example, sample
ferrum, -ī, n: iron, sword
forum, -ī, n: forum, open square, marketplace
gladius, -iī, m: sword
ingenium, -iī, n: talent, ability, nature, character

lupus, -ī, m: wolf

marītus, -ī, m: husband

odium, -iī, n: hatred

socius, -iī, m: ally, follower

tribūnus, -ī, m: tribune, representative

vōtum, -ī, n: vow, solemn promise

aetās, -ātis, f: lifetime, generation, age

agmen, agminis, n: stream, band, column, army in marching order

clāmor, -ōris, m: cry, shout

comes, comitis, m/f: companion, associate

conditiō (condiciō), -iōnis, f: stipulation, provision, state, condition

coniūrātiō, -iōnis, f: conspiracy

cor, cordis, n: heart

cruor, -ōris, m: blood, gore

delātor, -ōris, m: informer

flōs, flōris, m: flower

fūnus, fūneris, n: funeral, burial

laus, laudis, f: praise

līmen, līminis, n: threshold, entrance, home

necessitās, -ātis, f: necessity, need, poverty, difficult situation

nūmen, nūminis, n: divine spirit

ops, opis, f: power, means

ōrātiō, -iōnis, f: speech

ordō, ordinis, m: series, row, rank

sacerdōs, -ōtis, m/f: priest(ess), bishop

testis, -is (-ium), m/f: witness

PRONOUNS

quisquis, quaeque, quicquid or quidquid: whoever, whatever

ADJECTIVES

aeternus, -a, -um: eternal

castus, -a, -um: pure, chaste, innocent, virtuous

clārus, -a, -um: bright, clear, loud, distinct, distinguished

cunctus, -a, -um: all, the whole (in singular)

dexter, dext(e)ra, dext(e)rum: skillful, right (hand)

exiguus, -a, -um: small, scanty

inferus, -a, -um: low, southern

inimīcus, -a, -um (+ dative): hostile

īrātus, -a, -um: angry

perpetuus, -a, -um: continuous, uninterrupted

plēnus, -a, -um (+ ablative): full

posterus, -a, -um: following, next

praeclārus, -a, -um: bright, distinguished, excellent

quantus, -a, -um: how much

sanctus, -a, -um: virtuous, blameless

sānus, -a, -um: sound, healthy, sane

secundus, -a, -um: favorable

vacuus, -a, -um: empty, idle

commūnis, -e: shared, universal, general

difficilis, -e: difficult, obstinate

mortālis, -e: mortal, transitory, human

pauper (-eris): poor

suāvis, -e: sweet, agreeable, pleasant

VERBS

comparō, -āre, -āvī, -ātus: provide, furnish, prepare

creō, -āre, -āvī, -ātus: create, make

damnō, -āre, -āvī, -ātus: condemn, discredit

dōnō, -āre, -āvī, -ātus: present, bestow, award, consecrate

dubitō, -āre, -āvī, -ātus: waver, hesitate

existimō, -āre, -āvi, -ātus: value, esteem, judge, think

occupō, -āre, -āvī, -ātus: take possession, seize

orō, -āre, -āvī, -ātus: speak, beg

postulō, -āre, -āvī, -ātus: demand

prōnuntiō, -āre, -āvī, -ātus: declare

properō, -āre, -āvī, -ātus: hurry

sonō, -āre, -āvī, -ātus: resound, make a sound

stō, stāre, stetī, stātus: stand

doleō, -ēre, -uī, -itus: suffer pain, grieve

mereō, -ēre, -uī, -itus: deserve, earn, obtain

pateō, -ēre, -uī: lie open

persuādeō, -ēre, -suāsī, -suāsus (+ dative): convince, prevail upon

suādeō, -ēre, suāsī, suāsus (+ dative): advise, persuade, urge

accēdō, -ere, -cessī, -cessus: approach

addō, -ere, -didī, -ditus: bring, add, join, place

afficiō, -ere, -fēcī, -fectus: influence, affect

cōgō, -ere, coēgī, coactus: compel, force

compōnō, -ere, -posuī, -positus: bring together, collect, arrange, settle

corrumpō, -ere, -rūpī, -ruptus: destroy, weaken, mar, spoil

dēcernō, -ere, -crēvī, -crētus: decide, settle, propose

dēficiō, -ere, -fēcī, -fectus: fail, run short

descisco, -ere, -scīvī, -scītus: desert, withdraw, revolt, break away

dēserō, -ere, -seruī, -sertus: desert, abandon, leave, forsake

dīmittō, -ere, -mīsī, -missus: send away, lose

discēdō, -ere, -cessī: depart, go away

ēripiō, -ere, -uī, -reptus: snatch, tear away

fingō, -ere, finxī, fictus: shape, invent

fluō, -ere, fluxī, fluxus: flow

impellō, -ere, -pulī, -pulsus: incite, impel

impōnō, -ere, -posuī, -positus: place upon, impose

intendō, -ere, -tendī, -tentus: aim, stretch, strain, exert

parcō, -ere, pepercī (+ dative): spare, refrain from injuring

pendō, -ere, pependī, pensus: pay, weigh out

prōcēdō, -ere, -cessī, -cessus: proceed, advance

prōdō, -ere, -didī, -ditus: put forth, proclaim, abandon, betray

quaerō, -ere, quaesīvī, quaesītus: look for, seek

repetō, -ere, -īvī/iī, -ītus: seek again, recall

surgō, -ere, surrexī, surrectus: rise

tollō, -ere, sustulī, sublātus: lift up

trahō, -ere, traxī, tractus: draw, drag, derive, prolong

aperiō, -īre, -uī, apertus: uncover, lay open, reveal

conveniō, -īre, -vēnī, -ventus: come together, meet with

cohortor, -ārī, cohortātus sum: encourage, incite

queror, querī, questus sum: complain

absum, -esse, āfuī, āfutūrus: be absent, be removed

adeō, -īre, -iī, -itus: approach

conferō, -ferre, -tulī, -lātus: bring together, collect, apply, devote

exeō, -īre, -īvī or **-iī, -itus**: go out

supersum, -esse, -fuī, -futūrus: remain, abound

transeō, -īre, -īvī or **-iī, -itus**: cross

ait: he said (**aiunt**: they said)

ōdī, ōdisse (defective verb): hate, detest

PREPOSITIONS

adversus (+ accusative): against

prope (+ accusative): near (also can function as an adverb)

CONJUNCTIONS, ADVERBS

cūr: why

dēnique: finally, at last, further

dōnec: until

eō: there

fortasse: perhaps

licet: although, granted that

nē: lest, so that … not

p(a)ene: nearly, almost

priusquam: before

prōtinus: immediately

quamquam: although, however

quippe: certainly, to be sure

satis or **sat**: enough, sufficiently

scīlicet: evidently, certainly, of course

ubīque: everywhere

umquam: ever

ūnā: together (with)

ut/utī: as, like (with indicative verbs); so that (with subjunctive verbs)

-ve: or

velut: just as

CORRELATIVE EXPRESSIONS

cum … tum: both … and; not only … but also

eō … quō: the more … the more; there … where

tālis … quālis: such … as

tam … quam: as … as

tantus … quantus: so great … as

tantō … quantō: the more … the more

totiens … quotiens: so often … as

tot … quot: so much/as many … as

III: ADDITIONAL DRILLS

IIIA. Decline the following noun-adjective pairs. Consult the glossary above for the dictionary entries.

Case	gladius + Fut. pass. part. of **ēripiō**	hōra + Comparative of **suāvis**	nūmen + Positive of **īrātus**
Singular			
Nominative			
Genitive			
Dative			
Accusative			
Ablative			
Plural			
Nominative			
Genitive			
Dative			
Accusative			
Ablative			

IIIB. Give the requested forms of the following noun-adjective pairs. Translate the resulting phrases.

Noun	Adjective/Participle	Requested Form	Latin Form	Translation
flōs	**castus** Superlative	Accusative singular		
victōria	**dēficiō** Fut. act. part.	Genitive singular		
vōtum	**pendō** Perf. pass. part.	Ablative plural		
fūnus	**sanctus** Comparative	Nominative singular		
tribūnus	**parcō** Pres. act. part.	Accusative plural		
coniūrātiō	**aperiō** Perf. pass. part.	Dative singular		
anima	**difficilis** Positive	Genitive plural		

IIIC. Identify the following noun forms as directed. For ambiguous forms, give all possibilities. Give the correct form of *clārus* and *pauper* to modify each form.

Latin Form	Decl.	Case	No.	Gender	clārus	pauper
sacerdōtum (2)						
testibus (4)						
comae (3)						
ferrum (2)						

IIID. For each of the following nouns, select the adjective that agrees in case, number, and gender. Then translate the resulting phrases. You may use each adjective only once.

Adjective bank: **sānam, prōcedentī, aeternā, mortālibus, quaesītō, tollendōrum, quicquid, suāvis**

Noun	Case, No., Gender	Adjective	Translation
conditiōne			
exemplī			
sociīs			
aetātem			
corde			
clāmōrum			
līmen			
hōrae			

IIIE. Give the Latin for each of the following English phrases.

1. plots having been revealed (Ablative Absolute) _____

2. judging companions (Accusative) _____

3. of a common punishment _____

4. to/for a most difficult generation _____

5. perpetual praise (Nominative) _____

6. of doubting allies _____

7. O brightest flower! _____

8. with a full heart _____

9. a speech about to persuade (Accusative) _____

10. to/for rather scant powers _____

IIIF. Give a synopsis of the following verb. Translate each form.

pendō
conjugation _____
synopsis: 3rd person singular

INDICATIVES	Active	Translation	Passive	Translation
Present				
Imperfect				
Future				
Perfect				
Pluperfect				
Future Perfect				

SUBJUNCTIVES	Active	Passive
Present		
Imperfect		
Perfect		
Pluperfect		

IMPERATIVES	Active	Translation	Passive	Translation
Present				
Future			XXX	XXX

INFINITIVES	Active	Translation	Passive	Translation
Present				
Perfect				
Future				

PARTICIPLES	Active	Translation	Passive	Translation
Present			XXX	XXX
Perfect	XXX	XXX		
Future				

IIIG. Identify the following verbs as directed. Translate all forms. (Translate present tense subjunctives "let …" and imperfect, perfect, and pluperfect tense subjunctives "were/would that.")

Form	Person and No.	Tense	Voice	Mood	Translation
damnētur					
fingēminī					
sustulerim					
dēserueram					
pendēbāmur					
querēbātur					
supereris					
āfuissent					
cohortāta sīs					
impositus eris					
transīre					
prōdī					
surrectus esse					
impulsa es					

IIIH. Give the requested forms of the following verbs. Translate all forms.
(Translate present tense subjunctives "let/may …" and imperfect, perfect, and pluperfect tense subjunctives "were/would that.")

Latin Verb	Requested Form	Latin Form	Translation
doleō	Future active Infinitive		
trahō	first person singular Perfect active subjunctive		
occupō	third person singular Imperfect passive subjunctive		
mereō	third person plural Present active indicative		
creō	second person singular Future passive indicative		
repetō	Perfect active Infinitive		
parco	second person singular Present active Imperative		
conveniō	third person plural Perfect passive subjunctive		
aperiō	second person plural Pluperfect passive indicative		
pateō	second person plural Imperfect active subjunctive		
adeō	first person singular Future Perfect active		
conferō	Perfect passive Infinitive		

IV: ADDITIONAL PASSAGES

1. Apuleius, *Metamorphoses* 6.24. Cupid and Psyche are wed at last, with Venus's blessings (she literally dances at the wedding!) (see *NLP* 28.13–28.15).

Apollo cantāvit ad citharam, Venus suāvī mūsicae superingressa formonsa saltāvit. Scaena sibi sīc concinnāta, ut Mūsae quidem chorum canerent aut tībiās inflārent, Satyrus et Paniscus ad fistūlam dīcerent.

Notes: **cithara, -ae**, f: cithara, a stringed instrument; **mūsica, -ae**, f: music, art of music; **superingredior, -ī, superingressus sum**: "step lively"; **formo(n)sus, -a, -um**: beautiful; **saltō, -āre, -āvī, -ātus**: dance; **scaena, -ae**, f: theater, stage; **concinnō, -āre, -āvī, -ātus**: join, arrange, organize; **chorus, -ī**, m: dance; **tībia, -ae**, f: pipe, flute; **inflō, -āre, -āvī, -ātus**: blow; **Satyrus, -ī**, m: a demigod of the forest with a horse's tail and cloven hooves; **Paniscus, -ī**, m: a little Pan, a bucolic deity of the flocks and countryside; **fistūla, -ae**, f: pipe, reed, shepherd's pipe.

2. Tibullus, *Elegiae* 1.8.29–32. Tibullus here advises Phloe to put aside her pride and enjoy her affair with the young and handsome Marathus. Meter: elegiac couplets.

Mūnera nē poscās: det mūnera cānus amātor,
    ut foveat mollī frīgida membra sinū.
Cārior est aurō iuvenis, cui lēvia fulgent
    ōra nec amplexūs aspera barba terit.

Notes: **cānus, -a, -um**: gray, white-haired; **amātor, -ōris**, m: lover; **foveō, -ēre, fōvī, fōtus**: warm, caress; **frīgidus, -a, -um**: cold, chilly, lifeless; **lēvis, -e**: smooth, delicate; **fulgeō, -ēre, fulsī, fulsus**: flash, lighten; **amplexus, -ūs**, m: embrace; **asper, aspera, asperum**: rough; **barba, -ae**, f: beard; **terō, -ere, trīvī, trītus**: rub, wear away.

3. *de Rebus Bellicis* 17.3. *de Rebus Bellicis* is a late fourth century treatise of Roman imperial defense policy. Emphasizing current frontier dangers, the author describes a number of "essential" military machines. Here we have an invincible ox-powered warship.

Haec eadem tamen liburna prō mōle suī prōque māchinīs in sēmet operantibus tantō vīrium fremitū pugnam capescit, ut omnēs adversāriās liburnās comminus venientēs facilī attrītū comminuat.

Notes: **liburna, -ae**, f: a light warship; **prō** (+ ablative): according to; **mōles, -is**, f: mass, might, power; **māchina, -ae**, f: machine; **-met**: -self, own (an intensifying enclitic attached to personal pronouns); **operor, -ārī, operātus sum**: work, labor, be busy; **fremitus, -ūs**, m: roaring, growling; **pugna, -ae**, f: battle; **capescō, -ere, -īvī, -itus**: undertake, pursue, carry out, engage in; **adversārius, -a, -um**: opposed, contrary, "enemy"; **comminus**: hand to hand; **attrītus, -ūs**, m: rubbing, grinding, chafing; **comminuō, -ere, -uī, -ūtus**: enclose, combat.

4. Vergil, *Eclogue* 8.64–68. This Eclogue features a contest between two poets, whose songs are as powerful as Orpheus's. The first is a love song, the second a love spell to recall an errant lover. Each song consists of nine stanzas punctuated by a refrain (line 68 in our passage), enhancing the song's magical efficacy. Meter: dactylic hexameter.

Effer aquam, et mollī cinge haec altāria vittā,
verbēnāsque adolē pinguīs et mascula tūra,
coniugis ut magicīs sānōs āvertere sacrīs
experiar sensūs: nihil hīc nisi carmina dēsunt.
Dūcite ab urbe domum, mea carmina, dūcite Daphnim.

Notes: **efferō, -ferre, -tulī, -2lātus**: bring out, carry out; **altāria, -ium**, n (plural): altar; **vitta, -ae**, f: ribbon; **verbēna, -ae**, f: bough or twig of fragrant olive, laurel, or myrtle; **adoleō, -ēre, -uī, -ultus**: magnify, honor, worship, sacrifice, burn; **pinguis, -e**: fat, rich; **masculus, -a, -um**: male, manly, vigorous; **tūs, tūris**, n: incense, frankincense; **magicus, -a, -um**: magical; **āvertō, -ere, -vertī, -versus**: turn away, remove; **sacrum, -ī**, n: rite; **experior, -īrī, expertus sum**: try; **Daphnis, Daphnīdis**, m: the name of a legendary Sicilian shepherd, related to the Greek word for bay or laurel, Apollo's sacred tree (*Daphnim*: Greek accusative).

5. Ovid, *Metamorphoses* 11.537–45. Ceyx, king of Thessaly, and his wife were very happy together, even calling each other "Jupiter" and "Juno." Considering these bold nicknames an act of hubris, Jupiter struck Ceyx's ship with a thunderbolt. Knowing death is imminent, while some of his shipmates think of family members, Ceyx thinks only of his beloved Alcyone. When she learns in a dream that her beloved has drowned, Alcyone leaps into the sea, and the lovers are turned into kingfishers. Meter: dactylic hexameter.

Dēficit ars, animīque cadunt, totidemque videntur,
quot veniunt fluctūs, ruere atque inrumpere mortēs.
Nōn tenet hic lacrimās, stupet hic, vocat ille beātōs,
fūnera quōs maneant, hic vōtīs nūmen adōrat
bracchiaque ad caelum, quod nōn videt, inrita tollens
poscit opem; subeunt illī frāterque parensque,
huic cum pignoribus domus et quodcunque relictum est;
Alcyonē Cēÿca movet, Cēÿcis in ōre
nulla nisi Alcyonē est.

Notes: **totidem**: just as many; **ruō, -ere, ruī, rutus**: rush, hasten; **inrumpō, -ere, -rūpī, -ruptus**: break in, rush in; **stupeō, -ēre, -uī**: be stunned, be struck senseless; **beātōs**: e.g., men who die on dry land; **adōrō, -āre, -āvī, -ātus**: speak, address; **bracchium, -iī**, n: arm; **inritus, -a, -um**: void, useless, ineffectual; **subeō, -īre, -īvī** or **-iī, -itus**: approach, come to mind; **pignus, pignoris**, n: pledge, token, proof; **quodcunque** = *quodcumque*; **Alcyonē, -ēs**, f: a Greek name meaning "kingfisher"; **Cēÿx, Cēÿcis**, m: another Greek word for "kingfisher" (*Cēÿca*: Greek accusative).

6. Horace, *Carmina* 3.5.18–30. M. Atilius Regulus, consul in 256 BCE, was taken in battle in North Africa in 255 BCE during the First Punic War, and then returned to Rome to negotiate an exchange of prisoners—under oath (and on his honor) to return should his negotiations fail. Regulus faced a moral dilemma, the conflict of expediency (striking an easy treaty) versus his honor (he opposed the exchange) and knew that he would be tortured upon his return to Carthage. Here Horace, employing Regulus as his mouthpiece, condemns soldiers taken as prisoners for their cowardice (far better to die against a worthy foe). Meter: Alcaic strophe.

> "Signa ego Pūnicīs
> adfixa dēlubrīs et arma
>   mīlitibus sine caede" dixit

> "dērepta vīdī; vīdī ego cīvium
> retorta tergō bracchia līberō
>   portāsque nōn clausās et arva
>   Marte colī populāta nostrō.

> Aurō repensus scīlicet acrior
> mīles redībit. Flāgitiō additis
>   damnum. Neque āmissōs colōrēs
>   lāna refert medicāta fūcō,

> nec vēra virtūs, cum semel excīdit,
> cūrat repōnī dēteriōribus."

Notes: **Pūnicus, -a, -um**: Punic, Carthaginian; **adfīgō, -ere, -fīxī, -fixus**: fasten, affix; **dēlubrum, -ī**, n: shrine, temple; **dēripiō, -ere, -uī, -reptus**: snatch away from, tear down; **retorqueō, -ere, -torsī, -tortus**: twist; **bracchium, -iī**, n: arm, limb; **Mars, Martis**, m: the Roman god of war (metonym for the Roman army); **populō, -āre, -āvī, -ātus**: ravage, spoil, lay waste; **rependō, -ere, -pendī, -pensus**: repay, requite; **flāgitium, -iī**, n: shame, disgrace; **lāna, -ae**, f: wool; **damnum, -ī**, n: loss; **medicō, -āre, -āvī, -ātus**: drug, medicate, steep; **fūcus, -ī**, m: red or purple dye; **excidō, -ere, -cidī**: be lost, perish, disappear; **repōnō, -ere, -posuī, -positus**: put back, return; **dēterior, -ius**: inferior, weaker.

Crossword Puzzle.

Across

3. Caesar's Helvetian hostis
8. Apollo's belaureled lady
9. The symbol of the consul's absolute authority
12. Catullus's weapons of choice
14. The site of an historical powwow
16. The triplets who fight for Rome
17. The divine protectress of lovers
20. A very swift river
22. The first man in his family to attain the consulship at Rome
23. Rome's south-pawed hero
24. Cicero's loquacious neighbor
25. Ovid's disheveled lady
28. Avengeful wife
30. Apollo's sunny lady
34. A Metamorphic maga
36. Where Horace hopes to die
39. An ignominious Roman
41. He solved an Athenian murder mystery
43. They bring relief to Caesar's laboring soldiers
44. A disreputable Roman
45. Aeneas' young Greek friend
47. Caesar's outspoken opponent
49. A Catilinarian conspirator
51. A sweet child snatched by witches
52. He was among those who stripped Caesar of his command in 49 BCE
53. Aeneas' Greek ally in Italy
54. Caesar's naive lieutenant
55. Uttered by a rejected poet at his lady's door
56. The sequence of political offices at Rome

Down

1. Apollo's doleful lad
2. Caesar's Alesian adversary
4. A courageous Roman lady
5. Polybius's democratic branch of the Roman constitution
6. A country of conjurers
7. Caesar's distinguished lieutenant
10. An agrarian dictator
11. Tibullus's literary lady
13. Antony was even worse than this evil king
15. Propertius's literary lady
16. Ascanius's noble uncle
18. A beloved British saint
19. Horace's witch
21. A British bastion against burglary
23. Polybius's oligarchic branch of the Roman constitution
25. Polybius' monarchic branch of the Roman constitution
26. The most prestigious award for a Roman soldier
27. Birthday poems
29. Caesar's duplicitous Belgic foe
30. Odysseus' elegant necromancer
31. A venerable British bard
32. These creatures might eat me
33. A triune sorceress
35. His girlfriend is less than stunningly beautiful
37. He "restored" the Republic
38. A rusty ritual
40. A Pharsalian necromancer
42. Another Catilinarian conspirator
46. Catullus's literary lady
48. A Carolingian "very learned man"
50. Propertius's bawd

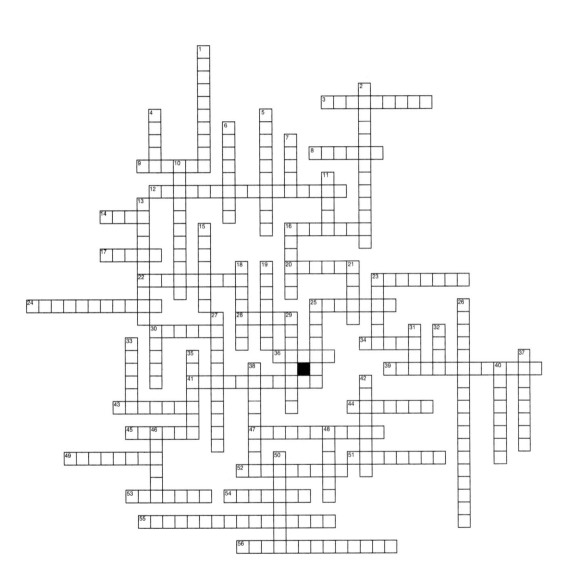

Indirect Questions

31A. Decline the following noun-adjective pairs.

Case	sensus, -ūs, m + Future passive participle of laedō, -ere, laesī, laesus	spēs, spēī, f + Comparative of rēgius, -a, -um
Singular		
Nominative		
Genitive		
Dative		
Accusative		
Ablative		
Plural		
Nominative		
Genitive		
Dative		
Accusative		
Ablative		

31B. Give the requested forms of the following noun-adjective pairs. Translate the resulting phrases.

Noun	Adjective/Participle	Requested Form	Latin Form	Translation
cāsus	lateō Pres. act. part.	Genitive singular		
iuventus	rārus Positive	Accusative singular		
spēs	requīrō Perf. pass. part.	Dative plural		
famēs	lēvis Comparative	Genitive plural		
mensa	alō Fut. act. part.	Ablative plural		
rēgīna	aeger Superlative	Nominative plural		
sensus	dubius Positive	Ablative singular		

31C. For each of the following nouns, select the adjective that agrees in case, number, and gender. Then translate the resulting phrases. You may use each adjective only once.

Adjective bank: **aegrōrum, rāram, insignis, dubiō, rēgiīs, varia, lēvī**

Noun	Case, No., Gender	Adjective	Translation
famem			
spēs			
iuventūtibus			
mensā			
cāsuī			
rēgīnae			
sensuum			

31D. Give a synopsis of the following verb. Translate each form.

alō, -ere, -uī, alitus
conjugation _____
synopsis: 3rd person singular

INDICATIVES	Active	Translation	Passive	Translation
Present				
Imperfect				
Future				
Perfect				
Pluperfect				
Future Perfect				

SUBJUNCTIVES	Active	Passive
Present		
Imperfect		
Perfect		
Pluperfect		

IMPERATIVES	Active	Translation	Passive	Translation
Present				
Future			XXX	XXX

INFINITIVES	Active	Translation	Passive	Translation
Present				
Perfect				
Future				

PARTICIPLES	Active	Translation	Passive	Translation
Present			XXX	XXX
Perfect	XXX	XXX		
Future				

31E. Identify the following verbs as directed. Translate all forms. (Translate present tense subjunctives "let/may ..." and imperfect, perfect, and pluperfect tense subjunctives "were/would that.")

Form	Person and No.	Tense	Voice	Mood	Translation
memorantur					
requisīta sint					
alēs					
latērem					
respexissētis					
tendāminī					
laesum erit					
effūserāmus					

31F. Give the requested forms of the following verbs. Translate all forms. (Translate present tense subjunctives "let/may ..." and imperfect, perfect, and pluperfect tense subjunctives "were/would that.")

Latin Verb	Requested Form	Latin Form	Translation
memorō	third person singular Imperfect passive indicative		
lateō	second person plural Future active indicative		
alō	first person singular Present passive subjunctive		
effundō	Present passive Infinitive		
laedō	third person plural Fut. Perf. indicative		
requīrō	second person singular Present active Imperative		
tendō	third person singular Pluperfect active subjunctive		
respiciō	first person plural Perfect passive subjunctive		

31G. Translate the following sentences into coherent English.

1. Consul frustrā rogat cūr puerī ōrātiōnem nōn audiant.

_____

2. Nunc memorāmus unde equī insignēs vēnerint.

_____

3. Mīrātī estis quam ingens urbs esset.

_____

4. Forsitan sciēbās ūtī Caesar castra posuisset.

_____

5. Nesciō autem quārē tribūnus pācem corrūperit.

_____

6. Requīrēmus dēnique quī līberōs laedant.

_____

7. Ōrēmus quō nocte pervēneritis.

_____

8. Māter igitur ā dīs petēbat quō puella pulchra īret.

_____

9. Quaesītum est quae rēgīna populōs semper dūcat.

_____

10. Dubius est utrum imperātor an consul in collī illō stet.

_____

31H. Translate the following sentences into Latin. Use the rubric below each sentence as a guide.

You (plural) ask where the legions are pitching camp.

Person, number, tense, voice, and mood of "you (plural) ask" _____

_____

Dictionary entry _____
Latin translation _____

What sort of clause is "where the legions are pitching camp"? _____

_____

Person, number, tense, voice, and mood of "(they) pitch" _____

_____

Dictionary entry _____
Latin translation _____

Latin translation of entire sentence _____

_____

The citizens recalled how Caesar killed the enemy in battle.

Person, number, tense, voice, and mood of "(they) recalled" _____

_____

Dictionary entry _____
Latin translation _____

What sort of clause is "how Caesar killed the enemy in battle"?

_____

Person, number, tense, voice, and mood of "(he) killed" _____

_____

Dictionary entry _____
Latin translation _____

Latin translation of entire sentence _____

_____

311. Word Find. The words may appear horizontally, vertically or diagonally in either direction.

VERGIL'S *AENEID*

```
N  Z  B  P  M  A  I  N  I  V  A  L  J  R  R  V  B  X  K  S
J  E  E  A  U  S  T  Y  J  U  N  O  F  H  T  X  V  Y  Q  B
D  B  F  L  Q  O  A  Q  M  S  D  I  I  T  V  K  E  O  S  P
A  R  N  I  O  G  J  E  U  E  R  D  H  L  T  K  O  S  R  W
H  J  I  N  D  M  J  I  N  D  O  N  P  B  D  P  C  I  Z  L
N  U  S  U  I  T  N  E  Z  E  M  M  P  I  E  T  A  S  H  C
Z  C  U  R  D  A  N  P  D  M  A  C  L  N  U  M  Y  K  E  T
G  E  S  U  C  T  R  F  F  O  C  P  A  R  A  X  F  J  C  Y
P  S  U  S  E  L  Z  L  S  I  H  T  N  G  F  S  F  S  T  K
G  A  A  L  L  I  M  A  C  D  E  U  R  Y  A  L  U  S  O  W
L  E  L  U  A  I  B  X  J  S  S  E  E  V  A  N  D  E  R  W
E  U  O  L  H  R  G  O  E  W  P  K  T  T  E  D  N  T  R  K
S  Q  Q  H  A  I  K  R  Y  B  J  E  I  V  I  P  E  A  X  C
S  R  Q  I  J  S  A  Y  E  R  Q  N  P  P  I  U  B  H  V  B
T  T  D  N  T  D  Z  W  I  V  U  N  U  H  C  G  M  C  M  N
P  L  K  I  T  O  W  C  J  S  E  C  J  E  U  Z  W  A  S  N
D  J  H  U  O  Y  G  B  Q  G  G  L  R  H  C  J  H  L  R  S
N  N  Q  T  X  D  S  V  U  K  N  U  W  E  D  L  A  O  K  A
M  B  L  I  I  H  R  Y  N  Q  C  V  W  A  M  T  N  D  N  Q
```

Achates	Euryalus	Nisus
Aeneas	Evander	Palinurus
Andromache	Hector	Pallas
Anna	Iarbas	Penates
Ascanius	Iris	Pergama
Camilla	Juno	pietas
Creusa	Jupiter	Priam
Cupid	Latinus	Teucer
Dares	Lausus	Turnus
Dido	Lavinia	Venus
Diomedes	Mercury	Vergil
Entellus	Mezentius	

Fear Clauses

32A. Decline the following noun-adjective pairs.

Case	cohors, cohortis (-ium), f + Positive of vagus, -a, -um	equitātus, -ūs, m + Present active participle of constō, -stare, -stitī, -stātus
Singular		
Nominative		
Genitive		
Dative		
Accusative		
Ablative		
Plural		
Nominative		
Genitive		
Dative		
Accusative		
Ablative		

32B. For each of the following nouns, select the adjective that agrees in case, number, and gender. Then translate the resulting phrases. You may use each adjective only once.

Adjective bank: **expectūra, monentī, praestantēs, nocturnum, pulsīs, vagae, institūtī**

Noun	Case, No., Gender	Adjective	Translation
frūmentī			
mundō			
mūrī			
ossa			
pecoribus			
tellūris			
terrōrem			

32C. Give a synopsis of the following verb. Translate each form.

vereor, -ērī, veritus sum
conjugation _____
synopsis: 1st person plural

INDICATIVES	Deponent	Translation
Present		
Imperfect		
Future	ˏ	
Perfect		
Pluperfect		
Future Perfect		

SUBJUNCTIVES	Deponent
Present	
Imperfect	
Perfect	
Pluperfect	

vereor, -ērī, veritus sum

INFINITIVES	Deponent	Translation
Present		
Perfect		
Future		

PARTICIPLES	Deponent	Translation	Passive	Translation
Present			XXX	XXX
Perfect			XXX	XXX
Future				

32D. Identify the following verbs as directed. Translate all forms. (Translate present tense subjunctives "let/may …" and imperfect, perfect, and pluperfect tense subjunctives "were/would that.")

Form	Person and No.	Tense	Voice	Mood	Translation
vetētur					
interficerēs					
ostendent					
pepulerim					
confecissētis					
circumveniāmus					
fatērī					
vereāminī					
statuī					

32E. Give the requested forms of the following verbs. Translate all forms. (Translate present tense subjunctives "let/may ..." and imperfect, perfect, and pluperfect tense subjunctives "were/would that.")

Latin Verb	Requested Form	Latin Form	Translation
constō	third person singular Pluperfect active subjunctive		
instituō	second person singular Future passive indicative		
expectō	third person plural Present passive subjunctive		
vetō	first person plural Perfect active subjunctive		
conligō	second person plural Imperfect passive indicative		
moneō	first person plural Future perfect active indicative		
fateor	second person singular Imperfect deponent subjunctive		

32F. Translate the following sentences into coherent English.

1. Caesar ergō metuit nē hostēs castra prope oppidum pōnant.

2. Timeō quoque nē consul vīcerit.

3. Parentēs enim metum magnum ut līberī constāre possent habēbant.

4. Verēbāminī ut sociī omnēs interfectī essent.

5. Rēgīna imperātōrī paventī nē exercitus pellātur parcit.

6. Terror maximus nē hostēs undique nōn circumventae sint nōs capit.

7. Dux epistulās cohortibus timentibus nē tempestātem dūram paterentur mīsit.

8. Puella timōre ab ingentī nē pecus etiam domō abesset capta est.

_____

9. Marītī uxōrēs monent nē timant nē vallum solvātur.

_____

10. Piget verērī nē poēna confecta sit.

_____

32G. Translate the following sentences into Latin. Use the rubric below each
    sentence as a guide.

It is impious to fear that the Romans may not prevail in the battles.

What sort of clause is "the Romans may not prevail in the battles"?

_____

Form, tense, and voice of "to fear" _____

Dictionary entry _____

Latin translation _____

Person, number, tense, voice, and mood of "(they) may prevail" _____

_____

Dictionary entry _____

Latin translation _____

Latin translation of entire sentence _____

_____

We feared that the horses could not cross the river.

Person, number, tense, voice, and mood of "We feared" _____

_____

Dictionary entry _____
Latin translation _____

What sort of clause is "the horses could not cross the river"? _____

_____

Person, number, tense, voice, and mood of "(they) could" _____

_____

Dictionary entry _____
Latin translation _____

Syntactic function of "to cross" _____
Dictionary entry _____
Latin translation _____

Latin translation of entire sentence _____

_____

32H. Give the Latin forms for the following English phrases. Then recombine the **double-underlined** letters to spell the name of a Roman who fomented civil war in the first century BCE.

the cavalry: __ __ __ __ __ __ __ __ __

feared: __ __ __ __ __ __   __ __ __

that the cohort: __ __   __ __ __ __ __ __

would dislodge: __ __ __ __ __ __ __ __

the wall (Accusative): __ __ __ __ __ __

ANSWER: __ __ __ __ __ __ __ __   __ __ __ __ __

Relative Clauses
with the Subjunctive

33A. Decline the following noun-adjective pairs.

Case	cibus, -ī, m + Positive of ūtilis, -e	pondus, ponderis, n + Positive of praecipuus, -a, -um
Singular		
Nominative		
Genitive		
Dative		
Accusative		
Ablative		
Plural		
Nominative		
Genitive		
Dative		
Accusative		
Ablative		

33B. Give the correct form of the specified adjective or participle to modify each of the following nouns. Translate the resulting phrases.

Noun	Case, No., Gender	Adjective/Participle	Latin Form	Translation
febrīs		**īrascor** Perf. dep. part.		
cinerum (2)		**aliēnus** Positive		
		aliēnus Positive		
venēnō (2)		**ūtilis** Comparative		
		ūtilis Comparative		
morbī (plural)		**careō** Pres. act. part.		
tergī		**quīcumque**		
tenebrās		**nesciō** Fut. pass. part.		
lībidinem		**praecipuus** Positive		
exercitātiōnēs (2)		**singulī** Positive		
		singulī Positive		

33C. Give a synopsis of the following verb. Translate each form.

careō, -ēre, -uī
conjugation _____
synopsis: 2nd person singular

INDICATIVES	Active	Translation
Present		
Imperfect		
Future		
Perfect		
Pluperfect		
Future Perfect		

SUBJUNCTIVES	Active
Present	
Imperfect	
Perfect	
Pluperfect	

IMPERATIVES	Active	Translation
Present		
Future		

INFINITIVES	Active	Translation
Present		
Perfect		

PARTICIPLE	Active	Translation
Present		

33D. Identify the following verbs as directed. Translate all forms. (Translate present tense subjunctives "let/may …" and imperfect, perfect, and pluperfect tense subjunctives "were/would that.")

Form	Person and No.	Tense	Voice	Mood	Translation
īrascēris					
nesciātur					
surgerētis					
quaeram (2)					
obtulerant					
cōgāmur					
addidistis					
cinxerim					
gāvīsa erat					
cecīdēre					
āmissus es					
sumpta erunt					

33E. Translate the following sentences into coherent English.

1. Medicum quī medicāmentīs mollibus ūtātur mālūmus.

2. Līberī febrēs quōs māter cūrāvisset gerēbant.

3. Epistulās maximē ūtilēs ad rēgīnam quae patriam dūcat mittētis.

4. Malus homo venēnō ā quō multī interficerentur caruit.

5. Pulchra est puella cuī poētae carmina hodiē cantent.

6. Cibum quō alitī essētis sine morā accēpistis.

7. Consul iuvenibus aliēnīs quibuscum pugnēmus nōndum crēdat.

8. Morbus quem bene cognoscam mē nōn caedet.

_____

9. Nesciō adhūc quae exercitātiōnēs puerōs fortīs faciant.

_____

10. Mulier cuius valētūdō optima quondam fuerit Rōmam veniet ut auxilium ā rēge doctō petat.

_____

33F. Translate the following sentences into Latin. Use the rubric below each sentence as a guide.

The informers, who were not men of great virtue, persuaded the citizens to abandon the republic.

What sort of clause is "who were not men of great virtue"? _____

_____

What is the antecedent of "who"? _____

Gender and number of the antecedent _____

Syntactic function of "who" in its own clause _____

Case, number, and gender of "who" _____

Latin translation _____

Syntactic function and case of "of great virtue" _____

_____

Latin translation _____

Person, number, tense, voice, and mood of "(they) were" _____

_____

Dictionary entry _____

Latin translation _____

Person, number, tense, voice, and mood of "(they) persuaded" _____

_____

Dictionary entry _____

Latin translation _____

What case follows "(they) persuaded"? _____

What sort of clause is "to abandon the republic"? _____

Person, number, tense, voice, and mood of "(they) abandon" _____

_____

Dictionary entry _____

Latin translation _____

Latin translation of entire sentence _____

_____

I lack friends, who would go with me into the gloom.

Person, number, tense, voice, and mood of "I lack" _____

_____

Dictionary entry _____

Latin translation _____

What case follows "I lack"? _____

What sort of clause is "who would go with me into the gloom"? _____

_____

Person, number, tense, voice, and mood of "(they) would go" _____

_____

Dictionary entry _____

Latin translation _____

Latin translation of entire sentence _____

_____

33G. A limerick to translate.

Ad hodiē medicum venīs

quī cūret morbōs atque febrīs.

Dat tibi venēnum.

Accipis id bonum.

Febre vītāque crās carēbis.

Conditionals

34A. Decline the following noun-adjective pairs.

Case	senex, senis, m + Superlative of tardus, -a, -um	aevum, -ī, n + Future passive participle of ēligō, -ere, -lēgī, -lectus
Singular		
Nominative		
Genitive		
Dative		
Accusative		
Ablative		
Plural		
Nominative		
Genitive		
Dative		
Accusative		
Ablative		

34B. For each of the following nouns, select the adjective that agrees in case, number, and gender. Then translate the resulting phrases. You may use each adjective only once.

Adjective bank: **ēlectī, translātā, perditae, probātūrum, fēlix**

Noun	Case, No., Gender	Adjective	Translation
arboris			
cupīdine			
hospitem			
aevum			
senēs			

34C. Give a synopsis of the following verb. Translate each form.

praesum, -esse, -fuī, -futūrus
conjugation _____
synopsis: 2nd person plural

INDICATIVES	Active	Translation
Present		
Imperfect		
Future		
Perfect		
Pluperfect		
Future Perfect		

SUBJUNCTIVES	Active
Present	
Imperfect	
Perfect	
Pluperfect	

praesum, -esse, -fuī, -futūrus

INFINITIVES	Active		Translation
Present			
Perfect			
Future			

PARTICIPLE	Active		Translation
Future			

34D. Give the requested forms of the following verbs. Translate all forms. (Translate present tense subjunctives "let/may ..." and imperfect, perfect, and pluperfect tense subjunctives "were/would that.")

Latin Verb	Requested Form	Latin Form	Translation
probō	second person singular Future passive indicative		
concipiō	third person plural Perfect active indicative		
ēligō	first person plural Present passive subjunctive		
perdō	third person plural Pluperfect passive subjunctive		
insum	first person plural Present active subjunctive		
praesum	third person singular Future perfect active indicative		
transferō	Perfect passive Infinitive		

34E. Translate the following sentences into coherent English.

1. Sī Caesar exercituī praeerit, semper vincēmus.

   _____

2. Sī arbor perdita erit, nāvis tardissimē perveniet.

   _____

3. Sī poētae carmina sua hodiē cantant, populī omnēs magnopere laetī erunt.

_____

4. Canis ad puerōs, etiam sī dormientem vocant, statim currit.

_____

5. Sī dux consilium melius concipiat, moenia quam celerrimē surgant.

_____

6. Sī uxōrēs marītōs fallant, īrascantur.

_____

7. Sī cīvēs lēgēs malās probārent, bellum cīvilem pugnārent.

_____

8. Sī rex gladiātōrēs hōs ēligeret, illī impetum in regnum facerent.

_____

9. Sī senex morbōs febrēsque ab hospitibus recēpisset, medicus īvisset.

_____

10. Sī medicus nōn īvisset, puella mortua esset.

_____

34F. Translate the following sentences into Latin. Use the rubric below each sentence as a guide.

If the troops will have been conveyed to the city, they will pitch camp.

What sort of conditional is this sentence? _____

Person, number, tense, voice, and mood of "(they) will have been conveyed" _____
Dictionary entry _____
Latin translation _____

Person, number, tense, voice, and mood of "they will pitch" _____
_____
Dictionary entry _____
Latin translation _____

Latin translation of entire sentence _____
_____

If ever you (plural) had wanted to speak on behalf of peace, you would have approved Caesar's plan.

What sort of conditional is this sentence? _____

Person, number, tense, voice, and mood of "you (plural) had wanted"
_____

Dictionary entry _____

Latin translation _____

Person, number, tense, voice, and mood of "you would have approved"

_____

Dictionary entry _____

Latin translation _____

Latin translation of entire sentence _____

_____

If you (singular) were not condemning your brother of the crime, he would be a happy old man.

What sort of conditional is this sentence? _____

Person, number, tense, voice, and mood of "you (singular) were condemning" _____

Dictionary entry _____

Latin translation _____

Person, number, tense, voice, and mood of "he would be" _____

_____

Dictionary entry _____

Latin translation _____

Latin translation of entire sentence _____

_____

If the general should do otherwise, we would drive him out of the town immediately.

    What sort of conditional is this sentence? _____

    Person, number, tense, voice, and mood of "(he) should do" _____
    _____

    Dictionary entry _____
    Latin translation _____

    Person, number, tense, voice, and mood of "we would drive" _____
    _____

    Dictionary entry _____
    Latin translation _____

    Latin translation of entire sentence _____
    _____

34G. A haiku to translate.

Sī Rōmam hospes

perveniat, moenia

alta mīrētur.

Haiku is a traditional form of Japanese poetry consisting of 17 syllables in three lines (5, 7, 5 syllables respectively). Adapt your favorite passage from *NLP* 34 into a grammatically correct Latin haiku featuring a conditional clause.

_____

_____

_____

Gerunds and Gerundives

35A. Decline the following noun-adjective pairs.

Case	arx, arcis (-ium), f + Gerundive of **prōpōnō, -ere, -posuī, -positus**	hēres, hērēdis, m + Future active participle of **vehō, -ere, vexī, vectus**
Singular		
Nominative		
Genitive		
Dative		
Accusative		
Ablative		
Plural		
Nominative		
Genitive		
Dative		
Accusative		
Ablative		

35B. Give the requested forms of the following noun-adjective or noun-participle pairs. Translate the resulting phrases.

Noun	Adjective/Participle	Requested Form	Latin Form	Translation
iūdicium	**nūdus** Comparative	Genitive plural		
hēres	**cōnfiteor** Pres. dep. part.	Ablative singular		
monumentum	**concēdō** Perf. pass. part.	Dative singular		
arx	**prōpōnō** Gerundive	Accusative singular		
iūs	**auferō** Perf. pass. part.	Accusative plural		
māteria	**vehō** Gerundive	Genitive singular		
lībertīnus	**rescrībō** Fut. act. part.	Dative plural		

35C. Give a synopsis of the following verb. Translate each form.

referō, -ferre, -tulī, -lātus
conjugation _____
synopsis: 3rd person plural

INDICATIVES	Active	Translation	Passive	Translation
Present				
Imperfect				
Future				
Perfect				
Pluperfect				
Future Perfect				

SUBJUNCTIVES	Active	Passive
Present		
Imperfect		
Perfect		
Pluperfect		

referō, -ferre, -tulī, -lātus

IMPERATIVES	Active	Translation	Passive	Translation
Present				

INFINITIVES	Active	Translation	Passive	Translation
Present				
Perfect				
Future				

PARTICIPLES	Active	Translation	Passive	Translation
Present			XXX	XXX
Perfect	XXX	XXX		
Future				

35D. Give the requested forms of the following verbs. Translate all forms. (Translate present tense subjunctives "let/may …" and imperfect, perfect, and pluperfect tense subjunctives "were/would that.")

Latin Verb	Requested Form	Latin Form	Translation
rescrībō	Infinitive Perfect active		
addūcō	first person plural Present passive subjunctive		
studeō	second person singular Future active indicative		
committō	third person singular Perfect passive indicative		
vehō	third person plural Future Perfect passive indicative		
consulō	first person singular Pluperfect active subjunctive		
subeō	second person plural Imperfect active indicative		
confiteor	Genitive Gerund		
interrogō	Dative Gerund		
referō	Accusative Gerund		

35E. Translate the following sentences into coherent English.

1. Poētae cantandō mulieribus aliquibus placent.

_____

2. Līberī omnēs discendō student.

_____

3. Lēgātī potestāte suādendī ūsī sunt nē quaedam puella crās āmitterētur.

_____

4. Ad cōnfitendum lībertīnus iste domum sē rettulit.

_____

5. Caesar ad hominēs interrogandōs vēnit.

_____

6. Rēx lēgātōrum rescrībendōrum causā cum imperātōribus dēnique conveniēbat.

_____

7. Cōnsul igitur patriam suam iūre concēdendō reget.

_____

8. Virī uxōribus cōnsulendīs semper crēdant.

_____

9. Utinam mīlitēs ad iuvenēs auferendōs bellum nōn gererent.

_____

10. Quippe carmina canenda mīrāminī.

_____

35F. Translate the following sentences into Latin. Use the rubric below each
        sentence as a guide.

My friend used to write many letters for the sake of encouraging his
parents.

Person, number, tense, voice, and mood of "(he) used to write" _____
_____

Dictionary entry _____

Latin translation _____

Case and number of "parents" _____

Dictionary entry _____

Latin translation _____

Verbal form of "encouraging" _____

Tense and voice of "encouraging" _____

Case and number of "encouraging" _____

Dictionary entry _____

Latin translation _____

Latin translation of entire sentence _____
_____

We will try to find material worthy for singing songs.

Person, number, tense, voice, and mood of "We will try" _____
_____

Dictionary entry _____

Latin translation _____

What does "worthy" modify? _____

Case, number, and gender _____

Dictionary entry _____

Latin translation _____

Syntactic function and case of "for singing songs" _____

Tense and voice of "singing" _____

Case and number of "singing" and "songs" _____

Dictionary entry of "singing" _____

Dictionary entry of "songs" _____

Latin translation _____

Latin translation of entire sentence _____

_____

35G. Give the Latin forms for the following English phrases. Then recombine the **double-underlined** letters to spell the name of the great compilation of Roman laws.

As a memorial for his heirs:

— — ═ — — — — — —

— — — — ═ — — ═ —

the emperor: ═ — — — — — ═ — —

conveyed his decision and:

— ═ — — — ═ — — — — — ═ — — — ═ —

brought together freedmen:

═ — — — ═ — — — ═ — — — — —

for displaying the laws:

═ — — — — — ═

— — ═ — — — — ═ — — —

ANSWER: __ __ __ __ __

— — — — — — — — — —

Future Passive Periphrastics, Supines, and Other Subjunctive Clauses

36A. Decline the following noun-adjective pairs.

Case	sors, sortis (-ium), f + Superlative of **aptus, -a, -um**	genitor, -ōris, m + Positive of **ēgregius, -a, -um**
Singular		
Nominative		
Genitive		
Dative		
Accusative		
Ablative		
Plural		
Nominative		
Genitive		
Dative		
Accusative		
Ablative		

36B. Give the correct form of the specified adjective or participle to modify each of the following nouns. Translate the resulting phrases.

Noun	Case, No., Gender	Adjective/Participle	Latin Form	Translation
collīs (2)		ferus Comparative		
		ferus Comparative		
rāmō (2)		removeō Perf. pass. part.		
		removeō Perf. pass. part.		
lūminī		pūrus Superlative		
religiōnem		aptus Positive		
tūra		mīrābilis Comparative		
vestium		arcessō Gerundive		
sors		ultimus Positive		
genitōribus (2)		ingrātus Comparative		
		ingrātus Comparative		

36C. Give a synopsis of the following verb. Translate each form.

arbitror, -ārī, arbitrātus sum

conjugation _____

synopsis: 1st person plural

INDICATIVES	Deponent	Translation
Present		
Imperfect		
Future		
Perfect		
Pluperfect		
Future Perfect		

SUBJUNCTIVES	Deponent
Present	
Imperfect	
Perfect	
Pluperfect	

INFINITIVES	Deponent	Translation
Present		
Perfect		
Future		

PARTICIPLES	Deponent	Translation
Present		
Perfect		
Future		
Gerundive		

36D. Identify the following verbs as directed. Translate all forms. (Translate present tense subjunctives "let/may …" and imperfect, perfect, and pluperfect tense subjunctives "were/would that.")

Form	Person and No.	Tense	Voice	Mood	Translation
ēductī sint					
immolet					
censērem					
superābēre					
arcessī					
arbitrāminī					
laborāvistī					
remōta erat					

36E. Translate the following sentences into coherent English.

1. Rāmī turpēs terrīs ā pūrissimīs statim removendī sunt.

2. Animālia mīrābilia arbitrātū mox inveniās.

3. Illī victum laborant, hī laborātum vīvunt.

4. Lūmen ubique addūcendum est ut tenebrae disiiciantur.

5. Ō liber grandissime! Mīrābile lectū!

6. Fera terram ad ultimam ēdūcenda esse arbitror.

7. Vestis tam ēgregia creanda erit ut ā rēgīnā sōlā gerātur.

8. Dummodo tūs optimum sit, bovēs quam plūrimās dīs omnibus maximīs et optimīs immolābimus.

9. Priusquam hostīs superāvissētis, sacerdōtēs arcessītī erant.

10. Dum rex religiōnem piissimē ageret, cīvitātēs valēbant.

36F. Translate the following sentences into Latin. Use the rubric below each
sentence as a guide.

The state must not be taken by the enemy.

What sort of verbal construction is "(it) must not be taken"? _____

_____

Syntactic function and case of "state" _____

Dictionary entry _____

Latin translation _____

Tense, voice, and gender of "taken" _____

Dictionary entry _____

Latin translation of "(it) must be taken" _____

Syntactic function and case of "by the enemy" _____

_____

Latin translation _____

Latin translation of entire sentence _____

_____

We summoned the senators to watch the show.

Person, number, tense, voice, and mood of "we summoned" _____

_____

Dictionary entry _____

Latin translation _____

List three ways to express purpose in Latin

1. _____

2. _____

3. _____

Which phrase in this sentence expresses purpose? _____

_____

Latin translation of entire sentence (three options)

1. _____
2. _____
3. _____

I think the branches ought to be moved back.

"I think" triggers what sort of clause? _____

Syntactic function and case of "branches" _____
Dictionary entry _____
Latin translation _____

Tense, voice, and mood of "ought to be moved back" _____

_____

Dictionary entry _____
Latin translation _____

Latin translation of entire sentence _____

_____

36G. A haiku to translate.

Librī studendī

tandem fīnem tangimus.

Mīrum locūtū!

Haiku is a traditional form of Japanese poetry consisting of 17 syllables in three lines (5, 7, 5 syllables respectively). Adapt your favorite passage from *NLP* 36 into a grammatically correct Latin haiku featuring a gerundive or supine (or both!).

_____

_____

_____

NLP Review F (Lessons 31–36)

I: CONCEPTS

IA: Latin Verbs: More clauses with subjunctive verbs.

- **INDIRECT QUESTIONS** (*NLP* 31) are triggered by verbs of asking, doubting, or knowing and are introduced by interrogative conjunctions (why? when? how?) and interrogative adjectives and pronouns (what? which?). Be careful here, as many of the verbs that can trigger indirect questions can also trigger indirect statements and indirect commands. Look for the special interrogative conjunction **and** the subjunctive verb.

  Amīcī <u>quam placentam socolātiam mālīmus</u> mīrantur.
  Our friends wonder <u>which chocolate cake we prefer</u>.

- **FEAR CLAUSES** (*NLP* 32) are introduced by **NĒ** for positive clauses (to emphasize what the speaker fears **will** happen, but hopes **will not** happen) and **NĒ … NŌN** or **UT** for negative clauses (to emphasize what the speaker fears will not happen but hopes will).

  Metuimus <u>nē</u> placenta socolātia dēsit.
  We fear **that** (*nē*) <u>the chocolate cake is gone</u> (but we hope it is not).

  Timēmus <u>ut</u> amīcī quid placentae socolātiae cēperint (= <u>nē</u> amīcī quid placentae socolātiae <u>nōn</u> cēperint).
  We fear **that** <u>our friends did **not** take any cake</u> (but we hope that they did).

- **RELATIVE CLAUSES WITH SUBJUNCTIVE VERBS** (*NLP* 33) give nuanced information about a particular noun or pronoun (instead of the statements of fact conveyed by relative clauses of description with indicative verbs). Most commonly they express general characteristics.

  Sunt <u>quī placentam socolātiam nōn ament</u>.
  There are some people <u>who do not like chocolate cake</u>.

- Latin employs several combinations of indicative and subjunctive verbs to express **Conditions** (*NLP* 34).
  - **SIMPLE**: If + indicative, then + indicative.

    Sī placenta socolātia <u>est</u>, <u>ēdimus</u>.
    If <u>**there is**</u> chocolate cake, (then) <u>we eat</u> it.

  - **FUTURE MORE VIVID**: If + future indicative/future perfect indicative, then + future indicative.

    Sī placenta socolātia <u>ēderimus</u>, <u>aberit</u>.
    If <u>**we will have eaten**</u> the chocolate cake, (then) <u>it will be gone</u>.

  - **FUTURE LESS VIVID** (should-would) **Conditions**: If + present subjunctive, then + present subjunctive.

    Sī placenta socolātia <u>relinquat</u>, prō ientāculō <u>ēdāmus</u>.
    If chocolate cake <u>**should be left over**</u>, (then) <u>we would eat</u> it for breakfast.

  - **CONTRARY TO FACT**: If + imperfect/pluperfect subjunctive, then + imperfect/pluperfect subjunctive.

    Sī placenta <u>esset</u> socolātia, <u>ēderēmus</u>.
    If the cake <u>**were**</u> chocolate (but it wasn't), then <u>we would have eaten</u> it (but we didn't).

The following table summarizes the common varieties of conditional clauses:

Type of Conditional	Verb Tense/Mood in Protasis ("if" clause)	Verb Tense/Mood in Apodosis ("then" clause)
Simple	Indicative (any tense)	Indicative (any tense)
Future More Vivid	Future or Future Perfect Indicative	Future or Future Perfect Indicative
Future Less Vivid (should/would)	Present Subjunctive	Present Subjunctive
Contrary to Fact	Imperfect or Pluperfect Subjunctive	Imperfect or Pluperfect Subjunctive

- For some other, less common, clauses with subjunctive verbs, see *NLP 36*.

IB: Gerunds (*NLP 35*).

- Gerunds are second declension neuter singular verbal nouns that only appear in four cases (Genitive, Dative, Accusative, Ablative).
- Review the tables in *NLP 35* for the formation of the gerund (look for the *-nd-*).
- Gerunds are translated as English *-ing* nouns.

  Conquendum amāmus.
  We enjoy <u>baking</u>.

IC: Gerundives (*NLP 35*).

- Gerundives (future passive participles) are 1st/2nd declension verbal adjectives.
- Review the tables in *NLP 22* and *35* for the formation of the gerundive (look for the *-nd-*).
- Gerundives take subjects (e.g., the nouns they modify): *ad Gadīs oppugnandas* ("for Gades to be attacked"), but are more smoothly translated into English by rendering the noun as a direct object ("for attacking Gades").

ID: Future Passive Periphrastic (*NLP* 36).

- The future passive periphrastic is formed with the gerundive (see *NLP* 35) and the verb "to be."
- The future passive periphrastic expresses necessity or obligation.

Carthāgō <u>delenda est</u>!
Carthage <u>must be destroyed</u>!

IE: Supines (*NLP* 36).

- The supine is a fourth declension neuter singular verbal noun formed from the fourth principal part of the Latin verb.
- Review the table in *NLP* 36.
- Supines occur only in the accusative and ablative singular.
- Supines in the accusative case express purpose, especially after verbs of coming and going.

<u>Vīsum</u> īmus.
We go <u>to see</u>.

- Supines in the ablative case often function as ablatives of specification after certain Latin adjectives (wonderful, horrible, worthy …).

Ō Rōma! Urbs <u>mīrābile vīsū</u>!
O Rome! A city **<u>wonderful</u>** <u>to see</u>!

II: VOCABULARY *NLP* 31–36

NOUNS

māteria, -iae, f: subject matter

medicīna, -ae, f: treatment, remedy

mensa, -ae, f: table, course, meal

mora, -ae, f: delay, hindrance

rēgīna, -ae, f: queen

tenebrae, -ārum, f (plural): darkness, gloom

aevum, -ī, n: lifetime, age

cibus, -ī, m: food

collum, -ī, n: neck

frūmentum, -ī, n: grain

iūdicium, -iī, n: trial, legal investigation, decision

lībertinus, -ī, m: freedman

medicāmentum, -ī, n: drug, remedy

monumentum, -ī, n: memorial,
monument

morbus, -ī, m: sickness, disease, illness

mundus, -ī, m: universe, world

mūrus, -ī, m: wall

rāmus, -ī, m: branch, bough

tergum, -ī, n: back

vallum, -ī, n: wall, entrenchment

venēnum, -ī, n: poison

arbor, -oris, f: tree, "mast" (of a ship)

arx, arcis (-ium), f: citadel, fortress

cinis, cineris, m/f: ash

cohors, cohortis (-ium), f: troop,
company, cohort

cupīdō, cupīdinis, f: desire

exercitātiō, -iōnis, f: exercise, practice

famēs, -is (-ium), f: hunger

febris, -is (-ium), m: fever

genitor, -ōris, m: father

hērēs, hērēdis, m: heir

hospes, hospitis, m: guest, host,
stranger

iūs, iūris, n: right, law

iuventus, iuventūtis, f: youth, the prime
of life

lībīdō, lībidinis, f: desire, lust, passion

lūmen, lūminis, n: light, eye

os, ossis, n: bone

pavor, -ōris, m: fear, dread

pecus, pecoris, n: flock

pondus, ponderis, n: weight

religiō, -iōnis, f: obligation, scruples,
observance of a religious ceremony

senex, senis, m: old man

sors, sortis (-ium), f: lot, chance, oracular response

tellus, tellūris, f: earth

terror, -ōris, m: dread, terror

timor, -ōris, m: fear, dread

tūs, tūris, n: incense, frankincense

valētūdō, valētūdinis, f: health,
soundness

vestis, -is (-ium), f: garment, covering

cāsus, -ūs, m: misfortune, fall

equitātus, -ūs, m: cavalry

sensus, -ūs, m: feeling, sense,
understanding

spēs, speī, f: hope

nefās (indeclinable): a violation of divine
law, an impious act

PRONOUNS

quīcumque, quaecumque, quodcumque: whoever, whatever

ADJECTIVES

aeger, aegra, aegrum: sick, weary

aliēnus, -a, -um: of another, strange,
foreign

aptus, -a, -um (+ dative): fitting (for)

dubius, -a, -um: doubtful, uncertain,
wavering

ēgregius, -a, -um: distinguished,
extraordinary

ferus, -a, -um: savage, wild

ingrātus, -a, -um: unpleasant, thankless

niger, nigra, nigrum: black,
dark-colored

nocturnus, -a, -um: by night, nocturnal

nūdus, -a, -um: plain, mere

praecipuus, -a, -um: particular, special

pūrus, -a, -um: upright, faultless

rārus, -a, -um: scattered

rēgius, -a, -um: royal

singulī, -ae, –a (plural): each, one by
   one, one each

tardus, -a, -um: slow, sluggish, dull

ultimus, -a, -um: farthest, most distant

vagus, -a, -um: wandering, roving

varius, -a, -um: varied, different

fēlix (-icis): fertile, favorable, lucky

īnsignis, -e: notable, remarkable

lēvis, -e: smooth, delicate

mīrābilis, -e: extraordinary, unusual

ūtilis, -e: useful, advantageous, helpful

VERBS

constō, -stāre, -stitī, -stātus: agree,
   stand together, stand firm

ex(s)pectō, -āre, -āvī, -ātus: await,
   dread

immolō, -āre, -āvī, -ātus: sacrifice

interrogō, -āre, -āvī, -ātus: examine,
   question

labōrō, -āre, -āvī, -ātus: work

memorō, -āre, -āvī, -ātus: remind,
   relate

praestō, -āre, -stitī, -stitus: offer, excel

probō, -āre, -āvī, -ātus: prove, approve

superō, -āre, -āvī, -ātus: overcome,
   conquer

vetō, -āre, vetuī, vetitus: forbid

careō, -ēre, -uī (+ ablative): lack,
   be without

censeō, -ēre, -uī, census: advise, resolve,
   think, express an opinion

lateō, -ēre, -uī: lie hidden

moneō, -ēre, -uī: advise, warn

paveō, -ēre, pāvī: be sacred (of),
   be terrified (at)

removeō, -ēre, -mōvī, -mōtus: move
   back, withdraw, be distant

studeō, -ēre, -uī (+ dative): strive for,
   be devoted to, study

addūcō, -ere, -duxī, -ductus: bring, lead

alō, -ere, -uī, alitus: nourish

arcessō, -ere, -īvī, -ītus: send for,
   summon

committō, -ere, -mīsī, -missus: join,
   entrust to, bring together in a contest

concēdō, -ere, -cessī, -cessus: yield,
   grant

concipiō, -ere, -cēpī, -ceptus: absorb,
   receive, grasp

conficiō, -ere, -fēcī, -fectus: complete,
   carry out

conligō (colligō), -ere, -lēgī, -lectus:
   gather together, collect, infer

consulō, -ere, -uī, -sultus: consult

ēdūcō, -ere, -duxī, -ductus: lead out,
   march out

effundō, -ere, -fūdī, -fūsus: pour out,
   squander, waste

ēligō, -ere, -lēgī, -lectus: choose, select

instituō, -ere, -stituī, -stitūtus: posi-
   tion, place, establish, decide

interficiō, -ere, -fēcī, -fectus: destroy,
   kill

laedō, -ere, laesī, laesus: hurt, wound,
   injure

ostendō, -ere, -tendī, -tensus: show,
   display

pellō, -ere, pepulī, pulsus: strike, drive away, dislodge

perdō, -ere, -didī, -ditus: destroy, ruin

prōpōnō, -ere, -posuī, -positus: expose, display

requīrō, -ere, -quīsīvī, -quisītus: seek again, search for

rescrībō, -ere, -scripsī, -scriptus: write back, answer a petition

respiciō, -ere, -spexī, -spectus: look back

statuō, -ere, -uī, -ūtus: establish, settle, decide

tendō, -ere, tetendī, tentus: hasten, direct

vehō, -ere, vexī, vectus: convey, carry

circumveniō, -īre, -vēnī, -ventus: surround, encircle

nesciō, -īre, -īvī, -ītus: not to know, be unfamiliar, be ignorant of

arbitror, -ārī, arbitrātus sum: think, perceive, judge

fateor, -ērī, fassus sum: confess, acknowledge

vereor, -ērī, veritus sum: revere, respect, fear, dread

īrascor, -ī, īrātus sum: be angry

cōnfiteor, -ērī, cōnfessus sum: confess, reveal, acknowledge

auferō, -ferre, abstulī, ablātus: carry away, take away, remove

īnsum, -esse, -fuī: be in

praesum, -esse, -fuī + dative: be in charge

referō, -ferre, -tulī, -lātus: bring back, return, report

subeō, -īre, -īvī or **-iī, -itus**: approach, undergo, endure

trānsferō, -ferre, -tulī, -lātus: transfer, carry over

PREPOSITIONS

circum (+ accusative): around

contrā (+ accusative): against, opposite (adverb and preposition)

CONJUNCTIONS AND ADVERBS

aliter: otherwise

dummodo: provided that

forsitan: perhaps

nōndum: not yet

quārē: why

quō modō or **quōmodō**: how

quō: where, to what place

seu: whether, or if

III: ADDITIONAL DRILLS

IIIA. Decline the following noun-adjective pairs. Consult the glossary above for the dictionary entries.

Case	vestis + Future passive participle of removeō	equitatus + Comparative of tardus	spēs + ultimus
Singular			
Nominative			
Genitive			
Dative			
Accusative			
Ablative			
Plural			
Nominative			
Genitive			
Dative			
Accusative			
Ablative			

IIIB. Give the requested forms of the following noun-adjective or noun-participle pairs. Translate the resulting phrases.

Noun	Adjective/Participle	Requested Form	Latin Form	Translation
arx	**dubius** Superlative	Ablative singular		
medicīna	**auferō** Perf. pass. part.	Genitive plural		
cibus	**aptus** Comparative	Dative singular		
tergum	**laedō** Gerundive	Accusative singular		
hērēs	**arbitror** Pres. act. part.	Nominative plural		
lūmen	**nocturnus** Positive	Genitive singular		
morbus	**superō** Fut. act. part.	Ablative plural		

IIIC. Identify the following noun forms as directed. For ambiguous forms, give all possibilities. Give the correct form of the gerundive of **arbitror** and the present active participle of **confīteor** to modify each form.

Latin Form	Decl.	Gender	Case	No.	arbitror (Gerundive)	confīteor (Pres. act. part.)
casūs (3)						
tellūre						
febribus (2)						
mūrī (2)						
mensā						
aevī						

IIID. For each of the following nouns, select the adjective that agrees in case, number, and gender. Then translate the resulting phrases. You may use each adjective only once.

Adjective bank: **praecipuō, institūtum, verenda, monentīs, aegerrimīs, superātārum, pūrae, requisīta**

Noun	Case, No., Gender	Adjective	Translation
sensibus			
terrōre			
sortī			
iūdicia			
rēgīnās			
vallum			
mōrā			
famium			

IIIE. Give the Latin for each of the following English phrases.

    1. to/for a queen to be approved _____

    2. of a summoning youth _____

    3. with heirs having been examined _____

    4. desire to be confessed (Accusative) _____

    5. O savage dread! _____

    6. a suitable land (Nominative) _____

    7. of citadels to be displayed _____

    8. with cohorts having been taken away _____

    9. to/for confessing guests _____

    10. fathers to be revered (Accusative) _____

IIIF. Give a synopsis of the following verb. Translate each form.

vehō
conjugation:_____
synopsis: 3rd person plural

INDICATIVES	Active	Translation	Passive	Translation
Present				
Imperfect				
Future				
Perfect				
Pluperfect				
Future Perfect				

SUBJUNCTIVES	Active	Passive
Present		
Imperfect		
Perfect		
Pluperfect		

IMPERATIVES	Active	Translation	Passive	Translation
Present				
Future			XXX	XXX

INFINITIVES	Active	Translation	Passive	Translation
Present				
Perfect				
Future				

PARTICIPLES	Active	Translation	Passive	Translation
Present			XXX	XXX
Perfect	XXX	XXX		
Future				

IIIG. Identify the following verbs as directed. Translate each form.
(Translate present tense subjunctives "let/may …" and imperfect, perfect, and pluperfect tense subjunctives "were/would that.")

Form	Person and No.	Tense	Voice	Mood	Translation
praesint					
censēbam					
alēris					
īrascerēminī					
consultus essēs					
ēlēgistī					
removērī					
interficiam					
ēducta erant					
effūderat					
exspectēmur					
confessa est					

IIIH. Give the requested forms of the following verbs. Translate all forms.
(Translate present tense subjunctives "let/may ..." and imperfect,
perfect, and pluperfect tense subjunctives "were/would that.")

Latin Verb	Requested Form	Latin Form	Translation
conficiō	Present passive Infinitive		
arbitror	Accusative Supine		
memorō	Ablative Supine		
subeō	Perfect active Infinitive		
conlīgō	Future active Participle		
interrogō	Perfect passive Infinitive		
lateō	second person singular Present active subjunctive		
arcessō	third person plural Imperfect passive subjunctive		
laedō	first person singular Present passive indicative		
fateor	second person plural Perfect subjunctive		
vetō	first person plural Future active indicative		
respiciō	third person plural Future passive indicative		

IV: ADDITIONAL PASSAGES

1. Quintilian, *Institutio Oratoria* 1.1.5. Learning starts early and it is important for children to have educated nurses.

Hās prīmum audiet puer, hārum verba effingere imitandō cōnābitur, et nātūrā tenācissimī sumus eōrum quae rudibus animīs percēpimus.

Notes: **hās**: referring to the nurses or nannies; **effingō, -ere, -finxī, -fictus**: form, fashion; **imitor, -ārī, imitātus sum**: copy, imitate; **tenax (-ācis)**: clinging, holding fast, resolute, tenacious; **rudis, -e**: rough, raw, ignorant, undisciplined; **percipiō, -ere, -cēpī, -ceptus**: learn, grasp.

2. Ovid, *Ars Amatoria* 1.417–18. Ovid here advises Roman men to treat their girlfriends' birthdays with all due religious respect—forgetting to give a gift could have dire consequences. Meter: elegiac couplets.

Magna superstitiō tibi sit nātālis amīcae:
    quāque aliquid dandum est, illa sit ātra diēs.

Notes: **superstitiō, -iōnis**, f: superstition, fanaticism; **nātālis, -e**: natal, related to a birthday (here used substantively, "birthday"); **āter, atra, atrum**: black, dark.

3. Suetonius, *Vita Neronis* 51. Despite an indulgent lifestyle, Nero fell ill rarely.

Nam quī luxuriae immoderātissimae esset, ter omnīnō per quattuordecim annōs languit, atque ita ut neque vīnō neque consuētūdine reliquā abstinēret.

Notes: **luxuria, -iae**, f: extravagance; **immoderātus, -a, -um**: exorbitant; **omnīnō**: altogether, entirely; **langueō, -ēre, -uī**: be unwell, lack vigor; **consuētūdō, -inis**, f: custom, habit, manner; **abstineō, -ēre, -uī, -tentus**: restrain, abstain.

4. Pliny the Elder, *Naturalis Historia* 6.91. In Taprobane, kings must maintain the highest sense of morality or risk suffering the most humiliating form of punishment.

Rēgem, sī quid dēlinquat, morte multārī, nullō interemente, āversantibus cunctīs et commercia etiam sermōnis negantibus.

Notes: construe this passage as depending on an understood *dīcunt*; **dēlinquō, -ere, -līquī, -lictus**: fail, commit a crime; **multō, -āre, -āvī, -ātus**: punish; **interemō, -ere, -ēmī, -emptus**: destroy, kill; **āversor, -ārī, āversātus sum**: turn away; **commercium, -iī, n**: trade, communication, correspondence.

5. Vergil, *Aeneid* 6.888–92. In the underworld, Anchises reveals the future glory of Aeneas' descendants. Meter: dactylic hexameter.

Quae postquam Anchīsēs nātum per singula duxit
incenditque animum fāmae venientis amōre,
exim bella virō memorat quae deinde gerenda,
Laurentīsque docet populōs urbemque Latīnī,
et quō quemque modō fugiatque feratque labōrem.

Notes: **incendō, -ere, -cendī, -census**: inflame, fire; **exim**: thence, thereupon; **gerenda** (*sint*): "ought to be waged" (future passive periphrastic); **Laurens (-entis)**: of Laurentum, a city near Rome; **Latīnus, -ī, m**: the king of the Latins.

6. Ovid, *Metamorphoses* 14.585–91. An affectionately manipulative daughter, Venus requests deification for her son Aeneas. Since the gods of Rome were so thoroughly anthropomorphized, it was easy for a human to attain divine status. At Rome, from the death of Aeneas' descendant Julius Caesar onward, a simple vote of the Senate granted divine status to good emperors upon death, including Augustus and Claudius, laying the foundation for the cult of deified emperors. Meter: dactylic hexameter.

Ambierātque Venus superōs collōque parentis
circumfūsa suī "Numquam mihi" dīxerat "ullō
tempore dūre pater, nunc sīs mītissimus, optō,
Aenēaeque meō, quī tē dē sanguine nostrō
fēcit avum, quamvīs parvum dēs, optime, nūmen,
dummodo dēs aliquod! Satis est inamābile regnum
adspexisse semel, Stygiōs semel isse per amnēs."

Notes: **ambiō, -īre, -īvī** or **-iī, -ītus**: canvass, embrace, visit in rotation; **circumfundor, -ī, circumfūsus sum**: pour around, surround; **mītis, -e**: mild, gentle; **avus, -ī, m**: ancestor; **inamābilis, -e**: disagreeable; **Stygius, -a, -um**: of the river Styx (the border between the worlds of the living and the dead), of the underworld; it was one of the quests of the great Greek and Roman heroes to visit the underworld while still living, as did Aeneas.

Crossword Puzzle.

Across

9. A Roman legal compiler
12. Rome's birthday celebration
13. Horace's verdant chartreuse
14. Pompey's double-crossing ally
15. Vergil's hometown
17. Civil War versifier
20. Citizen-maker
22. Pompey's stony lieutenant
24. Where Vergil dies
25. He travels to Hades for love of his wife
26. A member of Rome's divine trinity
29. Turnus's followers
30. Where Caesar saw Crassus
32. Venom vanquishers
34. He never called Martial
35. Lydia destroys him by loving him
38. The father of medicine
39. Festival days
40. The Etruscan art of liver-reading
41. A healing sanctuary
42. Senatorial decree
47. They dwell beyond the north wind
49. Caesar's Greek gal
50. Monster masher
51. A "constitutional" compendium
52. When Caesar was assassinated
53. Vergil's patron
54. A medical writer
55. Where Caesar declared war on Rome
56. Marcus Aurelius's personal physician
57. A popular physician at Rome
58. A father concerned for his son's education

Down

1. Caesar's belligerent lieutenant
2. Where Pompey was defeated
3. Cicero's Antonine tirade
4. His prayer: a healthy mind in a healthy body
5. Another member of Rome's divine trinity
6. Roman "mardi gras"
7. Where the Carthaginians intended to attack
8. A famous teacher
10. A legendary utopia
11. A divine healer
15. The one-eyed men
16. Peace with the gods
17. Caesar's retiring lieutenant
18. Another Roman legal compiler
19. Another Roman legal compiler
21. Another Roman legal compiler
23. Unfortunate in his heinous heirs
27. Bellicose beauties
28. Composite combative critters
31. Cybele's roaming Romeo
33. She labors in Cybele's leonine yoke
36. She curses Aeneas
37. Another healing sanctuary
43. The "butcher"
44. Ascanius' unlucky parent
45. The father of Latin literature
46. Jason's petulant paramour
48. Her husband loved her so much that he traveled to the land of the dead

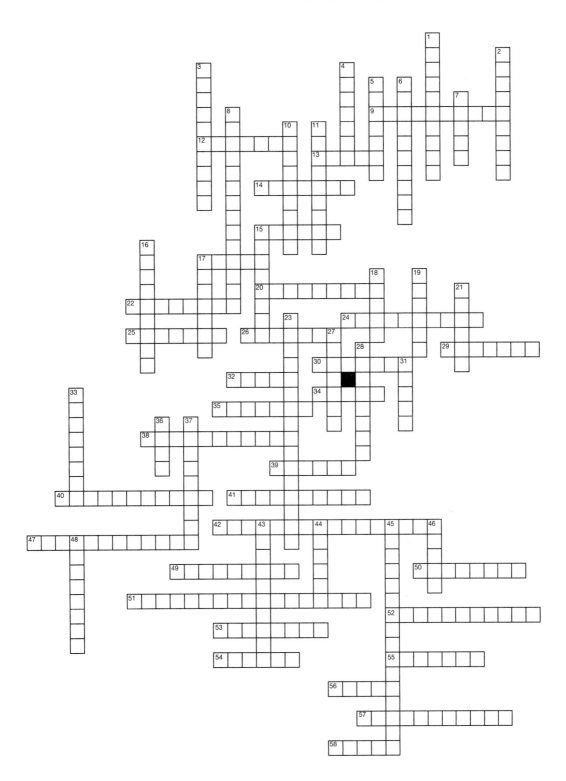

Answer Key for Crossword
Puzzles and Word Searches

REVIEW A

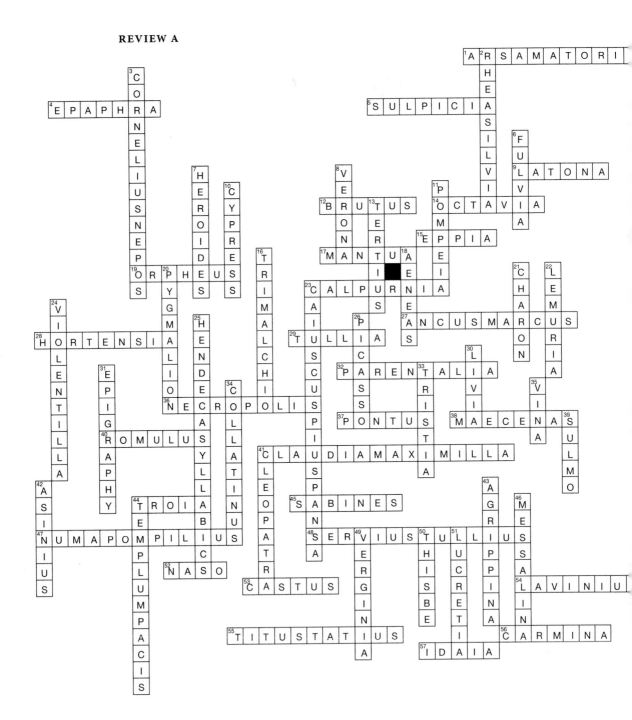

REVIEW B

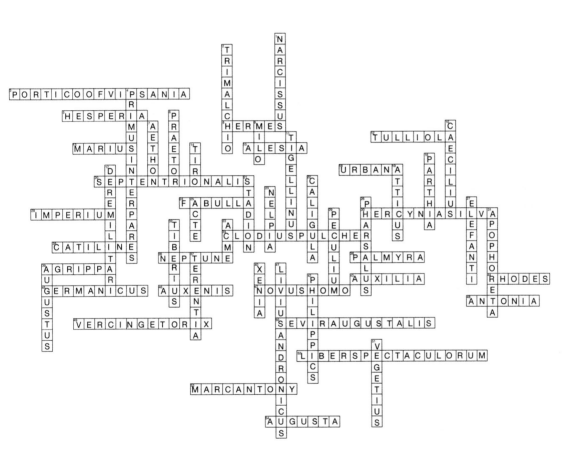

REVIEW C

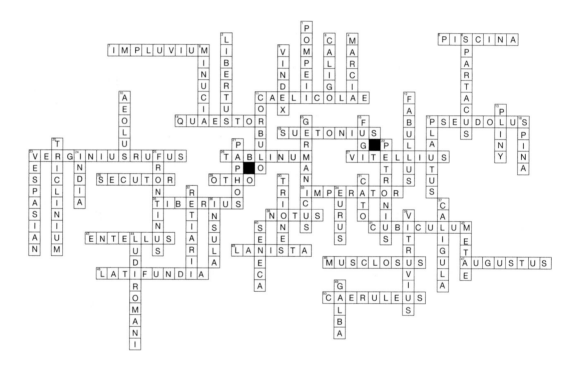

REVIEW D

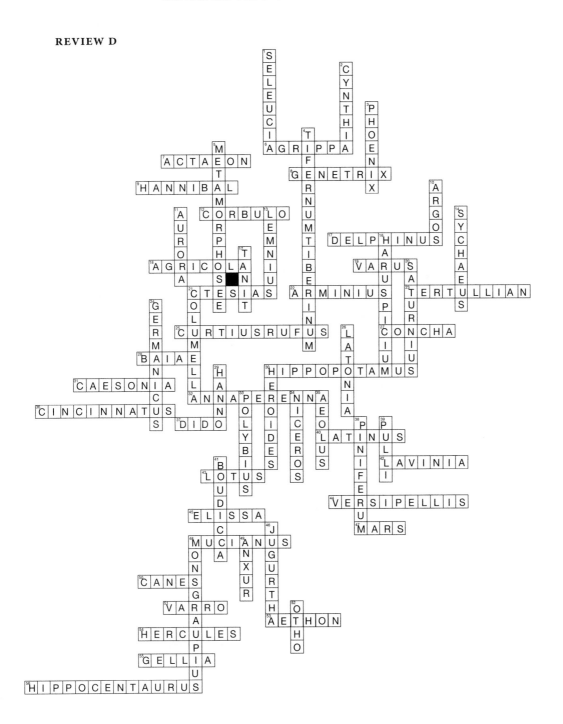

REVIEW E

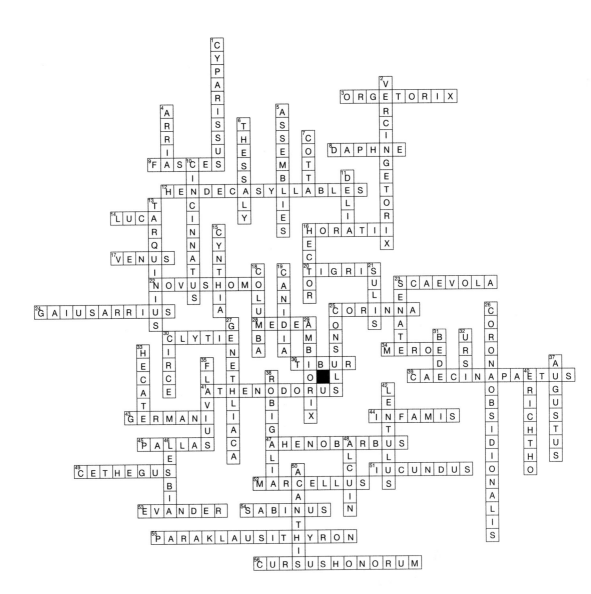

REVIEW F

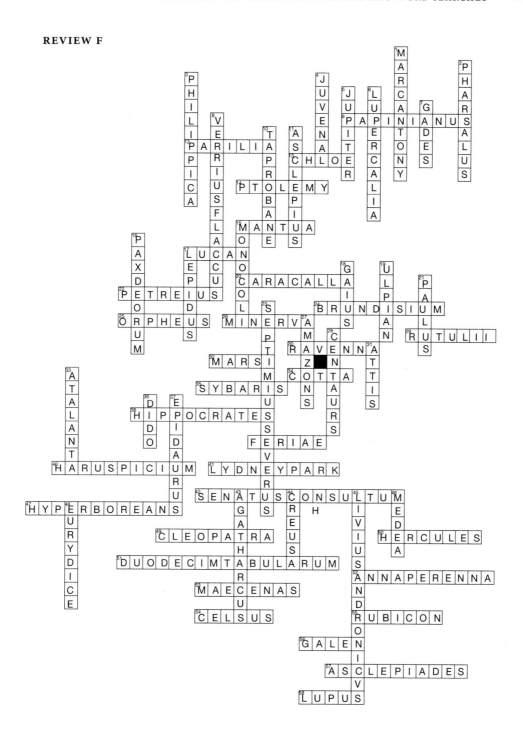

WORD FIND 9I

```
C  O  P  I  A  B  L  T  E  M  E  S  S  U  N  T
Z  N  P  H  V  X  K  A  U  T  E  M  O  G  F  T
X  Z  C  I  V  U  A  B  C  A  U  N  H  O  O  U
T  K  X  Q  U  I  O  S  E  R  V  U  S  T  I  D
F  H  S  O  Q  M  R  M  A  J  I  E  H  S  F  S
K  L  E  Q  B  A  M  I  Q  C  N  M  L  E  Z  W
E  C  J  W  B  E  P  I  S  T  U  L  A  E  H  P
K  C  U  S  M  O  D  R  E  V  D  E  U  H  L  I
S  U  M  E  C  S  O  N  G  O  C  S  G  T  E  U
P  I  O  N  A  C  T  Y  O  U  H  A  P  F  M  M
G  Z  N  T  L  I  D  B  C  P  P  N  W  C  J  B
Q  T  G  I  A  V  S  K  I  F  S  N  Y  V  A  K
R  G  M  E  F  I  L  M  P  U  H  E  T  I  X  T
V  O  R  T  N  T  N  A  B  E  D  A  R  T  C  L
J  D  S  I  B  A  T  I  G  O  C  O  I  A  O  C
W  R  M  S  J  T  G  C  C  Q  L  U  R  T  C  D
V  E  P  E  O  E  Z  I  H  G  Q  Z  N  E  X  W
N  Q  K  V  L  M  I  F  Q  N  Q  Q  R  I  D  O
O  M  P  X  K  F  S  F  I  T  K  Y  P  P  A  A
H  S  X  U  U  D  V  E  L  R  F  M  B  M  F  M
```

I shall be present: *aderō*	I shall respond: *respondēbō*	letters: *epistulae*
he said: *inquit*	moreover: *autem*	slave: *servus*
You (plural) will perceive: *sentiētis*	state (accusative): *cīvitātem*	of force: *vīris*
they were handing over: *trādēbant*	of no one: *nēminis*	a tear: *lacrima*
we shall understand: *cognoscēmus*	money (accusative): *pecūniam*	opinions: *sententiae*
you will think: *cogitābis*	with the laws: *lēgibus*	for duty: *pietātī*
I shall bring about: *efficiam*	glory: *glōria*	end: *finis*

WORD FIND 20I

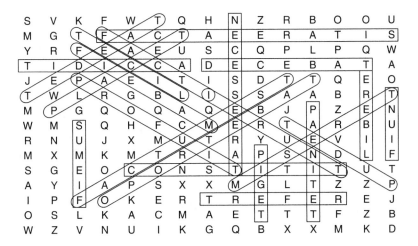

it was proper: *decēbat*	to be pleasing: *libēre*	it was fitting: *oportēbat*
it has been agreed: *constitit*	it causes regret: *paenitet*	it has benefited: *prōfuit*
it displeases: *piget*	it is agreeable: *placet*	it happens: *accidit*
it is permitted: *licet*	it distresses: *miseret*	it matters: *refert*
it disgusts: *taedet*	it shames: *pudet*	it was necessary: *necesse erat*
they become: *fiunt*	we shall become: *fiēmus*	I became: *fiēbam*
it has become: *factum est*	you (feminine, plural) had become: *factae erātis*	they (masculine) will have become: *factī erunt*

WORD FIND 25I

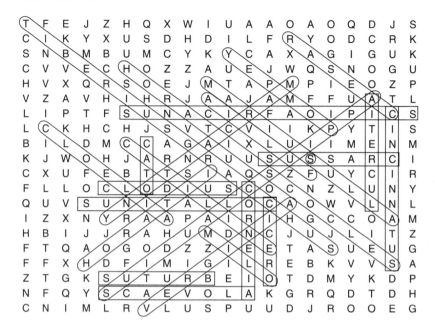

WORD FIND 31I

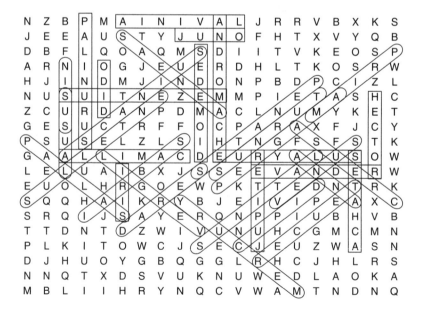